TALENT WANTS TO BE FREE

ORLY LOBEL

Talent Wants to Be Free

WHY WE SHOULD LEARN TO LOVE LEAKS, RAIDS,
AND FREE RIDING

Yale UNIVERSITY PRESS

NEW HAVEN AND LONDON

Published with assistance from the Mary Cady Tew Memorial Fund.

Yale University Press books may be purchased in quantity for educational, business, or promotional use. For information, please e-mail sales.press@yale.edu (U.S. office) or sales@yaleup.co.uk (U.K. office).

Set in Scala type by IDS Infotech Ltd., Chandigarh, India.
Printed in the United States of America.

Library of Congress Cataloging-in-Publication Data

Lobel, Orly.
  Talent wants to be free : why we should learn to love leaks, raids, and free riding / Orly Lobel.
    pages cm
  Includes bibliographical references and index.
  ISBN 978-0-300-16627-9 (cloth : alk. paper) 1.   Free enterprise. 2.   Entrepreneurship. 3.   Technological innovations. 4.   Ability.   I. Title.
  HB95.L63 2013
  330.12'2—dc23

                                                              2013011465

A catalogue record for this book is available from the British Library.

This paper meets the requirements of ANSI/NISO Z39.48–1992 (Permanence of Paper).

10 9 8 7 6 5 4 3 2

To my father, Dr. David Lobel, who combines the heart of a healer,
the mind of an inventor, and the soul of an artist

There is a crack, a crack in everything. It's how the light comes in.

—LEONARD COHEN

CONTENTS

ACKNOWLEDGMENTS

My debts to my many friends and colleagues who have generously contributed their minds and hearts to the creation of *Talent Wants to Be Free* are too great to list. Knowing it will ultimately prove impossible to relay how truly grateful I am for the contributions of others, I am happy to relate some of my deep gratitude here.

Talent Wants to Be Free is the product of years of research, teaching, collaborating, and consulting on the law, economics, and psychology of human capital. My personal trajectory—from Tel Aviv to Paris to Massachusetts, Connecticut, then Southern California, and around the globe again—brought to light how the freedom to flow, the ability of people to move, connect, and engage, shapes the success of markets and ideas. Along with my collaborators, psychologists, and behavioral economists I studied how motivation, relationships, and mobility are the crucial ingredients of successful innovation.

Reflecting the age of global exchanges, *Talent Wants to Be Free* has benefited greatly from numerous workshops I gave in the United States, Canada, Australia, China, Japan, Israel, Greece, Italy, France, and Germany. During all these travels I was fortunate to have the tremendous support of my mentors, friends, and family. My colleagues at the University of San Diego are my nuclear intellectual community. The life of research and innovation under the sun, against the ocean, and amidst natural beauty makes for particularly productive times. I am especially grateful to Larry Alexander, Jordan Barry, Lesley McAllister, David McGowan, Miranda McGowan, Lisa

Ramsey, Maimon Schwartzchild, and Ted Sichelman. Rich Paul was kind enough to teach my classes while I was on research leave and never fails to offer the best insights gleaned from the front line of the human capital wars. Laurie Claus and Mor Shori are friends upon whose wisdom and kindness I can always count. Dan Solove spent hours sharing his experience and insights. My colleagues at Tel Aviv University never rest. I am privileged to have many opportunities to join the law faculty's spirited intellectual exchanges. "If there is no flour there is no Torah" (Pirkei Avot 3:21). Deans Kevin Cole and Stephen Ferruolo generously supported my research and sabbatical to complete the book. My research on innovation has been supported by generous grants from the Kauffman Foundation, the Searle Center, and the Southern California Innovation Project. Many students have helped with the research of the book, and I am particularly grateful to Dave Angeloff, Adriana Macias, and Beth Rinehart. I also thank Karin Spidel, my dedicated and energetic administrative assistant. The editors at Yale University Press, Jaya Chatterjee, Bill Frucht, Alison MacKeen, and Mike O'Malley, offered invaluable guidance and support. Great thanks to my literary agent Lindsay Edgecombe for her enthusiasm and smarts.

My parents, Thalma and David Lobel, gave me the chutzpah to dream big and never cease to give me their friendship, judgment, and unconditional love. They are remarkably creative, active, and generous. Both combine science, art, and passion in their careers and lead lives that keep them engaged and young. Somehow they manage to do it all while caring selflessly for their family as full-time parents and grandparents. I am also grateful for the support of my in-laws, Orit and Zvika, my brother and sister-in-law, Dory and Keren, and my uncle and his partner, Raffi and Rick. My writing is always in memory of my brother Dani. *Talent Wants to Be Free* is about inspiration, creativity, and human potential. Dani died at the tender age of eighteen, and we lost greatly on all those fronts.

Among the debts I owe to all my loved ones, the greatest is to On Amir, my partner in every single way. He is my coauthor, my reader, my love. He pushes me to run up the mountain four days a week and he gladly holds the fort down when I write, teach, and travel. He has the unique ability to propel my ideas forward, and he challenges me to think deeper. Our daughters, Danielle, Elinor, and Natalie, make all the rest meaningful, and they never cease to amaze me. It is for their generation, the Innovation Generation, that we must take seriously the nourishment of our talent commons.

Introduction

CONTROL IS A DOUBLE-EDGED SWORD

The best way to send information is to wrap it up in a person.

—*J. Robert Oppenheimer, father of the atomic bomb*

BEYOND THE ZUCKERBERG VENDETTA

THE STORY OF ONE COMPUTER wiz's rise as the creator of Facebook, an Internet social network system of global renown, has become engrained in our modern mythology. In 2002, fresh out of high school, a young upstart named Mark Zuckerberg arrives at the wealthiest university on earth and soon becomes the youngest self-made billionaire of the twenty-first century. He does so not by going to class and drinking up the wisdom of the distinguished Harvard faculty but by using his computer skills to connect us digitally. Along the way, as he reinvents social networking, he makes some enemies, lays the groundwork for his future fortune, and becomes entangled in a few legal sagas. Now consider the ethics of Zuckerberg's path. As a geeky, socially awkward undergrad, he hacks Harvard's computers and posts pictures of all his female class-mates on his newly created Facemash, an interactive hot-or-not website, nearly getting him kicked out of school but also planting in his mind the power of online networking, digital pictures, and social commentary that entices our collective energies. A few weeks later, following his newfound notoriety at the college, Zuckerberg is approached by the twin brothers and future Olympic rowers Cameron and Tyler Winklevoss, who ask for his help in programming a network called Harvard Connection. Zuckerberg agrees and begins working on the Winklevosses' venture. At the same time and without their knowledge, he continues (or begins: you be the judge) to work on his own version of a social network. Less than a year later Zuckerberg releases Facebook, and the rest, as we say, is history.

Who owns the idea of Facebook? How would you interpret Zuckerberg's verbal agreement to work on Harvard Connection? Did Zuckerberg become an employee of the Winklevosses, and if so, should he have been prevented from working on a similar (but better) social network? What if he had signed, as many of us have, a contract with a noncompete clause, promising not to compete with the Winklevosses for the next three years? What if he had promised not to use any information or skill he learned during his time working for the Winkelvosses and had promised to assign all future inventions to their venture?

This book challenges the conventional responses to these dilemmas. We are at a critical moment in our history: the ways we organize, invest, and manage our economy have changed dramatically. While we've recognized that capital and intellectual capital must be critically replenished, our competitive edge is diminishing because we have stuck with archaic notions of how to nourish our human capital. While many authors, politicians, and concerned parents lament the education system or focus narrowly on each cyclical economic crisis, the missing link in every sector is our impoverished understanding of our talent pools.

The Winklevosses–Zuckerberg faceoff resulted in a cash and stock settlement worth $65 million. The Winklevosses' victory has been termed by critics "the Winklevoss Syndrome"[1]—the false belief that ideas are owned. Zuckerberg, as portrayed in the movie *The Social Network,* iterates a most powerful line: "If you'd invented Facebook, you would have invented Facebook!" Intuitively, we know that the abstract idea of a social network is very different from actually building one and that society is better off allowing talented people to freely compete and flow between creative ventures. But you may have a counterintuition. You might be thinking that Zuckerberg's actions were a clear betrayal. If you've ever hired anyone, you may strongly believe that companies should be able to restrict the talent they recruit from taking their ideas elsewhere.

If you've ever had an idea, held a job, or employed good folks, you probably have strong opinions about how talent should be governed. This book will challenge those opinions, and some of the conventional wisdom's most pervasive misconceptions. It doesn't matter if you're a business strategist, a company owner, an inventor, an artist, or a medical doctor—this book applies to your career. The talent wars are all the strategies, practices, laws, and disputes about controlling human capital in competitive markets. And the talent wars are not about to be fought— they are already being waged, with devastating consequences. In every industry and economic situation we battle to recruit, retain, and motivate the best people around us; but we're doing it wrong. We can do better.

This book is about how innovation happens and how talent wars, competition, and creative environments shape our quest for the extraordinary. Building on over a decade of teaching, researching, and consulting on human capital, I set out to write this book to help us see that in order for innovation to flourish we must learn to overcome our control mentality. Through my research and practice I've witnessed the deep tensions accompanying the essential need for brain power in today's markets. The lessons from the many battles over people, in and out of the litigation zone, are sometimes counterintuitive. Businesses often think that the best way to nurture talent is to keep it from leaving, fighting others who try to poach their best talent and fighting their own talented people when they leave. When it comes to owning people, we react emotionally and territorially. But what if the best course of action was to bid the employees a fond farewell and to later treat them as alums and potential rehires? What if the most effective strategies of motivating innovation in the firm were to allow the spilling of secrets and the shared ownership of ideas?

Facebook, a victim of its own success, has bigger fish to fry today than the Winklevosses. Facebook is competing with its largest rival, Google, over more than just social networking. Facebook is striving to recruit the best and the brightest employees, even if that means taking them directly from the Google ranks. To the most talented workers (call them human assets if you wish), Facebook has become, to cite one ex–Google employee, "a hell of a lot sexier" employer than Google, enticing a steady stream of Google employees to switch over. One in five Facebook employees is a former Googler. Google executives regularly strategize about the Facebook problem, the aggressive recruitment of Google's top performers. A former Googler and current Facebooker explains, "It's not just about the money. Entrepreneurs want to work at the hottest place on earth, and right now that's Facebook." In the Silicon Valley, where the two companies operate, these kinds of talent flows are common. Just a few years back Google was in Facebook's place and Microsoft in Google's. When Google approached Vic Gundotra, now Google's vice president of engineering, Microsoft vigorously sued, and in the end Gundotra was forced into a yearlong involuntary sabbatical from the industry. Companies like Microsoft, Google, and Facebook have become so reliant on new talent that they acquire (or, as the tech-buzz is now calling it, acq-hire) entire start-ups only to discard the product and keep the teams, founders, and engineers.

But in this archaic control mentality the costs are becoming evident. In 2010 the Department of Justice investigated Google and other tech giants, including Apple, IBM, Intel, and Adobe, for agreeing to mutual "do not touch" arrangements whereby the companies promise not to hire away competitor talent. These agreements would allegedly violate antitrust competition laws. But beyond their illegality, behind these strategic moves lie questions about the wisdom of such agreements. Many of our contemporary battles, even between industry giants, are still driven by a Winklevoss Syndrome—a false belief that we own ideas and people. Often, as we shall see, this mentality leads smart leaders into destructive battles. What happens to the market and our quest for innovation when talent moves are frozen? Can we bet on (and profit from) the next young Mark Zuckerberg?

While I was toiling away in classrooms and libraries at Harvard Law School and the Kennedy School of Government, deeply entrenched in labor market law and economics research, exciting rumblings from the college dorms were changing the ways we think about talent, competition, and the ownership of ideas. These rumblings were a prelude to the research that my collaborators and I launched on the nature of innovation, motivation, and the new talent market. Most of us in the 1990s bought into the anti-free-riding story: that we will lose out on important innovation if we allow our competitors to benefit from our investment in skill, knowledge, and research. Only recently, by bringing experimental and behavioral insights to bear on market realities, bridging the worlds of the law school and the business school, through my teaching of both law students and MBA students, through my consulting of business ventures and entrepreneurs, and through my many collaborations with management scholars, social psychologists, and organizational strategists, have I developed a new model for thinking about free riding and conquering the quest for talent. My collaborators and I, using key insights from law, economics, psychology, and business, launched interdisciplinary studies. We conducted experimental studies that demonstrated performance variances of people who were bound by contractual restrictions, mined empirical data on differences between regions that vary in their approaches to the talent war, and examined corporations' and industry leaders' new approaches to human capital. *Talent Wants to Be Free* fills the gap in our current debates about innovation and our competitive edge. While as a society we've paid significant attention to capital wars and intellectual property wars, we have accepted outdated and detrimental perceptions of human capital for too long. Once we understand the benefits that come with freedom, flow, and a healthy dose of free riding, we can learn, as businesses and as inventors and as a society, to choose our battles wisely.

THE MISSING LINK

Inextricably connected by their war over talent, Facebook and Google have also been locked in a conceptual debate over the essence of innovation. For years Google has had a reputation for encouraging employee creativity by allowing time for independent play and experimentation. Zuckerberg has publicly dismissed Google's approach to innovation, claiming that Facebook has, from day one (a tricky timeline to pinpoint given the Winklevosses' claims about the origins of the idea for a social network), been more focused and goal-oriented, directing its talent toward more concrete paths of innovation. Although the companies may adopt different approaches, each is trying to figure out the best ways to encourage their talent to be the most innovative and to think outside the box.

What is this box that we collectively struggle to think outside of? Has our creativity been so thoroughly tamed that we have to make targeted efforts to reach beyond it? These days, self-help books promise to teach us ingenuity, how to think outside the box, brainstorming techniques, and teamwork, all in the hope that we can turn those skills into money. Take, for example, the image of the boisterous meetings between creators with crumpled papers and smudged whiteboards, coffee stains on their shirts and ink stains on their fingers. Compare it with the quiet workroom of the solo inventor, toiling long hours into the night below a single swaying bulb. We all have a sense that innovation can be the product either of collaborative work processes within corporate research and development departments or of single eureka moments and the genius breakthroughs of individuals. These contrasting images have raised our collective interest, and recent years have seen great developments in our under-standing of the innovative process. Thoughtful studies about collabora-tive innovation have challenged the old individuated, lone-inventor ways in which we have thought about production and research and develop-ment. Books like Steven Johnson's *Where Good Ideas Come From* are helping us think about inventive environments from biological and cultural standpoints. Others, such as Larry Lessig's *The Code*, have power-fully argued against the grievous effects that overly strong intellectual property protections such as long copyright and patent ownership terms have on innovation.

Lacking in our debates is an understanding of how people and skills themselves become monopolized and depleted when we employ the wrong strategies. We've been missing insights on how people innovate differently under the constraints of human capital controls. An under-standing of how market norms concerning talent wars, ownership, and control of ideas and people impact innovation is the missing link. Could Facebook have been created under the leadership of the Winklevosses in Massachusetts? Or did it take Zuckerberg's genius, renegade attitude, and eventual move to California—a state that has a unique competition policy and an intellectual property system that encourage talent wars and human capital flows—to revolutionize the way the world interacts on the Internet? Should Google control the movement of its best workers (whether it is legally allowed to do so or not)? or should it approach the talent wars in the same spirit it approaches the challenge of motivating its creative talent from within, namely, by loosening controls and encour-aging flow?

Corporate incentives and strategic controls affect the likelihood of ingenuity and entrepreneurship in surprising ways. Many leaders in the field of innovation have contemplated the value of gym memberships and catered meals for their hired inventors and the ways in which surrounding them with an adult playground, an office full of high-tech toys, can enhance their creativity. Buzzwords about team-building, networks, and open innovation zip around, but too little is known about how work relations, contracts, and the background rules about intangible assets (people and knowledge) can enhance the innovative spirit of an organization. The time is ripe to bring the background to the forefront: the ever-present contractual fine print, litigious behavior, and organizational strategies that impact the ways in which individuals and businesses come together for successful innovation. In this book, we will learn about trade secrets, patents, copyright ownership, economic espionage, nondisclosure and noncompete agreements, duties of loyalty, and corporate reward systems. Each of these strategies attempts to control a company's greatest assets: its human and intellectual capital. These mechanisms affect the immediate and long-term capacities of firms and industries. A richer understanding of these effects will bring surprising lessons. We will discover that the default mentality of protectionism is frequently archaic and misguided. Counterintuitively, the way to gain is often by allowing tactical loss.

THE QUEST FOR THE HOLY QUEST

Innovation is commonly conceptualized as a quest.[2] The world has been sailed around and walked across, its mountains hiked, its caves explored, its terrain conquered, measured, and mapped. The exploratory spotlights of submarines have illuminated the depths of the sea, men have golfed on the moon, and our spaceships probe the dusty surface of Mars. Like the pioneers before them, modern inventors are the explorers of our time, forging the outer boundaries of the digital frontier, breaking new ground, calculating new formulas for energy-saving appliances, developing better ways to deliver medicine and food, and writing algorithms that hedge risks and convert old software so it applies to newer hardware. Though the terrain of modern expeditions is no longer icy rock faces or blistering deserts, an age-old problem endures: once new terrain is found, it is there for all to conquer. This is the inherent dilemma of the modern tools of innovation: knowledge, intellectual property, and human capital. These new currencies of economic competition are intangible and nonexcludable and can be widely replicated, consumed, and transformed, which makes them both extremely valuable and extremely vulnerable. Absent physical or legal protections, information spreads like wildfire to the outside world. If companies are unable to safeguard their information investments, then their information can be stolen in real time by their competitors, duplicated, tweeted about, and posted to YouTube instantly. In today's digital world, information is difficult and costly to create but easy and inexpensive to replicate. Lacking protection, a company may pay a heavy price now for the production of knowledge that will later benefit its competition. The disparity between costs of development and use is at the heart of the heated intellectual property debates.

The scope of intellectual property protections—patents, copyright, trade secrets, and trademarks—is a minefield of controversy. Ingrained in our beliefs is the idea that "the future of the nation depends in no small part on the efficiency of industry, and the efficiency of industry depends in no small part on the protection of intellectual property."[3] Yet even as intellectual property benefits its owners, its controls come at great cost. Policing usage, detecting infringement, and litigating disputes all consume vast amounts of time and resources. Most importantly and disturbingly, strong controls impede further innovation that would have built on the restricted knowledge. Too little air chokes the fire of innovation, and too much wind blows it out. Shaping policy and strategy in this area is like hitting a moving target while balancing on a ball.

Although the intellectual property wars are familiar to the public consciousness, the other half of our battles surrounding our new economic currencies of intangible assets—human-capital-talent-wars and employment restrictions on competition and use of skill—is just now beginning to reveal its magnitude and controversy. Human capital wars track many of the same concerns as intellectual property debates, but they are far less understood. Human capital controls have unique features that inevitably accompany any attempt to restrict people—the carriers of knowledge, or inputs if you are economically inclined, rather than knowledge, or output, itself. Human capital controls as they have risen in the talent wars attempt to restrict professionals from competing, competitors from recruiting, entrepreneurs from poaching, skilled and inventive workers from using their knowledge and experiences and from owning their ideas and creative aspirations. Our talent strategies concern the ability of people to pursue their passions and livelihood while establishing the professional and social connections needed for the advancement of their careers and the industry.

These strategies create systems in the market which determine how talented people construct their lives and their economic ventures.

Almost half a century ago the Nobel laureate Kenneth Arrow argued that competition, not central control, is what fuels innovation.[4] Writing specifically about human capital, Arrow observed that the "mobility of personnel among firms provides a way of spreading information."[5] In other words, Arrow believed that ideas travel with workers as they move between companies, thereby spreading knowledge and strengthening economies. Contemporary markets and new scientific studies provide empirical support for Arrow's assertion. We now know that innovation is a collective endeavor, and the ways in which it is spread through human interaction will determine its quality and growth. Simply put, movement and competition are good for innovation. New research confirms what forward-thinking businesses intuitively know: a touchstone of talent mobility is the interaction between inventive people. New data continue to reveal that when innovators collaborate they become greater than the sum of their parts. In this book, we will traverse the science of networks, the maps of inventor collaborations, and the geographies of competition policy to discover an updated wisdom: when it comes to the war for talent, we must choose our battles wisely. The departure of valuable employees can be a double blow to a company: the company loses a trained, talented individual, and its competitors gain from the loss by acquiring an insider as a new key player in their operation. This is corporate judo: using an enemy's own energy against him. As we shall see, clauses designed to restrict postemployment activities have become an almost universal feature of employment contracts. At the same time, while companies are buying into the control mentality, attempting to hide ideas and restrict their talent, this mentality conflicts with the fact that innovation universally depends on the flow of knowledge and people in a competitive market. As competitors and as a society, we must keep our eye on the nurturing of talent as a rivalrous yet common resource.

Several developments have coalesced in recent years to create new contemporary realities and redefine our conception of the talent wars and human capital controls. First, global competition, employment practices, teamwork, and labor market mobility have all challenged the way we think about a competitive edge in innovation. Second, we now have cutting-edge scientific knowledge that is revealing the foundations of successful innovation and is enabling us to assess more effectively the wisdom of different strategies and policies. Finally, the heightened significance of human capital and intellectual property has led to record numbers of disputes and conflicts. In some high-tech industries it is common practice to include litigation expenses when calculating the expected costs of a new start-up. Contributing to the already complex structure of these battles over the control of talent and knowledge, high jurisdictional variation and uncertainty about the scope of human capital and intellectual property rights raise serious concerns about the inefficiencies of current arrangements. Around the world policy makers and businesses are rethinking their innovation strategies, signifying the discontent with outdated and misguided approaches. At a time when the United States is facing its fiercest competition from Europe, China, India, and others, many countries and states are either in the process of reforming or are debating such reforms. Nevertheless, despite the consensus on the general goals of promoting entrepreneurship and development, there has been little agreement on how to achieve these goals. This book will demystify perceptions and false dilemmas in these debates and redirect us to a more informed conversation about smarter human capital strategies. In search of an updated vision that matches reality, we will be better equipped for the task of sustaining an innovative edge in contemporary competitive markets. I think you will find that this book helps you imagine better ways to manage ideas and the people who conceive them.

PART ONE THE HUMAN CAPITAL PRIORITY

IT'S A WAR OUT THERE. We need good employees, and we are fighting over the most talented people. Our natural reaction to loss is to try and hold on. Managers, CEOs, and even economists often have those same kneejerk reactions and default to a control mentality. But what does control really do? Are they guarding the castle or self-inflicting injuries? Here is the conflict: companies desperately need independent minds in order to be competitive, but the act of jealously guarding those minds wilts their independence and stagnates economic growth.

So how do we strike the right balance? We begin by looking at the different global efforts to win "the balance of the brains." President Barack Obama has declared this century's new Sputnik moment to be about future innovation. We recognize that the yet-to-be-invented depends on the ability of countries and industries to nurture and retain talent. But we don't know how to achieve this competitive edge. As the war over talent has become global, two important developments in the labor market collide: great expectations from workers at all levels and zero expectation of long-term employment. The only remedy for this inevitable collision will come from a deeper understanding of human capital management.

As the industrial era has given way to a digital era, we've loosened controls over the ways people work in their daily job routine, but not in how, where, and why they work. This gap is where the edge of innovation lies. I suggest that we have before us two paths, two competing models for thinking about the war over talent and human capital controls. The first, the Orthodox Model, tells us that to reap the fruits of innovation we must control. This sentiment runs though debates about ownership, intellectual property, corporate investment, finance, and economic growth. Even though it has been challenged on many fronts, it has remained in full force with regard to human capital development. The alternative path, the Dynamic Model, will serve us as we explore the wisdom of human capital strategies: innovation is positively linked to dynamic flows of information and people, stemming from motivational and aggregate benefits of the freedom to move among ventures. As we move along this path, we will consider new evidence about the benefits of looser controls—benefits that span inventors, companies, industries, and regions. In order for innovation to flourish, all of us, managers, competitors, economists, and lawyers, must learn to overcome our control mentality.

CHAPTER ONE

The Talent Wars

For a serial kidnapper, [the government headhunter] Philip Yeo looks harmless enough. But to hear some people tell it, he's a dangerous man. Over the past six years, Yeo has been roaming the world, trailing talented scientists in Washington; San Diego; Palo Alto, Calif.; Edinburgh and elsewhere, and spiriting them back to his home country of Singapore.

—*Time magazine*

THE BALANCE OF THE BRAINS

"TALENT HAS BECOME the world's most sought-after commodity," declared the *Economist* in 2006. Since then, the war to acquire talent has become even fiercer. As the workplace has changed, the global economic landscape has flattened. In the not-so-distant past, the developing world, including China, India, Brazil, Eastern Europe, and the Persian Gulf countries, supplied cheap labor, while North America and a handful of European countries dominated the high-end labor market. But not anymore! The so-called Third World is catching up and presenting unprecedented challenges and competition. One indication of these changes is that, despite past traditions of lifetime employment and worker loyalty, the "stick rate"—the length of time hired candidates stay at their jobs—is now lower in Asia than in the United States and Europe.[1]

13

Like venture capitalists (or vulture capitalists, as some managers perceive them when these investors are poaching their best workers), countries around the world are engaged in intense efforts to draw talent. Singapore, a rising high-tech hub in the global arena, has an international talent division within the government charged with finding ways to attract the most highly qualified people from abroad. Philip Yeo, characterized as the "serial kidnapper," heads Singapore's international talent division. More than a headhunter, Yeo prefers to describe himself as "a people snatcher." In an interview Yeo describes the changes in the American market atmosphere which help Singapore lure talent: "In the past, America was like a Golden Mountain. Now it is very forbidding. Every foreigner is a threat, and the whole atmosphere is changing."[2] In his book *Innovation Nation* John Kao calls for more attention to "the art of seduction" in global competition. According to Kao, talent is being lured to up-and-coming regions at alarming rates. New competition from Europe and the East has led the sociologist Richard Florida to sound similarly severe warnings about the United States becoming "a second-rate economy that cannot deliver economic opportunities for the vast majority of its people or the social welfare of Western European countries." And all the warnings point to one country that seems to be leaping forward to soon take over the lead as the world's strongest economy—China.

In January 2011 President Obama evoked the image of a new Cold War. As in 1957, when the Soviet Union launched the first earth-orbiting satellite, Sputnik, the United States now risks watching passively as a new empire, China, slowly but steadily becomes the dominant superpower in the global economy. Obama warned that China has "the fastest trains and the fastest computers in the world." And estimates abound that in just a few years other countries, not only China, will surpass the United States in vital technological fields. To catch up and take the lead, the United States must become more innovative in every field. The day after Obama made his remarks then Senator John Kerry reiterated and elaborated on the meaning of using the historical iconic image of the Soviet Sputnik for the twenty-first-century challenge of innovation: "We need R-and-D; we need science, technology, engineering, and math. We need to kick America into gear. This is our Sputnik moment. We've sort of seen Sputnik going across the sky, but we've done nothing similar to what we did in the 1960s to respond to it."

The Cold War's balance of power focused on a nuclear arms race, but modern international competition focuses on talent. And it is not just high-tech, biotech, and information markets that simmer with national and international movement. In *The Flight of the Creative Class* Florida warns that the nation's talent base is weakening in every field of the sciences, art, and economics ventures. Although American universities draw talented foreign students, many no longer seek to stay and work in the American market. According to the National Science Foundation, about half of the doctorate degree holders currently working in the United States in the fields of science, engineering, and computer technology are foreign born. Yet now we can no longer rely on the best of the best staying in the country as they begin their professional careers. In a dark ending to his latest book, *The Reset Economy*, Florida gives even stronger warnings: "We can then expect an ever-increasing malaise and depression in our R&D laboratories, ennui and apathy in our factories, and increased crime in our streets." Other authors, such as Amy Chua in her controversial *Battle Hymn of the Tiger Mother*, have further played into our fears of the new Sputnik-like rivalry with China to promote their tough-love style of parenting and careering. In her book Chua maintains that the Chinese parent their children in ways superior to those of Western parents, leading to a clear competitive advantage in the race for academic and professional success. In reality, the prognosis is not as grim as that of Florida, and the right cure is not as radical as that of Chua. Western parents certainly need not concede that they have become, in the words of the former governor of Pennsylvania Ed Rendell, "a nation of wusses." But there is truth in the notion that the United States is losing its competitive edge. Parenting in a certain style or churning out ten thousand extra doctoral graduates a year is not the way to regain our edge. Rather, our focus must be on the talent pool and our ability as businesses and as a society to nurture it.

OUR NEW SPUTNIK MOMENT

We all recognize that human capital and knowledge have become the dominant assets of the twenty-first century. But we have not yet figured out how to reconcile the key need for talent with the new realities of market competition. Companies must rely on strong, innovative people to maintain their edge, and workers must rely on their ability to change employers to remain in the labor force. We move among jobs far more frequently than we did just a decade ago, and most of us don't expect to stay at the same workplace for more than three or four years. More than that, the movement between jobs does not occur at random. Inventors of more valuable patents are more likely to move. A recent study finds that in many competitive industries one in three employees is approached by other firms attempting to recruit him away from his current job. Thomas Edison once modestly claimed that inventive genius is "99% perspiration and 1% inspiration." Yet the intensity of competitive bidding for super-stars in every market suggests that we believe talent is rare enough for business competitors to launch a full-on war to attain it. Companies will go so far in their efforts to collect talent as to acquire start-ups for multi-millions of dollars only to discard the purchased product and absorb the acquired team of people.

President Obama previously invoked the image of the Soviet Sputnik and the new race for innovation in a speech at the Forsyth Technical Community College in Winston-Salem, North Carolina, on December 6, 2010. He explained that he chose to speak at the tech college because it provides everyone, from high school graduates to laid-off autoworkers, new skills that enable them to work in the industries of the future. The pattern is set: re-skilling, moving to new jobs, and nurturing talent for the industries of the future. Today's market expectations, however, are in tension. While there is no longer job security, there is far more reliance on talent. This is our new Sputnik moment, but we have yet to under-stand how to get our talent rocket into space. The problem is that we've been focusing only on part of the picture. We're debating parenting styles and internal management styles, and we're thinking about colleges and training centers. But we have yet to think of ways to generate talent pools and then sustain them at the very core of economic production: within the market itself. Not just before entering the market or during junctures but over the course of lifelong careers, the key is that we need to under-stand how to fight over talent in lasting and productive ways.

LESS SECURITY, MORE TALENT

During the late twentieth century, as mass manufacturing was rapidly being transplanted to less costly facilities overseas, the United States and other developed countries experienced dramatic shifts in the way people work. We began focusing on specialization and advanced technology coupled with higher expectations of skill and adaptability to change. As industries came to rely on constant innovation and change to remain competitive, they transformed our expectations about employment longevity. During the industrial era, work relations were based on a social contract that promised secure, long-term, and full-time work. Promotion was internal, which assured long-term job security and progressive seniority-based compensation structures. At companies like Ford Motors, the iconic industrial-era company, workers expected to begin and end their adult working lives with the same employer. The postwar New Dealers relied on these assumptions of lifetime employment as they instituted a regime of collective bargaining through unions. Job security and stability continued to be the gold standard of employment until quite recently. IBM, one of the first megacompanies of the high-tech industry, was originally built on the same concepts of loyalty and long-term commitment as earlier industrial companies like Ford. So when IBM began laying off its employees in the early 1990s, it signaled a dramatic ground shift. The old expectations of long-term employment became apparent in the anger of IBM workers: "To be an IBM executive was to have great significance. 'We were part of a great big family,' said John Young, a tall, broad-shouldered man of 52. 'The manager was a father figure. In exchange, workers put in long hours and the spouses dutifully did their part.'" When asked about the layoffs, John's wife described a "sense of great betrayal."[3] In the two decades since IBM's startling layoffs, a new model of flexible relationships between employers and their employees has become the new gold standard for organizing work.

Boundaryless is the new buzzword of the modern work model, signifying the rapid movement of workers from job to job.[4] Workers can no longer expect to stay at the same worksite or with the same employer for more than a short period of their work cycle. Production is itself unbounded in the sense that it now occurs over long chains of subsidiaries, each step often taking place in a number of countries around the world. As businesses seek more flexibility in their hiring and production practices, they contract with employment agencies, themselves a booming industry dedicated to serving as intermediaries in the placement and recruitment of workers. Until recently we had two distinct circles of employees: the core insiders, working for large, stable firms, and the outsiders, part-time, temporary, seasonal, or simply atypical workers. The outsiders formed a secondary labor market typically employed in low-wage, low-skill, unstable jobs that disproportionately included minorities, women, and immigrants. These were the workers that were also more likely to be leased employees, working temporarily through an employment agency. Nowadays, insiders and outsiders mean something very different. Almost a third of all workers today do not follow the traditional full-time, permanent employee status. Even in established high-tech companies such as Microsoft, approximately one-third of the workforce is leased or employed as temporary employees or independent consultants. In short, the atypical worker of the past, the part-time, temporary, leased, and subcontracted worker, is becoming the twenty-first century's typical worker. The lines between insiders and outsiders have collapsed. Most important, even if you are a full-time employee hired directly by a large company, the likelihood that you will switch jobs within the next few years is high. From high-tech to entertainment, from services to sales, skilled workers are growing accustomed to moving between various short-term jobs.

"A MIND THAT'S WEAK AND A BACK THAT'S STRONG"

Winston Churchill predicted in a prophetic speech at an assembly in 1943 that "the empires of the future will be empires of the mind." Churchill's words resonate with what we expect today from the talent we employ; innovation must happen everywhere and depends on inspired people. A specialized research setting and the shop floor of a factory can both become creativity nurseries, but "empires of the mind" don't just happen by accident. Our ability to fan the sparks of productivity and creativity into raging fires of productivity and creativity depends on our ability to support these empires and thereby help workers reach their potential.

The recognition that we need to cultivate our workers' creativity has brought us to a startling point in history because for a long time most work was not conceptualized as being creative. It is illuminating to look back on how our expectations of our labor force have changed. Throughout the industrial era of the nineteenth and early twentieth centuries workers were not expected to invent, innovate, or be creative; they were expected to manufacture a widget and package it. As a result, work environments were not at all conducive to enhancing innovative capacities. The prevailing image of the worker was captured in lyrics by the country singer and songwriter Merle Travis describing the woes of his fellow coal miners: "Some people say a man is made out of mud/A poor man's made out of muscle and blood/Muscle and blood, skin and bones/A mind that's weak and a back that's strong."

Even further back, in the eighteenth and early nineteenth centuries, the imagery of workers resembled one of dependent children. They served their employers for a prolonged and in some cases involuntary period of time. Historians of this preindustrial era describe employment as being akin to family relations since employees often worked their entire adult lives for one employer. Status (work status *and* social status) was fixed and defined the entirety of work relations. In the legal world, rules about work were given a very appropriate title: master–servant law. Obedience was the iron rule. In return for obedience the master had an obligation to care for the worker's basic needs, including food and shelter. At the same time, although obedience was the rule, because of the more contained nature of early agriculture and artisan production, in which an entire product was made in the confines of one place, the actual workday was often less controlled than the industrial workday. The shift to mass industrialization during the late nineteenth century profoundly trans-formed the labor market. Work began to convert rapidly from small-scale production to large-scale manufacturing. The rise of commerce also produced increasingly complex employment relations. Layers of manage-rial and supervisory positions were invented and staffed; hierarchies were built. Now organized in large assembly-line factories, work became more and more impersonal. The modern corporation became the prevalent form of economic organization. By the early twentieth century, we had developed into what the historian Raymond Hogler terms "the Era of Management." In the Era of Management industrial production was centrally controlled, meticulously organized, and strictly supervised.

Henry Ford, the father of the Era of Management (or Fordism), implemented great control over the workers of the Ford Motor Company: rows of uniformed laborers performed identical movements in his auto-mobile assembly line. Under his leadership, the auto industry became the epitome of the industrial era. As in Travis's somber ballad, the paternal-istic image of the industrial worker was that of an individual with "a mind that's weak and a back that's strong." Leaders of the industrial revolution believed that the best way to define jobs was strictly and narrowly. Work on the assembly line at the Ford Corporation was standardized and isolated with clearly defined hierarchies.[5] Men would punch in at precisely 8 a.m. and, except for their designated breaks, stand at their post for nine hours. Assembly-line production was as revolutionary as it was central to the auto industry's ability to mass-produce affordable cars. Instead of workers working together as a team of skilled manufacturers building a complete car from beginning to end, Ford introduced the idea of the car coming to the worker: the worker remains at his fixed line location and performs the same task over and over. Such compartmentalization of roles was applied even across company departments, discouraging inter- action among coworkers. Frederick Taylor, the father of the early twentieth-century theory of scientific management (or Taylorism), provided the academic backing to Ford's practical reforms. Taylor believed that groups of people working together were less efficient than individu- ated, autonomous workers.[6] According to his theory, managerial plan- ning of the production must be strictly monitored from top to bottom. Tasks should be so specified and production steps broken down so finely as to eliminate the need for workers to think. Applying Taylor's scientific management theory, managers were trained to use time and motion studies, which measured the exact performance pavement and move- ment of an average worker, to develop the rules of performance for each step of assembly-line production. The ideal worker of the era was an unskilled cog in a machine, robotically performing the same task as effi- ciently as possible.

Naturally, Taylorism also involved strict hierarchies and rigid bound- aries between management and workers. Symbolic structures were put in place to make this line more pronounced. Workers were paid by the hour, while managers had salaries. Workers went to one cafeteria, managers to another. There were even separate entrances and parking lots. These distinct separations conveyed the message that talent and skill were not considered pervasively important across all ranks. Yet even then the great industrialists had a sense of the significance of their workers. One of the most prominent business leaders of the era, the steel legend Andrew Carnegie, said, "Take away my people, but leave my factories and soon grass will grow on the factory floors. . . . Take away my factories, but leave my people and soon we will have a new and better factory." Carnegie signaled by these words that steel was the raw ingredient, but his workers were the life of the industry. Still, the general state of mind of the industrial era was that workers were replaceable, needed to be controlled, and should be discouraged from engaging in creative activity.

LOOSENING CONTROLS: THE GIFT OF CONDUCTORS

The author A. A. Milne once said that one of the advantages of being disorderly is that one is constantly making exciting discoveries. Business leaders of the industrial era saw things differently. Order was an organizing principle, and hierarchy reigned. The boss was the boss, and most workers were discouraged from questioning orders or venturing beyond the narrow definition of their job. In the past few decades, however, as the nature of work and competition has changed dramatically, management theories have also evolved. What was once the conventional wisdom of management no longer holds true.

The pace of competition and production in the twenty-first century places demands on businesses that are different from those of the industrial era. In the postindustrial era, or what can be called the knowledge economy or the digital era, innovation is the lifeblood of corporations. Intangible assets—a company's ideas, people, and brand—are now the primary assets of many companies. Study after study shows that intangible assets are becoming the largest component of a corporation's asset base. But these assets come with built-in vulnerability. Even when innovation is protected as intellectual property, in the digital age duplication and dissemination can happen at the speed of light. Technology now enables competitors to swiftly find ways to copy, improve, and compete. Thus, rapid depreciation rates of innovation require the best and most innovative talent, and they require a management style that brings out the best of this talent.

Consider an orchestra and its conductor as a metaphor for the new workplace. An orchestra conductor is charged with creating perfect harmony via visual cues. The longtime conductor Itay Talgman, who has studied the styles of great conductors, concludes that the best conductor is the one who allows order to emerge from chaos. Without commanding, a great conductor creates the conditions for great music. Great conductors don't require musicians to connect the dots or paint by numbers. They radiate the joy of enabling multiple stories to be heard at the same time. The great conductor supports individual flow and facilitates the merging of each stream of creativity into harmonious success. And in the process, noise becomes music.

As a prelude to thinking about changing management styles, consider the contrast between two renowned conductors. The Italian conductor Riccardo Muti is an old-school conductor whose style of leading his orchestra involves command and control. You might say he is the Ford Motors of conductors. Muti has been called an autocrat, and although he is considered one of the truly great contemporary conductors, his career has not been without controversy. He frequently pulls out of productions when he disagrees with the orchestra's musical interpretations. As a boss, he seems to be rigid about accepting input from his team and resistant to any attempt by his musicians to think outside the box. In fact, in 2003 the world-renowned orchestra musicians of the storied opera house La Scala in Milan lodged a complaint against Muti, describing him as overly controlling. They complained that, as a conductor, Muti did not allow his musicians to develop creatively and refused to hire prominent guest conductors who he feared might threaten his reign. The musicians felt Muti was using them as instruments (or, rather literally, as an extension of their instruments) and not as partners. The most critical commentators describe Muti as "drunk with himself, drugged by his own art and his own personal vanity; he can only talk about himself; he's become a caricature of a conductor."[7] After years of conflict Muti eventually resigned from La Scala and in 2010 was appointed as the music director of the Chicago Symphony Orchestra.

Now, contrast Muti's style with that of perhaps the world's most famous conductor, Herbert von Karajan, who conducted the Berlin Philharmonic orchestra for thirty-five years. Karajan had the gift of commanding without controlling. One of his greatest skills was creating conditions that facilitated the creative process. He was not domineering; his musicians were not ordered to perform in a certain way. Under Karajan, their potential was allowed to flourish, and creativity was encouraged. In the music world the consensus is that Karajan had the ability to extract the most beautiful and harmonic music possible from his orchestra without being a taskmaster. Karajan closed his eyes when he conducted, signaling to his orchestra that the harmony should be found internally and that the connections would be found by listening. When asked about his conducting style, he mused that the most detrimental thing he could do to his orchestra members would be to give them very clear instructions. In Karajan's view, commands would prevent his musicians from listening to each other and finding the harmony; restraint would stifle the orchestra and mute the result.

In our new economy, as in the world of music, spontaneous and innovative activity from employees produces the most startling stories of success. Encouragement that reflects the desire for innovation pushes productivity beyond any specific role description. The best managers encourage their employees to do more than simply follow managerial orders. The mantra is to do more, be different, and be better. If the organizing principle of the industrial era was to command, the method of the new era is to coordinate.[8] As early as the late 1960s, Alfred Sloan, the celebrated longtime president of General Motors, suggested experimentation with "job enlargement." Under this new vision individual workers slowly but steadily began to receive far more autonomy. Sloan was a visionary, anticipating more than fifty years ago that workers needed more discretion and freedom to think in order to optimally perform.

Today, Sloan's experiment of allowing more discretion to ground-level employees has become the norm. Too much control snuffs out the flame of creativity. Talented workers exercising discretion and creativity at all levels of the organization are needed for competitive survival. While the old workplace was marked with boundaries and rigid lines, the new workplace is flatter in its structure and more open and transparent, allowing for more employee freedom and potential innovation. As companies face change at unprecedented rates, they feel the need to hire employees who are themselves willing to change along with the task at hand. The manager's role has shifted from that of boss to that of a coach or an orchestrator; she is more of a leader among equals than a controlling supervisor. As Marin Alsop, the conductor of the Baltimore Symphony, eloquently put it, "I'm blessed with 100 people who want to be the best they can be, and they're just waiting for me to enable them to do it."

Like great conductors, the best managers are great listeners, and their egos are tied to the success of the entire team they are leading. A great manager's goal should be to empower rather than control, to facilitate rather than micromanage. The smartest leaders recognize that authority need not be a zero-sum game. Freedom to flourish enhances a company—its ability to identify, absorb, and utilize information, knowledge, and skill. The twenty-first-century corporation thrives when the person at the top is a facilitator who coordinates and motivates the ranks, asking employees to think rather than simply take orders. Curtis Carlson, the chief executive officer of SRI International in Silicon Valley, has posited "Carlson's law" of innovation: "In a world where so many people now have access to education and cheap tools of innovation, innovation that happens from the bottom up tends to be chaotic but smart. Innovation that happens from the top down tends to be orderly but dumb." In the innovative company, coordinated chaos brings the most promising discoveries.

ACQ-HIRE: MAKING PEOPLE DECISIONS

We have loosened the controls of our management style, recognizing over the years that our competitive edge rests on independent thinking by our best talent. But we still have not given up the control mentality when it comes to our talent wars—our struggle to recruit, contain, and control human capital, its flow, and knowledge. If we take seriously the notion of freedom in nourishing talent, we must examine how talent is fought over, enlisted, and retained in an organization. Companies today are so focused on talent that those who can afford it are buying entire companies only to acquire human resources. The tech blogs are buzzing with *acq-hire* reports: "Google Buys Social Search Startup Angstro, Acq-Hires Co-Founder Khare";[9] "The team behind Brizzly, one of the better Twitter apps out there, is reportedly being acq-hired by AOL";[10] "Motorola Acqu-Hires Cappuccino Developers."[11] Still, despite inventing a new verb that signals the centrality of talent to a company, matching people to jobs remains one of the most challenging and underdeveloped aspects of management. In the words of one management expert, "Consider the way companies make their financial decisions: with rigor, professionalism and the application of advance knowledge. Contrast this with how people decisions are made. More often than not, the process is distinguished by a lack of rigor at every step, from figuring out when a change is needed all the way to the integration of the selected candidate."[12]

Decisions about hiring and retention involve evaluating a company's needs and direction; assessing existing workers and comparing them to potential hires; training and incentivizing their creativity; identifying when it is worth keeping employees and when it is time to let go; deciding when the time is right for a change; and knowing where and how to search for and attract new talent. There is a vast range of how systematically (or unsystematically) all of these decisions unfold. While some companies are utterly disorganized in their hiring practices, others are extremely methodical. Some companies go so far as to develop detailed schematics for the process: calculating the costs of recruitment from each college campus they work with and comparing it to the return on investment from that college, computing the yield rate, the relative progress of those recruits, and their retention rates.[13] When the time comes to evaluate existing talent, some companies, adopting the famous vitality model introduced by Jack Welch of General Electric, implement a formal "rank and yank" system, in which a percentage of low-performing employees are fired annually while the top performers are showered with rewards and promotions. Other businesses take a more intuitive process, allowing each recruit to be handled case by case by the people closest to the candidate's field. Either way, in the past, companies would go to great pains to avoid hiring the wrong person. But strategists warn businesses that, ironically, they may be eliminating some of their best candidates by overinvesting in the screening process. Instead, companies need to expedite their hiring and strengthen their retention processes. In other words, the default may be shifting to cutting red tape at the hiring stage—maybe even going so far as overhiring—and then keeping only the most outstanding.

However systematic or chaotic the decision about recruitment, hiring, and promotion is in your business or profession, the reality of simmering tension remains; the need for a constant stream of innovative insiders clashes with a surge in job mobility and battles over talent. Managers must face the dilemma of whether to train employees who are likely to move elsewhere rather quickly. Businesses are anxious about the fast turnover and zealous poaching of their best employees by their competitors. They also worry about whether their recruitment efforts will result in litigation. Beyond the tangible concerns, the anxiety around the clash between need and reality means that we have to grapple with the ways in which commitment has evolved. The dynamics of work commitment have changed, and performance is now decoupled from stability and long-term security. Workers who no longer receive the promise of job security wonder what type of reciprocal commitment they can expect from their employer. Focusing on management approaches within the organization, strategists are intent on understanding these new dynamics. Rosabeth Kanter of the Harvard Business School advises, for example, that employers build active commitment rather than loyalty; professional pride rather than long-term attachment.[14] Now that we see more clearly the patterns, the missing link appears before us: connecting the goals of commitment and innovation with the ongoing dynamics of the talent wars. Put more simply, the acute question on the minds of managers today is: How do we meet the challenge of keeping our best performers from leaving and taking their ideas and skills elsewhere? And how should we react when, inevitably, some of these most talented people become competitors?

CHAPTER TWO

Innovation's Edge

TWO COMPETING MODELS

IN EVERY INDUSTRY, managers I talk to say their most valuable assets walk out the door to go home every night. General Mills is one of the world's largest food companies, manufacturing and marketing such major brands as Betty Crocker, Cheerios, and Pillsbury. By the company's own estimation, the departure of a single senior marketing executive can cost the company millions of dollars as marketing knowledge, client contacts, and personal relationships walk out the door with him.[1] Not surprisingly, a natural reaction is to vigilantly protect against loss. The protectionist mentality, however, is dangerous because it automatically frames job mobility as a threat. Within this frame of mind, we see companies reducing efforts to develop their mobile talent; managers reacting irrationally to the departure of talent; and businesses locked in counterproductive battles in reaction to the flow of talent. Traditional economic analysis understands loss in the same flat way as the intuitive protectionist mentality: the orthodox economic view has been that human capital and intellectual property controls are necessary limitations stemming from the fact that, absent such protections, employers would underinvest in employee training. The view continues with the following idea: since employees generally lack the resources to self-finance their training and skill development, they will exchange their freedom in return for training.

In this view, mobility restrictions and information controls, through noncompete agreements, nondisclosure restrictions, and patent and copyright transfers, allow and promote efficient investment in human capital.[2]

In the 1960s the Nobel laureate Gary Becker distinguished between general and specific job training. General training includes skills that are valuable to many companies in a given industry, while specific training and skills are useful only within a particular firm. Becker understood that we "cannot separate a person from his or her knowledge and skills the way it is possible to move physical and financial assets while the owner stays put."[3] Still, Becker theorized that, in a perfect market, workers would pay for their general training and knowledge acquisition while firms would pay for specific training.[4] In this ideal world, the employer would not care if the employee left with information because the employee would already have paid for the value of training and any generally valuable information. In other words, Zuckerberg would pay the Winkelvosses for his exposure to their Harvard Connection project (and all the computing experience that comes with working on building a social network) at the moment he agreed to work on the project. Then, if he leaves to start working on his own social network ideas, no harm is done, as he has already paid his dues. If this were actually possible, there would be no need for restraints on worker mobility.

In reality, most employees cannot afford the cost of learning from their employer, be it general or firm-specific skills. Economic realities create an environment in which employees are almost always unable to pay for their own training and for learning valuable trade secrets, both because of the direct expense and because of the large pay cuts required to dedicate time to training. Most of the time it is impractical, even impossible, to assess the value of learning secrets within an organization before the secrets have been put to good use and translated into market value. As a result, according to the orthodox economic view, firms seek instead to restrict their employees' future opportunities to prevent appropriation of their investment. In other words, future restrictions on competition give present comfort. Allowing employers to implement such restrictions, goes the traditional economic story, encourages companies to foster investment.[5]

The classic model, which has informed (and has likely been informed by—a symbiotic reinforcement of alarms!) our control mentality, therefore predicts that without the protections afforded by noncompetes, trade

BOX 1

THE ORTHODOX MODEL

More company controls = more R&D and human capital investment.

secrets, and patent/copyright assignment agreements, employers would underinvest in people training, research, and development (box 1).[6]

Our journey into the world of the talent wars is aimed at enriching our understanding of the human capital–innovation nexus. It adds a dynamic perspective to the orthodox economic view by looking at the investment incentives of both businesses and talented employees over time. As we shall soon see, new evidence casts serious doubt on the assumption about decreased investment by firms under more mobile regimes. But our lessons will go further than that. We will see that the model is incomplete. It fails to take into account the impact over time of human capital controls as well as the effects of such controls on human motivation. Our quest to understand talent wars brings us to the lands of the science of innovation, creativity, and productivity. I invite readers to consider the tradeoff between controls and freedoms within these richer lands.

Before we delve into these tradeoffs, let us compare the traditional economic model that has long informed our control-bound mentality to the new model. The Dynamic Model differs significantly from the Orthodox Model because it captures insights about the complex workings of markets. Consider the motivation of inventors. Intuitively, we know that competition enhances motivation and excellence. Also intuitively, think about the multiplier effect of successful generations of economic growth: talent attracts talent; knowledge builds on knowledge; talent mobility enhances professional ties; and a virtuous cycle of innovation is set into motion. We recognize these effects in our daily lives, but for years the mentality of control has pervaded competition over talent.

While the remarkable benefits of loosening controls become clearer, our new model also acknowledges that companies have legitimate concerns. Companies rightly worry about the risks of leaking valuable information and ideas and about losing customers and employees. Our ultimate goal is not to deny the tradeoffs and the risks but to be smarter in how we deal with their overall implications. We will see how some controls are important while other control strategies have simply gone too far. I present here a graphic depiction of the model that we will soon examine more closely (fig. 2.1). You are probably familiar with many of the buzzwords in today's innovation debates: networks, collaboration,

---

THE DYNAMIC MODEL

Time 0 (During employment):

1) Controls encourage firms to invest in their employees' human capital.
2) Freedoms discourage individuals to invest in their own human capital.
3) Freedoms encourages alternative reward systems that effectively trigger innovation.

Time 1 (Post-employment):

4) Controls prevent loss of talent and secrets.
5) Freedoms enhance:
   - market competition
   - better talent-firm fit
   - reduced search costs for new talent
   - "new blood" moments
   - stronger inventor networks
   - richer talent pools
   - knowledge flows
   - entrepreneurship
   - regional "brain gain"

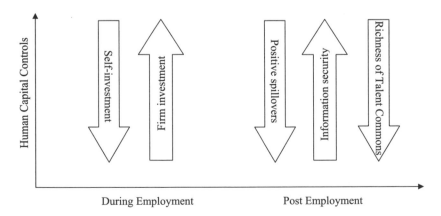

Fig 2.1. The Dynamic Model.

outsourcing, crowd-sourcing, flow, entrepreneurship, and social capital. The list goes on. While we know a great deal about how these ideas apply to current debates about management styles and even about intellectual property generally, our blind spot has been in our treatment of our new Sputnik—the quest for sustaining innovative human capital. Too often these abstract ideas fail to translate to actual strategies when it comes to the most important source of innovation: people.

TALENT IS ALIVE, LONG LIVE TALENT

The utopian cyber thinker Stewart Brand is famous for coining the phrase "information wants to be free." These words were instantly turned into the battle cry of the movements calling for the eradication of intellectual property controls. Activists decry the extent to which patent, copyright, trade secrets, and trademark laws have limited the use and reuse of ideas and information. A closer look at Brand's words, however, reveals that he understood the "desires" of information as being more complex than simple freedom, and the world of innovation as being full of conflicting pushes and pulls, costs and benefits. The phrase comes from the first Hackers' Conference in 1984, at which Brand stated, "On the one hand information wants to be expensive, because it's so valuable. The right information in the right place just changes your life. On the other hand, information wants to be free, because the cost of getting it out is getting lower and lower all the time."

Here lies the classic tension between the protection and promotion of the flow of knowledge. We want to ensure that information is produced, but we also want that same information to be put to good use once it is produced. When it comes to talent, the puzzle is more complex still. We want to invest in skill and professional growth, and we want the fruits of this investment to be used for our benefit. We want talent to be nurtured, but we also want talent to thrive. For a long time now economists have assumed that the objectives of labor mobility and human capital investment are fundamentally at odds: why invest in something (or someone) that will be leaving you? The bottom line has been that employers would be discouraged from investing in the training of mobile workers. But new hard evidence and a fresh intuition suggest otherwise. Our Dynamic Model suggests that the more flow and mobility, the greater the investment in human capital and innovation.

Understandably, this creates a puzzle for economists. The new evidence has led the prominent legal economists Richard Posner and William Landes, who were central in crafting modern intellectual property analysis, to discuss postemployment restrictions with a tone of uncertainty: "It is not even clear," they admit, "that enforcing employee covenants not to compete generates social benefits in excess of its social costs."[7]

We have long been aware of the troubling features of information monopolies; information, by its very nature, seems to demand freedom. If it does not flow naturally, we cannot progress as a society, build on generations of creativity, or use knowledge to promote innovation. But notice the key feature of the talent wars: human capital controls. Human capital controls, instead of targeting information itself (whether through patent, copyright, or locking up a secret formula in a vault), are about the carrier of the information. Mobility restraints target knowledge as embodied within a person. These controls also target interpersonal relationships. Human capital controls, including noncompetes, trade secrets, and preinvention assignment requirements, do not restrict just the use of information; they also restrict careers and connections that are born between people. Such is the innovation puzzle: we want to allow companies and individuals to reap the fruit of their investment, but at the same time we want to encourage the positive outcomes of the free flow of talent and ideas. The goal we strive for must be a balance between encouraging initial investment in human capital, training, and research and encouraging information sharing, further improvement, and growth. We don't want to deprive firms of their returns from their investment in people—but, as with information, even more so with people: incentives and benefits are complex. Stages are not sequential. Balancing occurs between the firm's interest and the motivations of its employees and competitors; between individual fairness and economic welfare; and between investment in innovation and subsequent flow. Although these pairs seem to be balanced—firm versus employee; industry growth versus corporate growth; initial innovation and subsequent innovations—they are not necessarily dichotomous. Often these goals and interests are not conflicted. Talent wants to be developed, but it also wants to be free and put to good use, and the most successful innovators are showing us that we can do both.

INVESTIGATING THE NEW MODEL

Below is a standard contract similar to one that many of you have required employees to sign or that you have been required to sign. Let's assume your company is BioGen, an up-and-coming biotech firm. BioGen's standard employment agreement states in its preamble that the company needs to protect its rights to confidential business and product information, inventions, and customer relationships. The contract contains dozens of provisions and legalese, but at the heart of the matter sit these restrictions:

1. *Restrictions on Competition:* While employed by BioGen, and for two years after, Employee will not be employed or affiliated in any capacity by, become an independent contractor or consultant for, or perform any services for a competing organization.

2. *Nondisclosure:* Employee agrees not to use or disclose any CONFIDENTIAL INFORMATION to or for the benefit of anyone other than BioGen, either during or after Employment for as long as the information remains confidential. Employee agrees and understands that this provision prohibits Employee from rendering services to a competing organization to the extent that Employee would use, disclose, rely upon, or be induced to use confidential information.

3. *Ownership and Assignment:* All inventions and ideas shall be the exclusive property of BioGen. Employee hereby assigns all inventions and future inventions to BioGen. Any INVENTION relating to the business of BioGen with respect to which Employee files a patent application within one year following termination of Employee's employment shall be presumed to be conceived by Employee during the term of Employee's employment.

The world of human capital controls—or employment intellectual property (EIP)—is revealed in these three clauses. Companies make regular use of these standard contracts containing noncompete, nondisclosure, and intellectual property assignment provisions. These EIP strategies—the laws, contracts, and norms that shape the field—are important to every firm, large or small, in every industry, and they affect one's likelihood of

Table 2.1

Schematic Table of Human Capital Tradeoffs

	CONTROLS	FREE FLOW ALTERNATIVE
Noncompetes	Protect Employer's Investment in Skills & Training	Protect Job Mobility and Freedom of Occupation
Nondisclosure Agreements & Trade Secrets	Protect Employer's Valuable Secrets	Protect Knowledge Dissemination
Invention/ Copyright Assignment	Protect Research & Development Investment	Allow Use of Inventions and Creative Expression

success in surprising ways. We know that human capital and intellectual property are inexorably intertwined with economic success. Under the Orthodox Model, though, strategies for controlling them have been understood to benefit companies while harming the individuals who embody them. Tracking many of the ways we traditionally debated intellectual property regimes more generally, human capital controls have been commonly understood to be helping the firm who invests in ideas, skill building, and innovation while limiting workers and future developers. These tradeoffs are illustrated in table 2.1, which begs the classic challenge: how to ensure that valuable assets are first developed (= allow control!) and subsequently put to good use (= allow freedom!).

FAIRNESS AND WELFARE

The firm, the individual, and the public good are the three forces that we constantly try to balance. The triangle of interests creates inevitable tensions. In the legal world we talk about two vectors that often need to be reconciled: fairness, focusing on the individual rights of employees and the individual interests of firms, and welfare, considering the overall gains and losses from a public perspective. For example, it may seem unfair that an employee is constrained and cannot pursue his professional career because of a postemployment restriction. But if it turns out that on the whole this constraint has led to progress in the industry, because firms confidently relied on their talent staying put, then we can say that welfare prevails.

It is easy to buy into this welfare/fairness division too much, believing that fairness and welfare must be polar opposites. The Orthodox Model suggests that welfare (that is, more overall innovation) comes from more controls. When judges feel uncomfortable with constraining talent none- theless, the majority of their concerns relate to issues of fairness toward the individual employee and her labor rights—an expression of the ever- present conflict between workers and capital. So courts and, sometimes, legislatures that seek to limit the control strategies employed in the talent wars turn to fairness justifications and posit their concerns as being about the weaker party, the worker. In response, classic economic analysis predicts that, absent severe market failure, wages will normally reflect the opportunity costs of any future contractual and regulatory restrictions on employee mobility, rendering judicial or legislative limitations on human capital controls unnecessary.[8] If you believe that people are adequately compensated for every future restriction they take upon themselves, then you might be convinced that, at least from the perspective of protecting workers, we can forgo any requirements that human capital controls imposed by business be reasonable (requirements which we will soon look at more closely) and allow human capital controls to exist as long as they fulfill the regular requirements of agreements: mutual assent and an absence of unconscionable terms. But judges and legislators have recognized that the theoretical analysis offered by economists—that compensation will follow restriction—often has little to do with market realities. Signing your life away for the proverbial lentil stew seems utterly unfair.

When I came to the United States for my graduate studies I received a Fulbright grant from the federal government. The grant required that I sign a contract, with the U.S. government no less, promising I would return to my home country upon completion of my studies at Harvard. The contract was a particularly harsh one in its terms, as one could not regain freedom by returning the grant, even with high interest. Employees encountering noncompete and other human capital restrictions face a similar feeling of a loss of freedom. The words of a recent graduate in private aviation management describing his decision to sign a noncompete reminded me of the process I encountered when signing the Fulbright contract: "It was a week away from college. I would sign anything—I would sign my life away. You don't think of those things when you're interviewing for the position. All you can think of is becoming the CEO of the company in ten years and staying with that company forever. And then reality sets in and you're underpaid and there are other companies out there."[9]

Field studies have revealed that a high percentage of employees feel compelled, perhaps even coerced, into signing a noncompete that was presented to them after they had already accepted a job offer. One recent study found that nearly 70 percent of those signing noncompetes were asked to sign them after they had accepted the offer, probably after turning down other offers. This led the lead researcher of the study to argue that "ceding the rights to one's expertise may hardly be a voluntary act."[10] Further complicating the matter is that much of the time employees sign or simply initial a general employee handbook rather than an individualized, negotiated contract. Similarly, nondisclosure agreements are riddled with information asymmetry and timing problems.[11] Normally, at the time of hiring, the employer knows far more than the employee about the material information that will be disclosed and the nature of its operation. There may even be an incentive for the employer to keep information vague in order to capture broad, uncertain aspects within the language of the restriction.[12] As a result, the employee is often asked to sign a nondisclosure agreement without first seeing the information that is the subject of the agreement as well as without knowing about the company and its likelihood to succeed.

Here, then, from the perspective of balancing interests, restrictions are a form of exploitation. Bargaining power when agreeing to restrict one's human capital becomes a policy concern for the courts. In the words of one court, "The average, individual employee has little but his labor to sell or to use to make a living. He is often in urgent need of selling it and in no position to object to boilerplate restrictive covenants placed before him to sign. To him, the right to work and support his family is the most important right he possesses. His individual bargaining power is seldom equal to that of his employer."[13] The primary concern of courts who take this perspective is the hardship that postemployment restrictions impose on an employee who wishes to leave his job, go else-where, or become independent. At their most dangerous, human capital controls such as noncompete agreements temporarily prevent workers who have trained and labored in a specific field with a specific set of knowledge from using their expertise in pursuing their passions and perhaps also from earning a living. Even the supposedly milder forms of control, such as nondisclosure agreements, can severely limit the inventor's available career options and inventive choices.

Confronting the question of labor rights and fairness produces heated debates. A handful of commentators criticize jurisdictions that limit the enforceability of noncompetes, arguing that such limitations reduce employee bargaining power by reducing employees' ability to contract for the sale of their human capital and, in turn, harming employees' wages and their employer's willingness to invest in devel-oping their skills.[14] But by far the majority of the commentators are concerned with exactly the opposite effect: that the enforceability of noncompetes from a fairness perspective limits employees' right to work and to freely choose their employer.[15] From the perspective of labor advocates, every man and woman should have the right to earn a living and pursue their profession, and noncompetes, expansive nondisclosure agreements, and other forms of human capital controls are heavy infringements upon the pursuit of that livelihood and therefore upon happiness.

One aspect of the relative bargaining powers of the two sides is worth further elaboration. Unlike my Fulbright grant, renegotiation of employment contracts is possible. And breach of an employment contract merely involves money, not deportation, as a contract with the federal government might. The Coase Theorem, a proposition by the Nobel laureate Ronald Coase, predicts that, regardless of the initial allocation of rights in society economically, efficient transactions will be reached in markets. The theorem thus suggests that if buying out of a postemploy-ment restriction is valuable enough, the former employee will renegotiate with her employer at the time of the possible breach. This analysis assumes, however, that renegotiation is available and frequent and that the cost of the breach can be covered. In reality, the costs of a breach can be sky-high. In 2005, in a highly publicized dispute, Nortel, a multina-tional telecommunications equipment manufacturer, agreed to pay

$11.5 million to settle a lawsuit with Motorola after hiring Motorola's president. Motorola launched the lawsuit just days after Nortel announced the recruitment of Motorola's former president as Nortel's new CEO. Motorola claimed that the former president's hiring was blocked for two years by his noncompete agreement. Following a contentious beginning, Nortel and Motorola negotiated a settlement. In addition, Nortel agreed to not recruit Motorola employees, to limit communications with Motorola customers, and to limit their new CEO's ability to advise Nortel on competitive strategy or analysis of Motorola. In this case, the departing employee was the highest paid, most powerful executive in the company, and his new employer had to pay millions of dollars to protect the new president's freedom. While it is unusual for the new company to go to such lengths to retain the restricted employee, the woes of the former Motorola president are not that unusual and highlight the norm. Most employees do not have the resources, information, and ability to test the validity of a restriction or to renegotiate its scope. Nor do they have the backing to risk significant monetary liabilities on a gamble if the court finds they have breached their contract. So in the end, more likely than not, most ex-employees will choose one of the survival strategies of lying low, taking a career detour, or going to a large company that promises to protect their freedom.

INNOVATIONOMICS: WHY FREE RIDING CREATES GROWTH

It is easy to fall into the business versus worker trap. As an employment relations and labor market scholar, I see this dynamic too frequently. Debates over the issue become flattened and distorted, as though we all know where each of us aligns before we have even heard the question. Are you for business or for workers? is the paradigm the popular debates seem to be creating for us. In truth, however, the economics of work and innovation reveal a story that is different from the simplistic and sometimes dangerously paralyzing adversarial capital/labor chant. To better understand the welfare equation—the question of the overall good that stems from controlling the flow of ideas and talent—we must dig deeper and immerse ourselves in the science of knowledge and innovation. We are in a perfect position to begin such a journey because we now know a great deal more than we knew in the past about the economies of invention and creativity, talent and competition, and geographies and growth, enabling us to reflect on how these ideas became so distorted. We are now able to utilize cutting-edge technologies and empirical studies to posit economic analysis against real data about how innovation happens. While the direct consequences of human capital controls have always been clear—for example, an engineer who promised his ex-employer to refrain from competing for two years will have to find alternative work or move out of town—the collateral damage has been less clear. We now need to understand how the talent wars and human capital battles affect innovation and markets. We now need to delve into the best evidence about the aggregate effects of the talent wars.

By looking at inventors, industries, and geographies, we can examine evidence of the ways in which talent wars affect our lives. New data allow us to assess how different strategies have impacted businesses and industries. The data provide the missing link between our talent wars and economic life. They explain the connections between our strategic choices and the surprising successes and, equally important, the failures of firms and regions. It explains, for example, why Northern California has taken the lead in the start-up world and why the fashion industry is organized differently from the publishing industry. While the meeting of innovation studies and the law is still very much in its infancy, a surge of research on innovation and entrepreneurship already offers a wealth of insights about the effects of talent wars on networks, knowledge production, inventorship, job mobility, and growth. As we shall see, the differences in how states frame the talent wars serve as a natural experiment. What we find clearly at every turn is that control is a double-edged sword. The first edge is unsurprising: information leakage and job hopping by talented workers provide competitors with an advantage. The second edge, however, is revolutionary: over the long run information leaks and talent spillovers foster new levels of creativity and innovation that benefit not only the best and most fearless companies but also the economy as a whole.

Every executive will admit this much: the most important way knowledge is diffused in the market is by the dynamic moves of people. Hiring employees from established rivals enables new companies to learn about industry technology most efficiently and rapidly.[16] Like dominos gracefully tapping each other and accelerating exponentially, workers engage with technologies, systems, and ideas and frequently move to new companies, triggering changes in the strategic directions of the hiring business. In the midst of the movement, how do businesses react to mobility and knowl-edge flows? Contrary to the assumptions of the Orthodox Model, a growing body of empirical evidence suggests that successful companies, particularly in high-tech industries, are more likely to increase their research and devel-opment efforts and expenditure when there are increased information spillovers within the industry. In fact, high employee turnover—talent moving fluidly among businesses—is positively correlated with produc-tivity, particularly in industries in which research and development are core activities.[17] These facts are ready to revolutionize our thinking: competitors such as Facebook and Google, Pepsi and Coca-Cola, and Southwest and JetBlue can zealously increase their investments, innovation, and bottom-line profits as their most talented players travel from competitor to compet-itor exchanging ideas and passion. So can smaller and newer firms. A virtuous circle is set in motion professionally and geographically; work mobility supports professional networks, which in turn enhances regional innovation and growth leading to increased opportunities and mobility. Have you ever felt that success is so present in your environment that it practically can rub off on you? As we shall soon see more closely, for all of these reasons entrepreneurs often seek to be in places where innovation is in the air. Simply put, localities with dense connections between innova-tors, knowledge flows, and human capital enjoy dramatically more innova-tion than smaller, protective, and more isolated settings. People who are creative and innovative thrive when they come into contact with other creative and innovative people. Talent attracts talent.

Beyond initial attraction, we also know now that mobile inventors are more productive than nonmobile inventors. The explanation for this fact is twofold. First, the more productive employees are also the ones who have more outside offers from other companies precisely because their talent is attractive. But, second and more important, when talented people move, their productivity gets a boost because their professional world expands and their innovation capacity grows. For comparison, studies find that mobile workers are more than four times as productive as nonmovers and that by contrast, the workers' level of education has no impact on productivity. Even historically, traveling and foreign-born inventors were significantly overrepresented among the great inventors.[18]

When companies are tempted to lament employees' leaving they might consider that the more an inventor moves between companies, the more active she stays in lifelong invention. Workers engage with new technologies, systems, and ideas when they move to new companies, which spurs original thoughts and forces them to keep up with their profession. So mobility has a tremendous positive effect on the localization of knowledge. Even after controlling for the benefits that stem from the agglomeration of industries, that is, the concentration of talent in productive regions, mobility has a significant positive effect on the likelihood that new patents will grow out of and build upon previous major patents from the same region.[19] The richer the local economy is with ideas, talent, and competition, the more likely it is inventors will have easy access to knowledge generated outside of their company. Economic hubs become unusually fertile places of entrepreneurial activity. Job mobility thus unleashes many of the positive qualities we seek in thriving markets.

CORPORATE WARFARE AND OTHER GOOD NEWS

Reflecting our fear of loss, one management strategist suggested that "a Nobel Prize–winning scientist may be a unique resource, but unless he has firm-specific ties, his perfect mobility makes him an unlikely source of sustainable advantage."[20] Wrong. If a Nobel Prize–winning scientist is part of your team, your advantages go beyond his or her mobility and your ability to control it. For markets, talent moves are a central way in which knowledge is diffused. Pioneering research shows that locations with greater mobility tend to have more local knowledge flows. The movement of a talented member of your team can actually help your mission to improve your company's status and product. Mobile inventors build upon the ideas from their previous firms far more often than other inventors.[21] Of course, mobility enhances a firm's access to the knowledge the new employee acquired before moving.[22] But such access often has positive effects on the sending company (the employer who has lost its employee to a competitor). When firms recruit inventors they increase the likelihood that the inventors' prior inventions will be put to use.[23] Companies learn by hiring, that is, they advance by acquiring new information via the hiring of inventors with prior knowledge they can share and expand on. Over time, the patents of those inventors who move become the most cited and valuable ones in the market.[24]

Lose the battle, win the war. What we are starting to realize is that the positive effects of mobility flow both ways. The win–lose state of mind that pervades much of the talent wars, as well as many other debates about intellectual property and human capital controls, is therefore misleading. The conventional wisdom that labels mobility as a negative event for the sending employer has been flipped on its head by new research. By their very nature, human capital and its ever-supportive sister social capital are a two-way street. In a repeat game, in which firms compete continuously in an industry, companies can learn to view many of their departing employees as continuing assets and employee turnover as a long-term strength. Clearly, companies gain when they hire their competitor's talent. But does a competitor's gain always mirror a loss on the other side? We can think of it this way: on the receiving side, companies gain both human capital—a talented individual—and social capital, that is, the ties between this individual and others. On the sending side, an employer loses human capital, but it too gains social capital and the thickening of its network as new employees fill the void. In the jungle, when vines are cut, they grow back with more force than before and in more directions. In industry, new connections and communications grow to replace the lost employee. Beyond the walls of work, the social relationships between people survive job and location moves, creating longer distance connections and more "bandwidth" to gain and share knowledge.

But in the face of this an important question lingers: are knowledge transfers truly bidirectional? Researchers at Wharton and the University of Maryland studied these questions, attempting to uncover the learning effects of "outbound mobility." That is, what learning processes can be detected at the losing firm, the business that sent its talent out into the world? They found that firms losing employees are more likely to subsequently cite patents (that is, use references to previous patents in their patent application) of those firms hiring their former workers and vice versa. In other words, not only the company gaining the new talent but also the company who lost it gained access and insight into the other's ventures. Other researchers looked at the question from a different perspective: the gains of the sending firm in their interactions in the greater market, such as representation on professional associations, technical committees, and lobbying efforts. In all of these areas companies find it easier to navigate the market and reach their goals when their footprint is broader than just their current talent. When representatives know each other and when ties are built, collaboration and even competition can become more effective.[25]

Outbound effects—the benefits of having former employees at other places—are most pronounced when an employee moves among geographically distant companies. While it is easy to cling to long-held beliefs that the loss of an employee is painful, the studies not only demonstrate the benefits of mobility for the losing firm, but also, surprisingly, show that these outbound mobility effects were not significantly different from those of the hiring firm. The employees may be gone, but they are not forgotten.[26] Sending companies gain access and possible advantages in future dealings. Both sides benefit greatly from the movement. Similarly, with regard to geographies, enduring social relations between inventors also benefit the sending region. Indeed, when an innovator leaves a region, the departure brings its own wealth of benefits. The departing inventor is more likely to cite to patents from her previous region, and the relationships formed within an institutional context may endure over time, space, and institutional boundaries.

Although the loss of talent cannot in itself become, for most companies, a widespread strategic mission, businesses can learn to react to such inevitable losses by reaping potential benefits. The new wisdom of smart businesses is to distinguish between direct competitors and other types of poachers: existing and potential cooperators, including customers and clients, suppliers and partners. These latter groups of poachers are no longer viewed as adversaries when they lure away talent. Like high-tech employees, so attorneys, accountants, and investment bankers all change jobs frequently. Examining the movement of patent attorneys in leading law firms over six years, research showed how the movement affected the law firms' connections to Fortune 500 companies, and one thing was clear: the departing destination makes a difference. The study shows that when an employee leaves to work for a client, the sending law firm gains. This is particularly true if the departure is amicable or not overtly contentious. Don't believe the statistics? Then consider this example. In 2004 some of the best traders of Goldman Sachs left the investment banking firm to start their own multibillion dollar hedge fund. Under the old framework this could be construed as devastating. An employer would likely have reacted in anger and burned the bridge. Here, however, Goldman Sachs didn't burn a bridge, and soon enough these departing employees became important clients of Goldman Sachs.[27] Similarly, the departure of a lead securities lawyer at the large firm Cooley Godward to a small, little-known auction website known as eBay was worrisome to the law firm. Less than a year later, their ex-employee, now the in-house counsel for eBay, knocked on Cooley's door and hired them to be eBay's counsel for its $1.3 billion IPO.[28] To the reader who might scoff and claim these are isolated incidents, Cooley Godward recently reported landing several more important clients referred by alumni. In fact, realizing these were not isolated losses but extraordinary opportunities, the law firm launched an alumni program. It holds cocktail receptions with hundreds of former employees, maintains an alumni contact directory on its website, and includes its alumni in some of its formal events. Additionally, in its monthly newsletter it highlights alumni profiles.

Importantly, these days it is difficult in many situations to tell the difference between customer, vendor, and competitor. A company that may be your competitor with one product line or service may well be your customer for others.

BOOMERANG HIRING

Acknowledgment of the value of former employees is reaching into every industry. Leading companies like Capital One, Microsoft, McKinsey & Co., Ernst & Young, Shell, and Procter & Gamble have all instituted similar alumni programs, which include events, conferences, and online forums. Professional social networks such as LinkedIn are facilitating these efforts. From this perspective again, we see the control mentality overshadowing beneficial practices for some businesses. Some companies administer strict policies of not hiring their former employees, no matter how talented they've proven to be. But others estimate that they save millions of dollars when they rehire their former employees.[29] It's called boomerang hiring. Embracing this new practice, Shell has a website, AlliancexShell, providing alumni with networking and information about rehiring opportunities. Leveraging the alumni resources of a company can be accomplished just as universities do with their alumni. Happy alumni become goodwill ambassadors of the company. Therefore, maintaining active relationships postdeparture can be a profitable endeavor for an efficient firm. In academia, the departure of colleagues serves as a signal of the quality and ranking of the school. At the University of San Diego we take pride in the number of faculty members who receive external offers from other schools. While we make efforts to keep them, some will inevitably be tempted, flattered, and lured away, and we make sure that those who do depart stay close friends. The university benefits and at times even strategically encourages some departures when such moves are likely to increase the visibility of the school and form new connections with other institutions.

In an era when we receive more information in one day than most people in the time of Shakespeare got during their entire lifetime, one of the greatest challenges of the information era is attention deficit. We are surrounded by 24/7 news alerts, research advances, budget cuts, and marketing buzzes. There is simply too much information to consume. Particular events, however, command our full attention. When an employee leaves a company, her departure can rein in our wandering attention and focus it on the outputs of competitors. Colleagues may see more clearly the gaps that led to the departure. They also begin to devote more attention to monitoring the firm for which their former coworker left.[30] Competitors become more salient when we know someone who joined them. But the losing company, too, can take steps to turn the loss into free publicity. If it plays its cards right, the losing company gains attention, public relations, and goodwill ambassadors in the industry.

The traditional response of companies experiencing high rates of turnover was to implement aggressive retention efforts, such as contractual restrictions on leaving and competing and threats of litigation. These traditional routes of defense and retaliation tend to create fear among the departing employees and the poaching firms and, worse yet, may not serve the company's best interests.

In the midst of what seems initially to be an upsetting situation, is it possible for companies to make the mental shift to look at the departure of key talent as a gain, and not necessarily a threat? Is it possible for them to learn to choose their battles wisely and to keep their eye on winning the war, that is, promoting innovation and economic growth over the long run? Moving from a win-lose to a win-win state of mind is not easy for anyone, especially market competitors. Competition and cooperation are dynamic as strategic alliances evolve, devolve, and re-form, often between competitors. But creative companies are adopting a more complete view. Thirsty for environments in which they can freely recruit talent in the market without operating in an atmosphere of control and protection, they also develop ways to turn loss into gain. Employing strategic approaches to prevent the loss of valuable employees, companies are creating environments that increase employee satisfaction and decrease employees' desire to leave. At the same time, they are learning how to turn inevitable losses into opportunities. They are learning how to choose their battles.

PART TWO CHOOSE YOUR BATTLES

Repression is not the way to virtue. When people restrain themselves out of fear, their lives are by necessity diminished. Only through freely chosen discipline can life be enjoyed and still kept within the bounds of reason.

—*Mihály Csíkszentmihályi, the father of positive psychology*

CAN WE DRAW A LINE between people and the knowledge they possess? Can the law protect secrets without restricting freedoms and mobility? Should we restrict those working for us from leaving and from developing ideas on their own? The truth of the matter is that companies must constantly search for new ideas outside their fields to serve as inputs into their internal research and development departments. For that to happen, though, firms must lower their guard to the outside environment, and that is easier said than done. As competitors, we face choices and conflicting pushes and pulls at every turn. This section is designed to help us better understand these choices and their implications on innovation and success. In the end, the evidence is nearly universal: excessive controls of talent and inventiveness are harmful to careers, regions, and innovation. As we shall see, the harm is caused both by the aggregate loss of knowledge, social ties, and talent flow and by the motivational effects that the talent wars, played out with a lingering mentality of control, have on inventive and creative talent as they interact with their environment.

This part of the book has several goals. Initially, it presents each aspect of the leading mechanisms of control employed in the talent wars. It then investigates the positive results that come from shifting our default mentalities and illustrates the benefits of human and cognitive flows. After reading these chapters, you will have a solid understanding of noncompetes, trade secrets, patent assignment clauses, copyright work-for-hire transfers, and so on. You will learn what questions to raise and what pitfalls to avoid when deciding whether to adopt or commit to these mechanisms. But, more than that, you will engage with the stories of success, failure, and change of companies, industries, cities, and societies. Knowing what we know about the astounding advantages spurred by innovative environments and design, questions about the operations of talent wars are crucial to making decisions about public planning, private investment, and management strategy. Perhaps the most exciting new data assess how differences in these strategies, in every aspect of the innovative process—the rates of participation in intellectual endeavors, human motivation, social networks, organizational behavior, and the flow of ideas—are affected by how we define the background rules of the game, the talent war game. Therefore, you are invited in each chapter to consider how creative leaders and innovators can balance their needs of nurturing their talent and developing their ideas and the benefits that come from collaborations, sharing, and flow.

CHAPTER THREE

Noncompete—Compete!

ACTING MUCH LIKE THE COMPETITIVE world of athlete poaching, software companies practice what the *Wall Street Journal* has termed guerrilla recruiting.[1] The best "athletes" of leading companies—their most talented managers, engineers, marketers, and designers—are approached, often in secret, and, in what appears to be a sudden coup, the player announces his defection to assume a key position with the competitor. In 2008 guerrilla recruiting struck at IBM when Apple approached one of its key managers, Mark Papermaster. Steve Jobs, who until his untimely death in 2011 had inspired the world by leading the way in innovation and the nurturing of talent, recruited Papermaster to work for Apple after twenty-five years of service at IBM, offering him an exciting position as head of its iPod and iPhone hardware engineering groups. IBM's reaction to Apple's offer? A lawsuit. IBM sought to enforce the noncompete agreement prohibiting Papermaster from working for a competitor for a full year after his departure. But was the new position at Apple a violation of his agreement with IBM? And was this agreement enforceable? Papermaster's experience at IBM was in the blade servers market. Blade servers are designed to minimize the use of physical space by stripping down server computers. In almost all commercial small high-tech devices like iPods, chip technology similar to that of blade servers is used. Papermaster was an expert in these types of microchips.

Papermaster and Apple argued that Apple and IBM were totally different businesses competing for different markets. IBM claimed that the position at the iPod division was a subterfuge, a job title concealing Apple's real plan to have Papermaster lead a new division of scalable processors, which are more directly in competition with IBM's blade server market. To convince the court to enforce the noncompete, IBM would have to show that Apple was a major competitor, not just generally but specifically in the blade server market. If the court found that Apple did not compete with IBM directly, then the noncompete restriction would not apply.

In the lawsuit IBM also argued that the noncompete agreement should be enforced because Papermaster had knowledge of highly confidential secrets about IBM's methods, systems, plans for acquisition and disposition of products, expansion plans, financial status and plans, customer lists, client data, personnel information, and trade secrets. But even if IBM could show that all the facts pointed to a breach of the noncompete, it still had to show that the noncompete was enforceable under the law. Apple argued that the noncompete was not enforceable in California, where Apple is headquartered. Unlike most other states, California law voids all noncompete agreements—a fact that, we shall soon see, pervades all disputes involving noncompete contracts that are signed under California's jurisdiction.

Along with the threat of litigation, IBM acted strategically to prevent Papermaster from accepting Apple's offer by counteroffering with a pay increase. Both sticks and carrots were employed, and the juxtaposition is striking: at the same time the company sued an employee who wished to leave, it offered him a raise. IBM even went so far as to offer a "garden leave": one year's salary for simply refraining from working for Apple, a paid sabbatical from the industry. In the end, as is often the case in litigation, neither side emerged as the obvious winner. After intense secret negotiations IBM and Apple settled the lawsuit: Papermaster could begin working for Apple six months after he left IBM, and all the information he learned at IBM would remain secret. Perhaps the only winners of the battle were the lawyers, who heavily billed their wealthy corporate clients.

Such are the realities of twenty-first-century noncompete disputes in the knowledge economy. The departure of a valuable employee is frequently a double blow to a company. The company loses a trained, talented individual, and its competitor stands to gain from this loss by hiring a former insider as a key player in its operation. Accordingly, noncompete clauses, designed to restrict an employee's postemployment ability to work for a competitor or start a competing company, have become a near-universal feature of employment contracts. Everywhere you look companies require at least some of their employees to sign noncompetes. Surveys show that nearly 90 percent of managerial and technical employees have signed them. Venture capitalists require them from the founders of the companies they finance.[2] This is true not only in the context of high-profile executives like Papermaster, but at every employee level. The cases of noncompete litigation involve workers from factory welders to CEOs, computer programmers to yoga instructors, doctors to bakers, lawyers to artists, marketing strategists to bioengineers. Noncompete agreements are also prevalent in the sports and entertainment industries. The National Basketball Association has strict rules about the transfer of players between teams. Musicians often must sign exclusive-dealing agreements with record companies to get signed.

Consider the absolute nature of these restrictions. Noncompetes will usually state that an employee of company *X* promises to not be employed or affiliated in any capacity by a competitor. For a person who has trained in a certain discipline, this means she essentially will have to take a career detour and find another professional position. Often these restrictions get signed in the first place because of leverage asymmetry. They are presented as do or die at the beginning of the employment relationship. Not surprisingly, in the past decade, as the number of firms using these restrictions has increased, the number of disputes and lawsuits involving noncompetes has doubled. In this chapter, I invite you to consider the controls (or sticks) of noncompete contracts and disputes around their validity. I will identify when their harm to the firm, its talent, the industry, and a region exceeds their immediate benefits.

A BRIEF HISTORY OF COMPETITION RESTRICTIONS, OR AVOIDING THE "INDUSTRIAL EQUIVALENT OF CAPITAL PUNISHMENT"

To understand why companies use noncompete agreements to prevent employees from working for the competition, it is useful to first consider why more restrictive contracts, such as a contract that would prevent an employee from leaving his job altogether, are unenforceable.

Imagine a business that requires its employees to sign a promise that they would stay at the company for ten years. Would the company be able to demand fulfillment of such a promise if the employee wishes to leave? For centuries, except under very special circumstances, it has been a well-established rule that courts will not order specific performance for personal service contracts. Specific performance of an employment contract, that is, ordering an employee to actually go to work for an employer he would like to leave, has been described as "the industrial equivalent of capital punishment," and courts often characterize it as reminiscent of slavery and involuntary servitude.[3] Therefore, a court will only rarely order a worker to perform a job no matter what his employment contract says. As a result, in modern times forcing an employee to remain at her job is no longer a viable legal option. Employees can almost always legally get out of an employment contract if they're willing to pay damages for its breach. Beyond dollar damages, a court will not order a return to work when the employee wants out.

That people cannot be enslaved to one employer is by now a universal truth. A few critics have argued that the unavailability of specific performance denies employees valuable bargaining leverage that comes with giving their employer the promise of absolute loyalty.[4] Yet most commentators today accept the logic of allowing an employee to free herself from her current boss as a fundamental liberty.[5] In all of the states and in most countries employees remain free to leave their employers at will at any point in the employment relationship. Because employers cannot require their employees to stay in their current position, they must find other ways to prevent their ex-employees from competing with them, whether by becoming their own bosses or by going to work for a competitor. The tool of choice is often the noncompete agreement.

Historically, under early English common law, all contracts restricting trade were void as a matter of public policy. This continues to be the logic of competition laws, or antitrust as it is termed in the United States, which prohibit arrangements such as cartels and price fixing among competitors. The early intuitive understanding of our ancestors was that noncompetes trigger the same problems as the business strategies that antitrust laws attempt to prevent. A noncompete agreement commits an individual to refrain from work and competition, thereby constituting a direct restriction of trade. The earliest known case in medieval England dealing with a noncompete covenant was in 1414, when a clothes dryer attempted to prevent his former worker from competing in the town for six months. In this first case, the court reprimanded the plaintiff because it viewed a request to restrict a fellow citizen from practicing his trade to be absurd, so much so that the court threatened the plaintiff with jail for initiating such a frivolous lawsuit.[6]

Much has changed since that first English case. As technology grew more valuable and information became a primary asset for industrial competition, courts began to allow noncompetes. In response, a few state legislatures passed laws declaring noncompete agreements unenforceable. Most notable among these states is California. California has been voiding noncompete agreements for over a century. Most other states allow noncompetes between employers and ex-employees, although each of these states subjects the agreements to a reasonableness requirement by restricting their scope. In other words, although restrictions on trade are generally unenforceable under the law and restricted by antitrust regulation, in most states noncompete agreements are excepted from the restriction but limited by a requirement that they be reasonable.

DROWNING IN THE SEA OF REASONABLENESS

To try to find a balance between allowing noncompetes to exist and restricting their expansion, most states use the overarching standard of reasonableness, otherwise referred to as the common law's rule of reason.[7] As any first-year law student learns and often comes to dread, reasonableness is a frequent presence in the law—a simple concept to understand but an incredibly difficult standard to apply. The reasonableness standard allows the courts to perform a case-by-case analysis of each contract, weighing all the positive and negative consequences to both of the disputing parties and to society. To judge a noncompete reasonable, the courts first look at whether the noncompete is reasonably necessary to protect the employer's legitimate business interests, for example, if the company needs to protect its client relations or its trade secrets. If so, a court may still decide that the agreement is unenforceable if the hardship to the employee or the injury to the public caused by the prevention of competition exceeds the employer's benefit. Put differently, if a contract hurts competition and efficient talent flows, the law may override the contractual agreement to prevent individual unfairness and public harm (or negative externalities, as economists would term it). Conceptually, then, the reasonableness of a noncompete is determined by a triangular inquiry:

1. From the company standpoint: is the restriction necessary to protect a legitimate business interest?
2. From the employee's standpoint, does the agreement impose undue hardship?
3. From a community standpoint, is the restraint contrary to the public interest?

A New York court explained the triangular balancing dilemma by noting that while "public policy favors economic competition and individual liberty and seeks to shield employees from the superior bargaining position of employers," the court must also consider the interests of "freedom of contract."[8] In this particular case, the employer's noncompete contract was deemed unreasonable when its overreaching terms prohibited the employee from having any contact, including purely social interactions, with the employer's customers or prospective customers or both, the employer's employees, and any entity that might be the subject of a future acquisition by the employer. The employer's interests were dwarfed by the hardship imposed on the ex-employee and the public interest in market interactions. The triangular perspective evaluating the balance of interests between the parties among themselves and in relation to society is paired with a second tri-inquiry of the more concrete aspects of the actual restriction: the reasonableness of the time, geography, and professional scope of the restriction. Put together, the enforceability of a noncompete agreement is judged according to the rationality, legitimacy, and fairness of the spaces implicated, the restriction's duration, and the realm of competitive activity that is curtailed (fig. 3.1).

If this seems a bit complicated to you, rest assured that it also seems so to the courts. While the double triangular balancing test is widely adopted, the determination of reasonableness is highly varied and fact intensive. To those familiar with the world of litigation this comes as no surprise. In general, the legal concept of reasonableness (and hardship and legitimate interest) is a standard that defies bright-line definitions. As applied to noncompete enforceability, in particular, courts have largely utilized a case-by-case evaluation that does not easily lend itself to

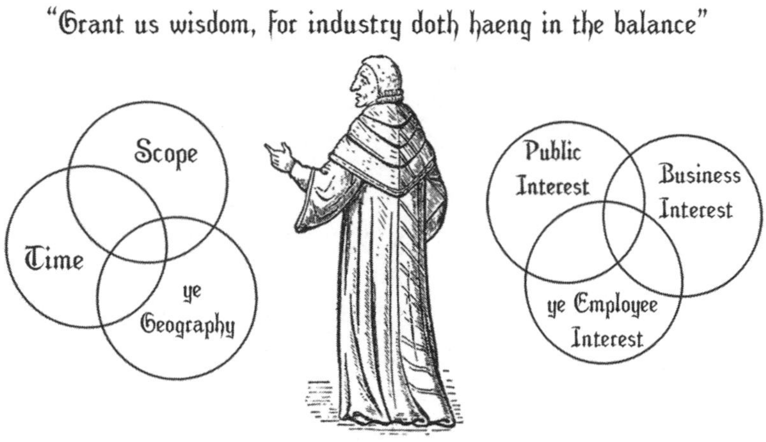

"Grant us wisdom, for industry doth haeng in the balance"

Fig 3.1. The reasonableness Venn diagram.

principled analysis. When courts are faced with determining the validity of noncompetes, each case is decided on its facts. The analysis is replete with open-ended standards and ambiguous balancing tests. One author describes the range of judicial interpretations of reasonableness in this fashion: "So disparate is the law concerning the legality of noncompetition agreements that, with respect to an identical clause, in one state it can be declared reasonable and be enforced, in a second state it can be declared unreasonable and unenforceable, in a neighboring state it can be declared unreasonable but modified to be reasonable and enforceable, and in a fourth state declared reasonable but not be enforced because it is deemed contrary to the forum state's public policy."[9] An Ohio court colorfully described the difficulty of determining whether a noncompete is enforceable as diving into the vast seas and drowning in the murky waters:

> No layman could realize the legal complication involved in [the] uncomplicated act [of signing a noncompete]. This is not one of those questions on which the legal research cannot find enough to quench his thirst. The contrary, there is so much authority it drowns him. It is a sea—vast and vacillating, overlapping and bewildering. One can fish out of it any kind of strange support for anything, if he lives so long. This deep and unsettled sea

pertaining to an employee's covenant not to compete with his employer after termination of employment is really Seven Seas and now that the court has sailed them, perhaps it should record those seas so that the next weary traveler may be saved the terrifying time it takes just to find them.[10]

The court then proceeds to call out the "sightings" in the "sea of periodicals," the "sea of annotations," the "sea of encyclopedias," the "sea of treatises," the "digest sea," the "restatement sea," and many more seas in the state law—certainly enough seas to drown the sharpest of legal minds! But why are the waters so murky? Part of the murkiness results from the reasonableness determination, which is multifaceted and complex. First, deciding whether or not a noncompete is reasonable is an intensely fact-specific exercise that is conducted on a case-by-case basis. Any small change in facts can completely alter the final decision. Coupled with changing fact scenarios, the reasonableness standard relies on judges' balancing of factors and interpretation of these facts and how much weight they decide to afford each issue. In reality, different judges come to entirely different conclusions based on the same facts and issues.

Out of the vast seas of variance, though, one can extract emerging patterns. Even though most states have adopted a similar framework of the rule of reason, the actual application of the doctrine by courts varies significantly. Most courts will proclaim that the mere goal of a noncompete to prevent competition is an insufficient reason for enforcement. So we need to look deeper to more specific and legitimate purposes. These are usually found in the protection of confidential information, secrets, and customer relations. As one court stated, "The employee does not come to a new employer as a *tabula rasa*—a blank slate—without experience and knowledge, but rather carries along former employer's secrets."[11] But, as we shall see in later chapters, trade secrets themselves are difficult to define legally. At the heart of the debate about trade secrets and in turn also about noncompete enforcement is distinguishing between general talent and skills and confidential information held in the mind of an ex-employee. In an attempt to classify skills and information, courts inquire into the nature of the employee's responsibilities, her level of skill, her value to the firm, and her value to the competitor. Very rarely will agreement emerge with respect to the ultimate conclusion on whether the noncompete is needed to protect secrets.

When it comes to justifying a noncompete the second most frequently used rationale (after protecting secrets) is protecting relationships with cherished clientele and preventing one's ex-employee from poaching those clients. Here again courts are often at a loss to draw distinctions between good and bad modes of competition.[12] In order to provide some kind of framework, judges will inquire into the importance of customer relationships within the particular industry. Illinois, for example, enforces noncompetes only if the employee will be threatening his employer's "near-permanent" relationships with customers.[13] As you can imagine, the actual labeling of client relationships with a firm as near-permanent raises an irony: Why is a noncompete necessary to prevent them from moving to a competitor if these relations are so strong? And shouldn't we be encouraging competition and consumer choice precisely where few choices existed? Other states, New Hampshire, for example, have a rule of thumb that allows companies to restrict their ex-employees from competing against them over clients with whom they directly dealt during their employment, but prohibits restricting contact with other customers. At the constrictive end of the spectrum sit states that allow more expansive restrictions, including defining all customers, sometimes including potential customers, as being off-limits to the ex-employee.[14]

TIME FLIES AS THE WORLD EXPANDS

A noncompete agreement must also be reasonable in its temporal and spatial limitations. The inquiry into time and space is fact specific, but courts have developed tools and rules of thumb to analyze the geography and time components of noncompetes. The time tables for restrictions vary dramatically. Some states, such as Pennsylvania, routinely enforce noncompetes that span three years and even longer, while other states will not enforce noncompetes that are longer than one or two years. Where geography is concerned, states have routine presumptions about the permitted scope of the territorial restriction. Virginia, for example, will allow a noncompete to span only the areas in which the employer is currently in business. Missouri takes a different approach and allows a broader reach, extending noncompetes to places where the employer has no current business presence.

In our competitive, fast-paced economy, time and geography are inter-twined. Time frames are shortening while spatial boundaries are expanding. Global commerce and international markets allow us to compete more quickly and on far larger scales. An Internet company based in Germany, for example, can successfully compete with a rival based in California. Advances in technology, as in cell phone and circuit design, occur so rapidly that knowledge in a field may become obsolete within a few months. Courts therefore increasingly consider the speed with which technology changes in a particular field and are skeptical of lengthy time restrictions when the industry is one that moves at a fast pace. In fact, in the Internet industry, noncompetes spanning only one year have recently been deemed too far-reaching. On the other hand, the geography of noncompetes has expanded. Competition used to be local—one hardware store against another down the street. Slowly, as cities grew and transportation became more efficient, competition became regional, then national, and now, in many cases, global. As a result, we are seeing courts enforce the broadest noncompetes ever, which define the prohibited territory of competition as an entire state, region, and even country and continent. Recently, trying to ride this wave of expansion, companies have tried to define noncompete areas as any place where the firm may have a business interest. In one such case, the court struck down this noncontained competition, referring to it as an amoeba, a shapeless creature with infinite expansion potential.[15]

Further complicating the inquiry into a noncompete's validity, beyond time, geography, and the firm's legitimate business interests, the noncompete must also withstand the test of being a reasonable burden on the employee. I hope at this point some of you are asking yourselves, is it ever reasonable to prevent an employee from working in his field? For states that enforce noncompetes, the inquiry has become ever more fine tuned. The courts evaluate the moment of the signing of the noncompete, the event triggering the departure, and the postemployment realities. Each of these aspects of reasonableness reveals a great disparity between jurisdictions. Should the noncompetes be in writing and signed by both parties? Should there have been adequate compensation or a valuable promise to the employee such as a raise or promotion or training in return for the signing of the limiting agreement? Should the noncompete be enforced only against an employee who voluntarily quit or also against a fired employee? The courts' answers to all of these questions have differed widely. Some courts will void a noncompete if the restriction will take away an employee's sole means of support, while others enforce the noncompete while emphasizing the importance of enforcing contracts and keeping promises.

In light of all the variables in motion and the varying weights afforded to them, it is easy to see why predicting whether a noncompete is reasonable is difficult even for the most experienced lawyers. One court's attempt at determining an agreement's reasonableness illustrates just how difficult the prediction is. This particular court announced that there are no fewer than forty-one questions to be considered (box 2).[16]

BOX 2

41 QUESTIONS: ONE COURT'S ATTEMPT TO BRING ORDER TO REASON

1. Does the employer have a protectable interest?
2. Is the noncompete ancillary or incidental to some other transaction?
3. What is the object of the parties?
4. Is the real object merely to remove a competitor and ordinary competition?
5. Is the real object just to prevent the employee from quitting, or to suppress or discipline him?
6. Is the real object to cause the employee to withdraw from all business?
7. Is the real object merely to prevent employee from using the skill and intelligence acquired or increased through experience or instruction received in the course of work for employer?
8. What is the nature and extent of employer's business?
9. What was the nature and extent of employee's work in employer's business?
10. How long had employee worked for employer?
11. Are employee's services unique in character, or can employee's place be readily filled?
12. Did employee's work give him opportunity to become acquainted with employer's customer?
13. How many of employer's customers did employee come to know?
14. Was this particular employee practically the employer's sole and exclusive contact with the customer?
15. Was employee's contact with employer's customers a regular, reoccurring contact?
16. Was employee's contact with employer's customers a close, personal, direct, and ingratiating contact that gave employee such a hold on customers that they would follow him to the rival?

---

17. Would employer's customers know that employee had quit and joined the rival?
18. What is the distance between the business place at which employee worked for employer and the business place at which employee works for rival?
19. Does employee contact and serve customer at customer's premises or at employer's premises?
20. Is employee's work a route or nonroute type?
21. Does employee's work involve solicitation, i.e., seeking out people to procure them as customers?
22. What is the nature and extent of employee's work for rival?
23. On behalf of rival, did employee solicit and attempt to entice away the patronage of customers that he had served for employer?
24. Did employee actually entice away and divert to rival the customers he had served for employer?
25. How many of such customers did employee lure away?
26. Did employee obtain and is he using employer's secret customer list?
27. Have employer's trade or business secrets been confided to employee?
28. Was the purpose of employee's subsequent employment by rival the obtaining of such secrets?
29. What territory does employer's business cover?
30. What territory did employee cover for employer?
31. From what territory does the covenant bar employee?
32. Is employee barred from territory in which employer has no business?
33. Is employee barred from territory in which he never worked for employer?
34. What is the size and condition of the area over which the prohibition extends? Is it urban or rural? Is it metropolitan or small city? Is it thinly or densely populated?
35. What is the duration of the prohibition?
36. What is the character of work from which employee is excluded?
37. From what persons or class of persons is employee excluded from doing business?
38. Are the circumstances such as to require radius protection or merely nonsolicitation of employer's customers that employee had served?
39. Has employee been guilty of deception, bad faith, fraud, or specific misconduct?
40. What actual business loss was caused to employer by employee's working for rival?
41. How many other rivals are engaged in the same business in the community? Is the business common or unusual in nature?

But these complex inquiries and sets of questions still do not mark the end of the investigation into whether a noncompete will be enforced. Remember the tri-circles above: reasonableness is not simply a matter of balancing the interests of firms and their employees. It is also a question of the effect of the restriction on the public interest. Does the public lose too much when people cannot pursue their profession after they leave a job? Following is a tale of doctors and lawyers that illustrates our general ambivalence about the validity of noncompetes and their challenge to the public interest.

WHAT WE VALUE: A TALE OF TWO PROFESSIONS

Imagine arriving one rainy winter day with your sick child at your pediatrician's office, desperate to see the doctor, and being told your and your child's favorite pediatrician has left the practice. You make inquiries to determine the whereabouts of the doctor, but once you've found him he informs you that he cannot continue to treat your child as a patient because of a noncompete agreement signed with his former clinic. The doctor has known your child since birth and watched her grow and has earned your trust and the trust of your child. No one else will do. Now imagine a parallel situation, this time at your office. You call your company's law firm with an urgent matter concerning an important deal that is on the brink of materializing. The final legal matters must still be ironed out, but you are told by the law firm that the attorney who was working with your office has moved to another firm. This attorney knows your company inside out. You want to continue to work with her because you trust her, you've been working with her for months on the deal, and at this point no one else will do. After the experience with your child's pediatrician, you brace yourself for another blow. What happens if she has signed a noncompete with her former firm?

Noncompetes and the rights of consumers to freely choose a trusted professional make the debate more personal when we remember that *we* are the patients and clients of these professionals. These questions set us sailing once again on the vast seas of reasonableness. Lawyers and clients; doctors and patients—which relationships are most valuable from a societal perspective? The American Bar Association (ABA) has adamantly opposed noncompetes between lawyers. In fact, the ABA's ethical rules prohibit noncompetes completely. For many decades the ABA has steadily maintained that employment agreements restricting the ability of lawyers to practice and compete postemployment are unethical.[17] The Model Rules of Professional Conduct state that a lawyer shall not participate in "a partnership, shareholder, operating, employment, or other similar type of agreement that restricts the right of a lawyer to practice after

termination of the relationship."[18] The ABA explains that such agreements violate public policy because they restrict lawyers' professional
autonomy and limit the freedom of clients to choose representation. The
professional association for lawyers has always felt that the public has a
right and an interest in having the largest possible pool of lawyers from
which to select representation. In practice, noncompete arrangements
among lawyers are generally found to be invalid, and some courts ban
even indirect restrictions, such as agreements to withhold departure
compensation from lawyers who leave to a competing firm.[19]

In contrast to the bar's approach, doctors routinely employ noncompetes in their practice. The American Medical Association (AMA) has
declined an outright prohibition on noncompete agreements despite
repeatedly taking the position that such agreements harm the public
interest and negatively impact patient care. Early in 1933 the AMA
declared that employment clauses interfering with competition in the
marketplace or preventing the free choice of a physician were unethical.[20]
By 1960, however, the association seemed to waver in its stance against
noncompetes. The official opinion was revised to state that reasonable
agreements not to practice in certain geographical areas or for particular
lengths of time should not be flatly prohibited. Although the AMA recognized that such agreements might not be in the best interest of the public,
it expressed a belief that they are not necessarily unethical. This decision
was reaffirmed in 1971 at a meeting of the association's House of
Delegates, which declared that "there is no ethical proscription against
suggesting or entering into a reasonable agreement not to practice within
a certain area for a certain time, if it is knowingly made and understood."[21]
In 1980 the AMA issued an opinion that noncompete agreements among
physicians are contrary to the public interest, but it stopped short of
calling the arrangements unethical. The current manifestation of the rule
found in the National Code of Medical Ethics states that "restrictive covenants are unethical if they are excessive in geographic scope or duration
in the circumstances presented, or if they fail to make reasonable accom-
modation of patients' choice of physician."[22]

In practice, noncompetes are very common in physicians' employment and partnership agreements. Generally, courts have been unwilling
to rely on the AMA Code of Medical Ethics' ambivalent statements
concerning noncompetes as a basis for invalidating such controls. The

tide, however, may be turning in some states. Colorado, Delaware, and Massachusetts have outright declared noncompetes among physicians to be void.[23] Other states, including Arizona, Ohio, and North Carolina, allow them very narrowly.[24] Recent decisions in Tennessee, Iowa, and Illinois suggest a growing willingness among courts to invalidate restrictive employment agreements among physicians. In 2005 the Tennessee Supreme Court found no reason to distinguish between human capital controls of doctors and those of lawyers because both professions implicate significant public policy considerations.[25] The court embraced the freedom-to-choose concept used in attorney cases by stating that "the right to freedom of choice in physicians . . . and the benefits derived from having an increased number of physicians practicing in any given community" outweigh the business justifications of individual employers.[26] The decision caused a stir within the medical community in Tennessee, and after two years of deliberation the Tennessee General Assembly developed a law designed to allow certain kinds of physician to enter into noncompete agreements.[27] The assembly determined that the agreements must be reasonable, and, specifically, they must be (1) set out in writing and signed by both parties; (2) not exceed two years; and (3) be limited in scope.[28]

Although physician noncompete agreements have seemingly been revived in Tennessee, other states are following the lead of the Tennessee Supreme Court in finding such contracts invalid. A good example is Iowa, which has allowed noncompetes among physicians since the early twentieth century, and Iowa courts reaffirmed their validity in the 1960s.[29] But in 2008 the Iowa Court of Appeals refused to enforce a noncompete agreement against a departing physician at the University of Iowa.[30] The Iowa court determined that the university had not spent time and money training the physician and, more important, patients should not be forced to travel great distances for cancer care, particularly in light of the fact that the region was designated as an underserved area.

The dissimilar attitudes that the medical and legal communities have adopted toward talent wars and competition between professionals reveal the essential dilemma of the triangular struggle: talent wants to be free and so does the public. Consumers, clients, and patients value the ability to choose among professionals. On the other hand, firms often cling to the protectionist mentality and engage in attempts to restrict these choices. As we will now explore, in the long run these firms fighting so desperately to restrict their talented people would likely benefit from the very movement they are attempting to limit. All too often firms become myopic and find themselves locked in a protectionist mindset, an unhealthy equilibrium in which they need an outside push, such as policy, to jolt them awake and set them on the right road. Effectively crafted policies can set an industry on a win-win track. Enter the Californian-style game.

ZERO TOLERANCE: THE CALIFORNIA WAY

There are serious problems with the vast sea of uncertainty and gross variation between states when it comes to handling noncompetes—but all is not lost. One benefit is a natural built-in experiment: if states have different stances on noncompetes, then we can study how these differences affect the societal goals we want to promote, namely, innovation, growth, and talent. The idea of comparing states began with one state that has provided the most obvious landscape for a natural experiment for comparing different systems of managing the talent wars: California. For over a century, dating back to 1872, California has held a steadfast aversion to postemployment restrictions.

The California Business and Professions Code voids "every contract by which anyone is restrained from engaging in a lawful profession, trade, or business."[31] The statute embodies California's policy of favoring open competition and its citizens' right to pursue the employment and enterprise of their choice. The California judiciary has emphasized that employee mobility is paramount to the state's economy and that the law must protect "the important right of persons to engage in businesses and occupations of their choosing."[32]

The ban on noncompetes in California is as old as the state, implemented at a time when laws were rapidly developing in the quest for statehood.[33] Among legal historians there is a debate about whether California's early ban was simply a historical fluke or an intentional economic policy. In passing the law, the California legislature stated that "contracts in restraint of trade have been allowed by modern decisions to a very dangerous extent." At the time, however, the aversion to "restraint of trade . . . by modern decisions" was more likely based on an intuitive inclination for openness and employee mobility rather than on a deep understanding of the importance of central coordination and how it encourages knowledge and talent flows.

Nonetheless, while the ban may have come about in a serendipitous manner, throughout the decades California has embraced its exceptional stance. The California legislature refused to alter the state's ban on noncompetes, and the California courts have repeatedly affirmed the ban as fundamental policy. In some cases California courts have been so adamant about enforcing the state's prohibition of noncompetes that they have held that companies who do not hire or promote talented employees who refuse to sign a noncompete (which would in any case be void if taken to court) are liable in tort and should be subject to punitive damages. Similarly, both an employer who requires a noncompete and one who respects another employer's unenforceable noncompete can be found by Californian courts to be liable in tort suits.[34] For example, when a sales representative was hired by a competitor and then fired out of "respect and understanding" for colleagues in the industry (meaning that the new employer got a threatening call from the ex-employer about a noncompete), the court announced that such termination was wrongful.

Still, through the end of the twentieth century and until very recently, confusion about the proper interpretation of the California law prohibiting noncompetes pervaded the courts. The California courts interpreted the ban to prohibit all agreements that do not fall under one of the statutory exceptions. By contrast, the federal Ninth Circuit Court of Appeals, interpreting the same California law, construed the prohibition to allow a "narrow restraint" exception to the general rule voiding noncompetition agreements.[35] Basically it introduced something of a reasonableness standard, allowing noncompetes in California when they were designed to protect trade secrets. In 2008, however, the California Supreme Court reaffirmed the state law that prohibits any noncompete agreement between an employer and employee.[36] The court spoke strictly, rejecting the Ninth Circuit's approach; even a merely partial or narrow restriction on an employee's ability to practice her trade or profession will not be allowed. The case responsible for this holding from the California Supreme Court involved an accountant for the mega-accounting firm Arthur Andersen who had signed a noncompete contract during his hiring process. After having been implicated in the Enron debacle as the enabling accounting firm, Arthur Andersen announced it would sell some of its practice groups to HSBC, a multinational banking and financial services company headquartered in London. HSBC required Andersen's employees to sign a "Termination of Non-Compete Agreement" that required employees to release Andersen from any and all claims, give up any indemnification rights, and continue indefinitely to preserve confidential information and trade secrets, all in return for revoking their noncompete agreement. When the ex-accountant refused to sign the release, HSBC withdrew its offer of employment. When the case reached the California Supreme Court, the court confirmed the California principle that an employer cannot, by contract, restrain a former employee from engaging in his or her profession, trade, or business. The court flatly validated the long-standing California rule and rejected the reasonableness standard applied by most other states.

California continues to strictly stand by its rejection of noncompetes as a method of control in the talent wars. Notably, however, noncompetes are enforceable in California against former partners or owners (as opposed to employees) when selling a business or a partnership interest. If you set up shop and buy out your competitor, you can make him sign a binding agreement whereby he promises to move away and to not open up a competing business down the street from the one you just bought. With respect to partnerships, the partnership needs to be a substantial one. For example, employees given insubstantial stock are not considered partners or owners, and using such stock to attempt an end run around California's noncompete policy has been deemed a "sham" by California courts.[37]

California's unique approach frequently leads to jurisdictional battles and conflicts of laws. For example, an employer located in Virginia can require its employees to sign a noncompete, which, geographically, will also cover the state of California. From the perspective of Virginia's contract law, the noncompete is enforceable as long as it is reasonable. But the California courts routinely refuse to enforce noncompete agreements formed outside of California.[38] They also reject contractual clauses that agree that the choice of law will be that of another state. The result is that if you are working in California or want to move to California to work, even if your ex-employer is located in another state, California policy will allow you to work despite a noncompete agreement to the contrary.

THE NATURAL EXPERIMENT: A TALE OF TWO CITIES

Eppur si muove (And yet it moves).

—*Galileo Galilei*

California views its strong stance as an overall gain for its economy, and the data confirm this intuition. This outlier western state that fiercely protects the ability of talent to move among competitors is therefore a good place to begin our query of the effects of such a stance on innovation and growth. "And yet it moves," Galileo rebelliously exclaimed (although his words are thought to be apocryphal) after signing a recantation of the Copernican theory that the sun was the center of the solar system. Galileo had a correct theory about the sun, and although in the minority and forced to recant he stood strong in his belief. California is in the minority among states in its belief in talent mobility. Other states assert that noncompetes are essential and without them their state would grind to a halt, and yet California, which doesn't allow noncompetes, still moves. Not only does California continue to move, it thrives. It is home to some of the world's most successful industries. Despite not having the ability to require noncompetes from their employees, companies in California compete vigorously and successfully on a global scale. The Silicon Valley is legendary for its stories of employees leaving stable, lucrative positions, working out of their garage, and perhaps even moving back in with room-mates and resuming the embarrassing practice of bringing their dirty laundry home to mom, only to become highly successful industry leaders when the gamble pays off. These talented entrepreneurs, the creative and innovative workforce of the Silicon Valley, could not have moved with such ease in any other state.

A famous duo through which to posit a comparison between California and a state that enforces noncompetes is the Silicon Valley and the high-tech hub of Massachusetts Route 128. Each of the regions bene-fits from having established cities (San Francisco and Boston), strong nearby universities (Berkeley/Stanford and Harvard/MIT), and large pools of talented people. Despite the similarities and despite a stronger start for Route 128, which began its high-tech region with more than three times the jobs available in the Silicon Valley, within a few decades in the second half of the twentieth century the Valley overtook Route 128 in number of employees, its local rate of growth being three times greater than that of its eastern counterpart. The distinguishing factor for the development of the Valley is how much it values openness, change, and mobility. The economic geographer AnnaLee Saxenian, who has compared the two areas, observes that the Silicon Valley is more open and networked and more likely to rely on the outsourcing of its core functions. In Massachusetts, firms were more likely to be vertically integrated—large companies that internalized most of the production functions—and employee movement among firms occurred less frequently than on the opposite coast. Subsequently, Massachusetts firms developed a culture of secrecy, hierarchy, protection, and a certain conservative spirit. The open structures of innovation in the Valley have an immediate impact on its market. Its openness allows for dramatically reduced time-to-market frames when companies introduce new technologies, allowing the industry to develop and grow at unprecedented rates.

Building on its culture of openness and mobility, a rather unconventional interpretation of market forces took root in the Silicon Valley—an ethos that perceives business failure as a positive step in high-tech entrepreneurship.[39] The exchanges and vibrancies of the Valley give it an edge over the autarkic and isolated environment of its East Coast competitor. Saxenian cites an engineer who explains, "Here in Silicon Valley there's far greater loyalty to one's craft than to one's company. A company is just a vehicle that allows you to work. If you're a circuit designer, it's most important for you to do excellent work. If you can't succeed in one firm, you'll move on to another one." In a very practical sense innovation is favored over the control and ownership of talent.

The first scholar to suggest that California's aversion to noncompetes is at least partly responsible for the Silicon Valley's success was the Stanford law professor Ron Gilson. Gilson hypothesized, without much empirical evidence to back it up, that the Silicon Valley experienced greater growth than Boston's high-tech area because of the differences in enforcement of noncompetes.[40] He suggested that beyond the Silicon Valley's economic and cultural advantages, it was California's refusal to enforce noncompetes that brought success to the Valley. In the absence of noncompetes, talent mobility accelerates and spurs new companies. Free from restriction, innovators and ideas are free to blossom into a powerful, healthy industry. But is the Silicon Valley really different in its rates of job mobility, start-up, and innovation?

Yes. We now have the data to back up the intuition that the early California legislature developed over a century ago. Studies examining high-tech industries across the country show that the Silicon Valley indeed has more job hopping than any other high-tech region. In fact, even high-tech communities in California outside of Silicon Valley have greater job mobility than parallel communities in other states. In one study the Federal Reserve and the National Bureau of Economic Research examined job mobility in the nation's top twenty metropolitan areas. The study relied on a large population survey data set and found higher intra-regional employee mobility in the California computer industry as compared to any other state. But, perhaps most important, the report also finds that other high-tech communities in California outside of Silicon Valley have greater job mobility than similar communities in other states, suggesting that it is California's exceptional stance on noncompetes that makes increased job-hopping a statewide phenomenon.

Since patents are inventions that must be filed and granted, the relationships between inventors are connections that can be mapped by using the database of the patent registry. Mapping the network of connections between inventors also reveals that the Valley has rapidly developed denser inventor networks than other high-tech hubs. Until recently, network analysis had not scrutinized claims about the Valley's regional advantage, but a new study sheds light on the region's development, examining three decades of patenting inventors. The U.S. patent registry includes all inventors' last names, hometowns, and the patent owner (usually the employing company) of every patent. The database enables researchers to construct inventor networks, where a link exists between two inventors who have coauthored a patent. Researching over two million inventors and almost three million patents, a Harvard Business School study observes a dramatic aggregation of the Silicon Valley regional networks at the beginning of the 1990s (fig. 3.2).[41] Comparing Boston and Northern California, the study finds that the Silicon Valley indeed mushroomed into a giant inventor network, a Voltron superstructure, as small, isolated networks came together. By the beginning of the twenty-first century almost half of all inventors in the area were part of the supernetwork. By contrast, the transition in Boston occurred much later

Fig 3.2. Silicon Valley's inventor network in the 1990s (from "The Evolution of Inventor Networks in the Silicon Valley and Boston Regions," Lee Fleming and Koen Frenken, *Advances in Complex Systems* 10, no. 1, ©2007 World Scientific).

and was much less dramatic. The study suggests that it was the specific patterns of labor mobility in the Valley, particularly the movement from established firms like IBM to its competitors, that were most significant to interorganizational networking.

BEYOND SUNSHINE: NATIONWIDE EVIDENCE

The causal connection between the Silicon Valley miracle and intense talent flows is difficult to prove. In comparing California to other states, there are thousands of factors and variables that make it difficult to pinpoint a single cause-and-effect relationship. California always seems to us too unique to be compared along just one axis. We have to look at the data in many different ways; one important viewpoint is the comparison of a region to itself.

Michigan is a natural experiment of such a longitudinal study—a before-and-after study of a single place that underwent legal reform. In 1905 Michigan passed a statute similar to the contemporary California ban on noncompetes, declaring any restriction on employment to be against public policy, illegal, and void. The law was enforced until 1985, when the legislature repealed the statute as part of an overall antitrust reform. From the mid-1980s on, Michigan adopted the reasonableness doctrine applied in most states. Research initiated again by Harvard Business School professors observed this change and its effect on the mobility of Michigan workers.[42] Using the U.S. patent database, which lists the names of individual inventors and their location, they found that after noncompetes became enforceable, there was a large decrease in mobility, and, significantly, the decrease was most strongly found in valuable or star inventors. In general, inventor mobility in Michigan dropped by more than 30 percent once noncompetes became enforceable. With respect to specialist inventors and highly cited star inventors, the decrease was even steeper, 45 percent.

Another way to move beyond the California miracle as the outlier state that prohibits noncompetes is to compare patterns of enforcement across all states. Recently, researchers have coded the strength of noncompetition enforcement across the states, resulting in a state-by-state index of noncompete enforcement of the fifty states and the District of Columbia. California scores 0 in enforcement, but most states score between 1 and 9. Since all states require reasonableness, no state blindly enforces all noncompete contracts without restriction, which would produce a score of 10 on the scale. Several recent studies use this code to identify differences with respect to the measures we've been exploring: mobility, inventor networks, innovation rates, and economic growth. In a manner similar to that of the natural experiment in Michigan, the UCLA professor of management Mark Garmaise researched three states, Texas, Louisiana, and Florida, that changed their attitude toward noncompetes markedly during the 1990s and 2000s. By studying changes within one state one can observe exogenous shocks, that is, independent changes that affect a single environment. Garmaise's study found that stronger enforcement of noncompetes significantly reduced mobility even with just small tweaks in the employment of the reasonableness standard. In other words, it's incremental, not an on-off switch. Mobility is reduced whether a state moves from a 0 to a 3 or from a 5 to a 7.

Garmaise also studied these questions by looking at all fifty states as coded on the scale of noncompete enforcement. In addition to finding higher mobility rates in lower-enforcing states, he also discovered, even more strikingly, that tougher enforcement reduces research and development spending and capital expenditures per employee, decreases executive salaries, and shifts compensation from bonuses and performance-based pay to a heavy reliance on a base or fixed salary.

In a study similar to Garmaise's, in 2010 researchers from Yale examined over three hundred metropolitan areas and found great advantages for states that weakly enforce noncompetes. Using the same code for weak and strong enforcement of noncompetes, the study found that states where noncompetes are not enforced or are weakly enforced have higher levels of patenting and employment and are better positioned to support entrepreneurship and start-up ventures. To remove concerns about a California effect, the research replicated the results but excluded the Silicon Valley area, and the findings remained consistent. We will examine these remarkable findings more closely in later chapters, but for now the message is clear: even among states that allow noncompetes, narrower enforcement produces many of the benefits that one aspires to see taking hold in a region.

DARK MATTER AND THE TIP OF THE NONCOMPETE ICEBERG

How should we interpret these findings about the many benefits of increased mobility and talent competition? The Boston attorney Gabor Garai analogizes the impact of noncompetes to the appearance of an iceberg. A few cases attract media attention, but they are just the tip: "The bulk of it is under water," he says. "That's where you have all the people who don't even try to leave or try to start a company because of their fear of being sued." Entrepreneurs describe their frustration with the counterproductive fear of employees who are willing to forgo job opportunities and interactions with potential clients to avoid even the appearance of impropriety. "Dark matter" is another metaphor referring to the same concern: "The pervasive use of non-competes in Massachusetts is part of the dark matter of the legal landscape in the state. You know it's there; exerting some gravitational force, but you can't see it or measure it. You never really know how many employees didn't move to another job, didn't start their own companies, and didn't take the risk of challenging their non-compete agreements in court."[43]

A small but growing minority of states are following the California way. Colorado now prohibits most noncompete restrictions and even has criminal sanctions for an employer that requires its employees to sign noncompete agreements. The state is not quite at 0 yet because there remain certain permissible exceptions for contracts that allow companies to recover the expense of educating and training an employee. In particular, it continues to allow noncompetes for employees who received training as "executive and management personnel and officers and employees who constitute professional staff."[44] In other words, Colorado draws a distinction between types of employees, allowing only higher skilled white-collar employees to be restricted by a noncompete. North Dakota and Oregon also have near-complete bans on noncompetes.[45] In Oregon the adoption of this new stance on noncompetes in 2008 was a response to the state legislature's concern about "a dangerous expansion in the use of non-competition agreements." Similar to the law in Colorado, the Oregon law allows enforcement of noncompete restrictions only against highly paid managers and professional staff. The law has a number of additional restrictions: first, it requires that the employee be informed about the noncompete in writing *before* the employee begins working for the company; second, the restriction to not compete can extend only up to two years; and, third, it must be designed to protect a company's trade secrets.

In 2009 a bill titled "An Act to Prohibit Restrictive Employment Covenants" was introduced in the Massachusetts legislature. It would void all noncompetes. Massachusetts already has a statute prohibiting noncompetes in the broadcasting industry that was passed as a result of strong lobbying efforts by the American Federation of Television and Radio Artists (AFTRA).[46] The bill was introduced as an initiative of the Alliance for Open Competition, a group of venture capitalists, executives, and entrepreneurs, which described it as dedicated to fostering innovation throughout the country: "We seek to break down a major barrier to entrepreneurialism: the use of non-competition agreements mandated by employers that force employees to sign away their rights to engage in any business of a competitive nature when they leave their present jobs. Today Massachusetts, New York, and Michigan are among dozens of other states that still enforce non-compete clauses."

The alliance's campaign to seek passage of legislation modeled after California's eradication of noncompetes emerged from its sense that noncompetes impede start-ups, thereby "forcing innovative entrepreneurs to take on tremendous legal and financial risks, and hampering the ability to meet our fullest economic potential as a nation." Richard Tibbetts, a software architect and start-up founder in Massachusetts, describes the initiative as "a simple legislative change which will cost the government little and have a big impact on Massachusetts competitiveness." The alliance passionately advocates that successful high-tech companies naturally perceive themselves as breeders of multiple start-ups, leading to a multiplier effect across successive generations of technology companies. It warns that a legal regime that enforces noncompetes is, in effect, the silent killer of the multiplier effect, retarding innovation and reducing the creation of start-ups. Paul Maeder, a general partner at Highland Capital Partners in Lexington, Massachusetts, explains simply, "Noncompetes make states, well . . . noncompetitive. It looks like California has taken another step to reinforce their leadership in the innovation economy." Notably, the group states that it opposes noncompetes but supports the continued use of trade secret protection, nondisclosure agreements, and other forms of restrictions.

Those who favor the tools of restriction have resisted the Massachusetts bill. Since it was introduced, it has undergone considerable review. The bill now allows noncompetes in certain instances for higher paid jobs but limits those agreements to one year. Over the past few years the efforts to enact legislation that would prohibit or significantly restrict noncompetes in Massachusetts have continued. In 2011, at a legislative hearing, the governor issued a statement in favor of restricting noncompetes, stating that economic research has shown that they can have a "demonstrable negative effect on the mobility of technology workers, especially those with advanced, specialized skills" and that the reduced mobility of these skilled employees may "adversely affect our innovation economy." The statement suggests that noncompetes are often unfairly imposed and advantage established large employers while hindering new entrepreneurship. The governor ended his statement by calling the change a pressing need for Massachusetts's economy.

With Massachusetts lobbyists leading the way, state legislatures elsewhere have begun proposing similar amendments. At the same time, other states, including Texas, Georgia, and Florida, are enacting laws to reverse the historical judicial hostility of their courts to noncompetes. In addition, countries as diverse as England, China, Israel, and Japan have been debating reforms—in discussions much like those in the

United States surrounding the enforcement of noncompetes—to create the optimal conditions for innovation and growth. The research points strongly to the many benefits of weaker noncompetes. We've seen already that the data support the intuition that more competition and less control of talent flow encourage job growth, start-ups, and regional development.

CHAPTER FOUR

Competition and the Miracle of Place

INNOVATION IN THE AIR

IN THAMES VALLEY, near London, is the world-renowned Motor Valley. What the Silicon Valley is to high tech, the Motor Valley is to race cars. The Motor Valley is responsible for the newest, most advanced high-end racing and sports cars. The region dominates the industry by producing Formula One cars, Indy cars, and the best sports cars in the world.

Formula One has a history of radical innovation, and each year its new advances spread across the industry. This history coincides neatly with high rates of talent flow. It is common for drivers, designers, and engineers to move from one team to another. Within the industry, leading engineers and designers move an average of eight times during their career. This means that approximately every three years they find a new employer. If this were a region with noncompetes, information wouldn't spread and talented people would be forced to sit on the sidelines while their contracts forbade them to work. They would miss out on innovations and industry advances, and when they finally got back "in the driver's seat," so to speak, they would be behind the times and much less competitive candidates. As the talent moves around the industry, it inevitably brings with it crucial information about what makes a race car the fastest it can be. Industry insiders have commented on the phenomenon that some teams, "somewhat cynically, employ people on short term contracts to extract what they know from other teams."[1] And yet here, in this highly mobile industry, we see some of the most significant technological advances and economic success. Despite (or quite possibly because of) this constant flow of personnel, companies choose to stay within the region, and the agglomeration dominates the worldwide auto industry. The region, with its culture of fierce talent poaching, remains home to the best-selling sports car companies in the world. A close study of the industry has led the British economists Nick Henry and Steven Pinch to conclude that "as personnel move, they bring with them knowledge and ideas about how things are done in other firms, helping to raise the knowledge throughout the industry . . . this 'churning' of personnel raises the knowledge base of the industry as a whole within the region."[2]

In 1920 the British economist Alfred Marshall developed the theory of local knowledge. Marshall argued that if one looks closely and compares regions, "the mysteries of the trade become no mystery, but are, as it were, in the air."[3] Since then, the body of empirical evidence about how geography matters has expanded significantly. The connections between place and business success are unraveling, and the reasons are manifold. Usually we think that factors in the equation of success of businesses are internal to the company: its business plans, assets, and people. Rarely do we consider the importance of the external environment. But the reality is that places have characteristics that induce or inhibit growth. Environments with "innovation in the air" form a virtuous cycle: innovation accelerates near innovation. Proximity to talent is a catalyst for more talent.

What is it that makes an economy thrive? Is it a region's natural resources? Is it the funneling of local capital investment? The quality of the region's education system? And why are innovative activities concentrated in certain areas? The answer lies first and foremost in the people who inhabit the region. Successful regions depend on a population of skilled and talented workers, and in turn these workers learn more quickly when they work in successful areas. The converse holds true as well: less successful regions produce slower-learning workers.[4] We now know that nearly identical places will succeed or decline depending on their human capital.

Marshall hypothesized that firms cluster together in certain locations instead of spreading out because clusters provide lower costs for goods, people, and ideas. In economic jargon, these three factors correspond to the benefits of capital, labor markets, and knowledge spillovers. A half century after Marshall hypothesized that innovation "is in the air," the Nobel laureate economist Kenneth Arrow explained that competition spurs industry advancement. Arrow argued that competition, not central control, is what fuels innovation.[5] Focusing on human capital, Arrow observed, "Mobility of personnel among firms provides a way of spreading information."[6] Arrow theorized that ideas travel with the movement of people between firms and that this movement accelerates progress and growth. Fast-forward to twenty-first-century network science: new studies provide the empirical evidence for Marshall's and Arrow's assertions and demonstrate the many positive effects of innovation-inducing environments.

Arrow predicted that once a company becomes a monopoly it has fewer incentives to undertake the risks of improving successful inventions. A company that maintains a dominant market position will measure the costs of investing in potential innovation against the profits that the company already receives through its current product line. The Arrow Effect predicts that in a monopoly situation innovation will only lead the monopolist to replace its own market share, leading to only marginal gains over current profits. In other words, the monopolistic company is competing against itself—not the best motivator for a market actor. In contrast, when competitors enter the market they calculate greater profits from innovative improvements because, initially, their profit baseline is set much lower. Thus competitors have sufficient incentives to make drastic improvements that larger monopolistic firms might not consider worth their while.

The Arrow Effect explains why companies need competitors to incentivize more innovation. Yet the geographic effect on innovation is greater than the direct effects of competition. When companies of the same industry are geographically close, an intermediate set of support services and related industries provide better choices and lower costs. In turn, thriving local economies attract bigger and better pools of workers. Potential employees are drawn to vibrant cities. The city, by its diversity and size, serves as an insurance policy for both companies and individuals against job loss and industry crisis. In a city, workers can always find a life raft when their boat sinks. Conversely, a small, one-company town creates huge risks for its workers. If the town's principal company goes under, the lack of other opportunities offers little insulation to the worker.

By drawing talent, vibrant cities gain the self-reinforcing advantage of deep labor markets. Built-in pools of skilled workers not only serve as buffers in economic cycles, but also allow companies to exchange personnel for work on certain projects, even as each employee remains employed at the original company. Regional density allows economies to become more specialized—more suppliers exist, and intermediaries provide problem solving and other services at a lower cost. The inherent advantage of cities also results in metropolitan areas having more inventors and generating more patents per capita than towns and rural areas, and the larger the population of a city, the more innovation is likely to occur. In a dense metropolitan area the number of patents per person is about 20 percent higher than in a metropolitan area half as dense.[7]

Combining the two aspects of geography and industry competition, the economist Paul Romer brought together the insights of Marshall and Arrow (economists now refer to their combined insight as the MAR effect, after the initials of each of these leading thinkers). According to Romer, because knowledge is predominantly industry-specific, geographic concentration will create positive growth for the entire specialized economy. A region dense with companies operating in the same field will be rich with knowledge exchanges and will grow exponentially. While these macro-predictions are useful, the MAR effect still doesn't explain exactly how large talent pools, mobility, and competitive raiding help industries and regions grow. Economists talk about knowledge spillover, the movement of valuable information within a market, but we need a better illustration of how this knowledge actually travels. To gain a more complete understanding, we must look closer into the ways in which knowledge is embedded in our talent and flows in the market. Specifically, we must consider how relations between professionals contribute to innovation. Further clues to the miracle of place lie in overcoming the stagnation effects of static groupthink, Not Invented Here, and other innovation traps to be explored below.

SIX DEGREES OF KEVIN BACON
In a savvy move in 2007, at the opening weekend of the Sundance Film Festival in Park City, Utah, Kevin Bacon announced the launch of SixDegrees.org. The actor, who has given his name to the popular game called six degrees of Kevin Bacon—the search for connections between

the movie star and all other Hollywood personalities in six steps or less—put the surprising popularity of the game to good use. Six Degrees is a charitable social network based on the insight that Bacon and the rest of us are connected to any other person on this planet through six or fewer relationships. The first experiments testing the veracity of six degrees were done in the mid-1960s when the American sociologist Stanley Milgram randomly selected a sample of people in the Midwest and asked them to deliver packages to a stranger in Massachusetts. He told the senders the recipient's name, job, and general location and then asked them to deliver the package to someone they knew personally who was most likely to know the recipient. The findings were extraordinary. The chains of delivery were far shorter than expected. On average each chain had five intermediaries, leading to the notion of six degrees. The experiment received new life in the twenty-first century when, in 2001, professors at Columbia University recreated Milgram's experiment using e-mail messages. The electronic experiment included 48,000 senders and 19 recipients in 157 countries in total. Remarkably, the World Wide Web of the new century is also connected by six degrees of separation!

It really is a small world after all. Indeed, *small world* has become a scientific term describing "fast-paced Darwinian environments in which ideas are cheap, knowledge flows freely, and talent seeks opportunity."[8] When people move more often and more freely, worlds become smaller. In truly small-world environments, the average links between two people can be considerably fewer than the standard six, and the interactions within the network can be richer and more frequent. Small worlds trim the number of intermediaries between professionals and enhance the quality of exchange. A wealth of new insights has come from new research on how small worlds operate and evolve. In both artistic and scientific networks, friendships and prior ties are of fundamental importance. In professional settings an important and at first glance counterintuitive insight is that weaker ties tend to matter more than strong ones. A strong tie is one that connects a person to a social network through multiple acquaintances. Your close friends and family members—the people you celebrate birthdays and holidays with and see at soccer and poker games—most likely know each other and have multiple ties between them. Those are your strong ties. Weak ties, on the other hand, are more likely to connect us to other circles and expand our network. Weak ties are formed with the person you meet at a trade show, a conference, or a fund-raiser. The story of one person, Ego, illustrates the power of his weak and strong ties:

> Ego will have a collection of close friends, most of whom are in touch with one another—a densely knit clump of social structure. Moreover, Ego will have a collection of acquaintances, few of whom know one another. Each of these acquaintances, however, is likely to have close friends in his own right and therefore to be enmeshed in a closely-knit clump of social structure—but one different from Ego's. The weak tie between Ego and his acquaintance, therefore, becomes not merely a trivial acquaintance tie but rather a crucial bridge between the two densely knit clumps of close friends.[9]

The hero of our story, Ego, benefits more from the weaker ties in his network. Weak ties have a greater likelihood of being bridges than strong ties precisely because they connect people to social circles different from their own. One would think that when you are looking for a job it is best to approach your closest friend or your weekly tennis partner for leads, but chances are you and your best friends have circles of friends and connections that mostly overlap. In fact, study after study shows that weak ties are more powerful for economic purposes and lead to better job opportunities than strong ties. Generally, the more appealing the job, the more likely it is that weak ties rather than immediate close connections will help you find that job. Low-skilled workers are more likely to rely on strong ties—think of the unemployed handyman asking around for some work—while skilled workers benefit from their looser ties even more than from their direct, close connections. In university settings, these loose but numerous ties are referred to as the invisible college; through cooperation, professional meetings, and conferences, collaborators gain a web of professional and societal connections linking researchers across institutions.[10] This is the concept behind LinkedIn, a professional network linking you with your friends' second-degree contacts. LinkedIn currently reports more than 120 million registered users, spanning more than 196 countries and territories worldwide.

Networks are the great equalizer of professional growth. If someone was born into a poor environment and received little guidance from her immediate network of close kin, professional networks can serve as a substitute for family ties. A recent study examined the question of how the likelihood of entrepreneurial activity of one individual is impacted by the prior family experiences or by the career experiences of that individual's coworkers.[11] The study found that a person's peers increase his or her likelihood of becoming an entrepreneur in two ways: by enhancing the capacity to perceive entrepreneurial opportunities and by increasing motivation to pursue those opportunities. Both of these effects are strongest for those without exposure to entrepreneurship in their family, suggesting that market ties can serve as substitutes for community ties.

THE GOLDILOCKS SHAPE OF NETWORKS

The story of Ego illustrates the economic value of networks for individuals, particularly for the most sought-after talent: high-skilled workers, inventors, and executives. Networks consist not only of people but also of firms. In one famous study the economic sociologist Brian Uzzi examined how social structures affect economic life. Uzzi found that the structure of a company's ties impacts its chances of survival. The ties between a company's suppliers must be neither too strong nor too weak to promise success.[12] In other words, the best-performing companies are those that have multiple ties but are not so reliant on close connections that they are suffocated by such dependency. Uzzi argues that corporate "embeddedness," the shape of a company's social relations, explains its economic strength. Uzzi's field study of social connections in the apparel industry demonstrates that, naturally, embeddedness within tight networks is beneficial to a company. At the same time, perhaps paradoxically, too much embeddedness or, as we have seen with individuals, too much reliance on close ties can reduce a firm's adaptive capacity. For example, if a distributor has a connection to a supplier that is socially strong, it interferes with the distributor's ability to act rationally and choose a rival supplier with a lower price. Firms need to be like oak trees and have a deep network of roots but still be flexible enough to bend in the winds of change.

Accordingly, individuals and firms each need strong *and* weak connections to thrive. Up to now I have emphasized the benefits of these connections in enabling more successful job searches. Perhaps even more exciting are the ways in which networks spur creativity and innovation.

We need diverse social and professional connections to innovate. In every field, human interaction is necessary to seed the first ideas for groundbreaking inventions.

How many Kevin Bacons away are we from our next breakthrough? How important are past ties for forming successful collaborations? Recently, a team of researchers examined the ways in which friendships and personal connections help artistic as well as scientific production. The team compared veteran professionals who have already participated in collaborative networks with rookie first-timers attempting to market their research and plays. What the team found was surprising. Prestigious, high-impact scientific journals have a high percentage of incumbents. We could expect that much. But, at the same time, the researchers also found that working with too many former collaborators reduces the placement ranks.[13] This means that forming the next winning team is a matter of having highly networked and experienced collaborators but not necessarily the same ones you worked with previously.[14] Rather, introducing new blood into a creative team enhances the likelihood of success. Recall our observations on the necessity of both strong and weak ties and the need to expand one's network to avoid overreliance on one's closest connections—this principle isn't limited to job seekers.

We have always intuitively known that human knowledge is a collective endeavor. Still, tracking the birth of an idea poses a central challenge for research. One of the difficulties with capturing the proliferation of an idea is finding a paper trail. Can we observe the spread of innovation in the same way we witness the spread of a virus? Today, science offers us new tools to test the connections among individuals and their relations to human activity.[15] Network science can teach us about the connections between millions of individuals via our communications over the web, professional interactions, search patterns, and even our consumption habits. Network theorists apply mathematical models to study relationships between objects or subjects. Networks consist of links (or edges) between people or firms (nodes) and centers (hubs), showing the connections between individuals through professional ties, friendships, communication, and commerce.

If it is true that ideas can spread like viruses, then the study of real viruses, the infectious kinds we want to halt, is a good place to begin to understand the spread of ideas. Scientists engage in network mapping of viruses for a very practical reason: to assist social planning and policy in controlling the spread of epidemics such as HIV. When scientists map networks, from person X to Y to Z, they usually take on a similar shape. In the network, most people have only a small number of sexual partners—the network edges. A small number of individuals are different, though, as they stand out for having hundreds of sexual partners (leading some advocates to call for a separate crime of "reckless sex").[16] Mapping the connectivity nodes and hubs as well as the spread of the virus can help policy makers plan programs for distributing condoms and testing to prevent further infection. Network science and modeling patterns of interactions, for example, through the use of computer simulations, not only provide clues about the past spread of a virus but also enable the prediction of future flows. These maps can help regulators control the spread of dangerous viral infections and disease outbreaks and help educators create programs to prevent sexually transmitted diseases. Recently, network analysis has even been applied to show the dating and mating habits of users of Facebook, suggesting that the rates of syphilis increase in places with high rates of social network users. If science can show us the love/disease connections between thousands of Internet users, can the science of networks also help us predict the links between talent flow and innovation?

PATENTS AND THE PAPER TRAIL

For research on innovation, patent registries are fruitful archives for mapping inventive collaborations. Innovation includes but is broader than inventions that can be patented. An invention is a concrete new product or device that is original and novel. Innovation encompasses such inventions but also includes improvements and any change that adds value in the market. Innovative information can be the subject of intellectual property protections, including patent, copyright, trademark, and trade secrets. But innovation also includes nonprotectable improvements and changes such as the development of better processes, business strategies, research patterns, and the effective absorption of knowledge. Because of its diffuse and incremental nature, the origins of innovation are usually difficult to pin down and measure, but patents are a different story. Patents open a window on innovation; they leave a trail.

For the purposes of patent filing, every inventor must be given credit (even if, as we shall see later, ownership is transferred to the employer).

Therefore, each patent record contains information about the inventor's home address and employer. In patent network imaging, the nodes of the network can be the patents issued, and the links are citations of one patent by another.[17] Alternatively, the nodes can be the inventor who invented the patent, and the links are the collaborations between different inventors. If inventors *A* and *B* worked together on one patent, and *B* and *C* on another, then *A* and *C* are part of a network, and inventor B is the node of the network. Thanks to advanced network analysis techniques and newly introduced electronic filing systems at the patent office, when these data are filtered, invention networks reveal the connections and collaborations among millions of individual inventors. Patent data now afford us an invaluable way to track inventor collaborations and movement.

Network imaging helps us to actually visualize human relationships. After gathering the data, network researchers use inventor-matching algorithms to assess rates of collaboration between other inventors. The first important finding of the studies of inventor networks is that the density of a network is highly correlated with the number of inventions in that network. This means that the more people are in contact, the more creative *each* person becomes. The connections between innovators increase the overall numbers of patents as well as the number of coauthored patents in an area. Put simply, a dense network is more collaborative and more productive as a whole. The ripple effect happens when, for example, a group of nanotechnology scientists relocate to San Diego, where there are dozens of biotech researchers. Suddenly the likelihood of interactions followed by interdisciplinary breakthrough grows exponentially. Just as streets connect houses in neighborhoods, these invisible ties operate as innovation catalysts between people.

Network studies of patent citations (references to existing patents in newly filed patents) also reveal that inventions that start in places that are more industrially diverse receive more than twice the number of citations than those developed in smaller or more homogeneous towns. While patent citations are an imperfect way of measuring innovation, such citations have been shown to be correlated with patent value as well as with the market value of the firm that owns the patent. Put differently, if you invent something while working in a vibrant and diverse place, your invention has a greater likelihood to soar and succeed. This last observation leads us to the importance of diversity and interdisciplinarity in the art and science of innovation.

TWENTY-FIRST-CENTURY RENAISSANCE

> What we need in America is a renaissance. We need to go forward by going backward.
>
> —*Stanley Crouch, novelist and critic*

Born in 1452, the illegitimate son of a notary and a peasant woman, Leonardo da Vinci embodied the concept that "a man can do all things if he will."[18] In the age of the Renaissance, those who were found to be gifted (unfortunately, mostly men and few women at the time) were encouraged to develop skills in all areas of knowledge, both science and art. Da Vinci was what we moderns call a Renaissance man: he was a scientist, engineer, anatomist, botanist, painter, sculptor, architect, mathematician, writer, and an inventor. Da Vinci traveled in Europe throughout his early adulthood, apprenticing with different artists and thinkers. Along the way he invented, designed, and theorized such diverse novelties as helicopters, hang gliders, solar power, musical instruments, cannons, tanks, and advancements in hydrodynamics. Thousands of pages of notebooks record Da Vinci's tremendous ingenuity and amazing range of interests.

Versatility and interdisciplinarity were the hallmarks of the Renaissance. But these ideas precede fifteenth-century Italy. Most ancient Greek inventors were polymaths: they embraced a comprehensive approach to education and refused to restrict their knowledge to a single subject. But many believe that da Vinci was the last true Renaissance man. As technology became more advanced and complex, modern times demanded specialization. No longer could one person hold the key to all sciences and crafts. And yet, even today, the fact that the best breakthroughs occur between technically distant fields echoes the Renaissance emphasis on multidisciplinarity and reinforces its importance. In the modern era of integration, twenty-first-century innovation becomes ever more fine-tuned and sophisticated; no discipline is isolated from others. Nanotechnology is an example of a field that emerged from the cross-pollination of mechanical engineering, semiconductor technology, and molecular biology, and it has applications in fields as diverse as medicine, pharmaceuticals, electronics, and energy production. When asked how he defined creativity, Apple's Steve Jobs, who was the beacon of high-tech innovation until his untimely passing, responded that creativity is connecting things. Jobs exemplified this belief through the passions of his life by studying new and seemingly unconnected areas; he developed expertise in fine cars, calligraphy, meditation, and Eastern philosophy.

The payoffs of diversity and multidisciplinarity are real. A group of Harvard Business School professors wondered about the value of teams from various disciplines working together. They compared cross-disciplinary team inventions to those of more homogeneous teams, finding that inventions from very diverse cross-disciplinary teams are on average less promising than those made by people who are from similar disciplines. But then they looked at the likelihood of a major breakthrough and found that it was higher in a more diverse creative team: "As the distance between the team members' fields or disciplines increases, the overall quality of their innovations falls. But . . . the breakthroughs that *do* arise from such multidisciplinary work, though extremely rare, are frequently of unusually high value—superior to the best innovations achieved by conventional approaches."[19]

This means that merging diverse disciplines is a high-risk, high-reward business. Uncertainty is similar in that way: the higher the uncertainty in the search for innovation, the more likely radical and unexpected ideas are to occur. Reinforcing the importance of diversity and uncertainty, new studies of innovation conclude that it is not simply the number of new ideas introduced in a company or a team that will lead to a breakthrough, but also the levels of disparate and diverse ideas. Knowledge does not restrict itself to residing quietly within the bounds of a company but spills across companies and across sectors.[20] Multiplicity in fields, diversity of teams, and expanding connections between the inventive individuals yield many failed ideas, but these processes are also more likely to yield the grand prize—that one-in-a-million invention that becomes engrained in the history of human progress. The diverse engagement litters the ground and fertilizes the soil from which breakthroughs grow. As in many other aspects of our lives the maxim the higher the risk, the greater the reward holds true here.

Over time, innovation can be understood as happening on a larger scale, beyond any one person, one company, or even one industry. Zooming out, a similar centrality of diversity emerges in the interactions between talented collaborators within work teams, at a company, within an industry, and within a region.

BUBBLING HUBS

> A poem compresses much in a small space and adds music, thus heightening its meaning. The city is like poetry: it compresses all life, all races and breeds, into a small island and adds music and the accompaniment of internal engines.
>
> —*E. B. White*

Da Vinci's multidisciplinary accomplishments were not fueled in a vacuum. The powerful Medici family passionately sponsored Renaissance arts, and their patronage radically transformed Florence into a bubbling creative hub. The economic support of the Medicis allowed artists such as Leonardo and Michelangelo to thrive. Like Leonardo, Michelangelo was an archetypal Renaissance man—a painter, sculptor, architect, poet, and engineer. In the fifteenth century Italy's high level of urbanization and particularly the city of Florence's unique political, social, and civic features fostered the eruption of an intense, long-lasting cultural movement. The Medicis' influence created a thriving hub for new thought, and Florence's density of talent sparked revolutionary creations.

The new science of networks confirms what the Medicis knew all along: bring creative and inventive people together and each will become even better. With a nod to the past, the entrepreneur and writer Frans Johansson refers to the phenomenon of bringing people together from a wide range of disciplines as the Medici effect. Today, five centuries removed from the Renaissance, we still find that hubs of innovation boost their inhabitants. If da Vinci is the archetypical Renaissance man, the design company IDEO is the contemporary model of a Renaissance company. Cofounded by a Stanford professor, the company has been called by the *Wall Street Journal* "Imagination's Playground." *Fortune* calls it "Innovation U." IDEO is full of designers who are engineers, but the company also includes anthropologists, psychologists, artists, and musicians. IDEO has been responsible for the Palm Pilot, the Apple and the Microsoft mouse, the Leap Chair, the Twist 'N Go cup for Pepsi, and thousands of other designs, including toys, furniture, and medical and digital equipment. The start of IDEO's interdisciplinarity did not randomly occur in Palo Alto, California. Seated along the pulsing veins of the Silicon Valley, the company soared to new heights. Its success has been remarkable by any measure, and it now has additional offices in New York, Chicago, Boston, London, Munich, and Shanghai. The Silicon Valley is the twentieth century's Florence.

Thousands of start-ups inhabit the Silicon Valley. During the mid-1990s the region became the home of over 20 percent of the world's largest high-tech companies, including Internet, software, computer design, and gaming and biotech companies. Despite the burst of the high-tech bubble in the early 2000s, the Valley's reign continues, and the region has one of the highest average incomes in the country. New companies in the area continue to be founded at an impressive rate. Unsurprisingly, many regions have attempted to duplicate the Silicon Valley's success. Economists and sociologists continue to try to decode its secret.

Although the Silicon Valley is the paradigmatic example of a high-tech cluster, other industry clusters and Florence-like bubbling hubs are easy to find. Economists call them agglomeration economies—spatially connected industries. We witness such clusters all around us: Hollywood rules the movie industry; Nashville has become the metonym of country music; New York City is the hub of financial and legal services; Hartford, Connecticut, is the nerve center of the American insurance industry; in San Diego, where I teach, biotech companies have mush-roomed, placing the city on the global map for pharmaceuticals and applied life sciences.

Even finer maps can be drawn within the contours of cities. Manhattan naturally springs to mind, where, for example, on a single block—Forty-Seventh Street between Fifth and Sixth Avenue—there are almost three thousand diamond businesses.[21] A few blocks on Broadway define the present and future of theater and music. On other streets one can find suppliers of fashion, electronics, apparel, accounting, and soft-ware. In a little swath of New York City, centralized and isolated on an island, there is something for everyone. If you can make it there, you can make it anywhere. E. B. White, a longtime fixture at the *New Yorker* maga-zine, wrote about his beloved city in 1949:

> Commuters give the city its tidal restlessness; natives give it
> solidity and continuity; but the settlers give it passion. And
> whether it is a farmer arriving from Italy to set up a small
> grocery store in a slum, or a young girl arriving from a small
> town in Mississippi to escape the indignity of being observed by
> her neighbors, or a boy arriving from the Corn Belt with a
> manuscript in his suitcase and a pain in his heart, it makes
> no difference: each embraces New York with the intense
> excitement of first love, each absorbs New York with the fresh
> eyes of an adventurer, each generates heat and light to dwarf the
> Consolidated Edison Company.

What A. A. Milne said about chaos, that it carries the advantage of constantly sparking exciting discoveries, goes beyond the organizational level of creative playgrounds among coworkers. As captured in the words of White, positive chaos fuels an entire city. Disorder creates excitement and spurs human capacity.

The Nobel laureate economist Robert Lucas explained people's will-ingness to pay high rents in bustling cities very simply: they want to be near other people. Lucas asked, what could people be paying Manhattan or downtown Chicago rents for, if not for the proximity to others? This is the bright side of congestion. Cities allow people to connect on a daily basis and augment each other's talents and skills. "New York City's garment district, financial district, diamond district, advertising district and many more," writes Lucas, "are as much intellectual centers as is Columbia or New York University." The high priestess of urban studies, the sociologist Jane Jacobs, viewed the chaos of cities as the lifeblood of blossom and change. Jacobs describes cities as idea incubators. Recall the economic analysis embedded in the MAR effect: that firms concen-trated near others of the same industry will experience economic advantages. The MAR effect is incomplete. Jacobs's research adds the dimension of diversity and cross-industry fertilization: "The diversity, of whatever kind, that is generated by cities rests on the fact that in cities so many people are so close together, and among them contain so many different tastes, skills, needs, supplies, and bees in their bonnets."[22] And just as we saw that a tipping point of close ties, when they close in on a business, creates dependency and stagnation, according to Jacobs there is such a thing as overefficiency, overorganization, and order in cities, where economies and ideas stagnate when diversity is lacking.

The geography of innovation confirms that inventive activities in geographic isolation are less frequent, and, subsequently, are less likely to have an important impact. Although companies that choose to relocate near their competitors incur congestion costs, they often gain more than they lose from proximity. Economists refer to this as benefits of agglomeration and localized knowledge spillovers. We've already seen that there are multiple advantages of clustering geographically. Overall, economic clustering raises the rate of innovation and growth. Where companies agglomerate, the supply of talent, technologies, and possibilities for collaborations expands exponentially. Competitors, through close observation, adopt best practices when they are in proximity to other industry leaders. Grouping can lower transaction costs for clients and customers as well because they have easier access and more choice when they visit a business cluster. Simply put, you go to the garment district for a dress; you fly into the Silicon Valley for a microchip. It costs less to have more choice. Marshall predicted the following chain of events in a place where innovation is concentrated: "Good work is rightly appreciated; inventions and improvement in machinery, in processes and the general organization of the business have their merits promptly discussed: if one man starts a new idea, it is taken up by others and combined with suggestions of their own; and thus it becomes the source of further new ideas."[23]

And, as we've seen, it's not just that similar companies located in proximity have a competitive edge. Some of the most important knowledge spillover occurs between different but complementary (rather than identical) industries. For example, when regions like the Silicon Valley house active software, biotech, microchip, and venture capital firms, these diverse industries complement one another, and each becomes stronger. Complementary knowledge across diverse industries and skill sets triggers innovation by connecting ideas and leading to new fields and experiments. Empirical evidence supports both threads of economic predictions—the MAR effect's focus on industry concentration and

Jacobs's focus on diversity. Industry clusters and diverse dynamic markets each have positive effects on individual firms' success. The research is quite conclusive: the more diverse the area is and the more competitors there are in each industry, the faster the economy grows.[24]

THE INDUSTRY–UNIVERSITY NEXUS

One of the most important characteristics of a geographic area is the presence of educational institutions, which complement a culture of innovation in a region. Related to the success of the Silicon Valley and its high flow of talented and mobile people are the knowledge spillovers and partnerships between universities—like Stanford, UC Berkeley, and UC San Francisco—and private sector companies. Interestingly, Stanford University was faster to promote industry–university collaboration than its counterparts Harvard and MIT in the Massachusetts high-tech hub. Stanford signaled an openness to the industry and to diversity in goals— not-for-profit higher education and for-profit marker ventures—that was very much in line with the culture of openness and noncontrol that boosted the Valley. The benefits of such partnerships are clear: universities nurture the fundamental research that becomes the basis for applied innovation in the private market. Nowadays, alliances between universities and private industry have become central in certain high-density innovation localities.

In 1989 the economist Adam Jaffe wrote, "A state that improves its university research system will increase local innovation both by attracting industrial R&D and augmenting its productivity."[25] In pioneering empirical research, Jaffe studied the number of patents of each state as a function of the research and development performed by local universities. Jaffe found that academic institutions create positive spillovers into local businesses, so that greater university research expenditures correlate with greater local patenting rates. Here, too, proximity matters. Several studies have used patent filings to examine citations of university research by corporate R&D departments. The studies find that firms are more likely to quote research from universities that are nearby than from universities located farther away.[26] Recent technology booms have occurred in cities as diverse as San Diego, Seattle, Austin, and Chapel Hill. The Durham–Chapel Hill industrial corridor of North Carolina has been dubbed the Silicon Triangle because it enjoys proximity to Duke

University and the University of North Carolina and has evolved into one of the prominent high-tech clusters in the country.

We can see this centrality of the university–industry nexus in studies about particular industries as well. The success of biotechnology companies has been clearly linked to the total number of articles written by their own scientists in collaboration with the local university's star scientists. However, it is notable that the number of academic publications alone, as a general figure, absent collaboration with industry, does not predict the success of an industry. In other words, unlike the raw measure of patenting rates, which inherently reflect active collaboration in the industry, the raw measure of university publishing does not reflect success of an industry like the booming field of biotech. It is active scientific collaboration with universities, not simply the presence of a university nearby, that helps the biotech firms.[27]

A BOHEMIAN INDEX

If you build it, they will come.

—*Field of Dreams* (1989)

Modern cities are magnetic. In the new world of urban living, many of us want balanced, *prêt-à-porter* doses of learning institutions, arts, Italian food, and spiritual centers. In high school tech-geeks and artsy bohemians don't mix. But in postadolescence, in cities, they are drawn together. And they aren't just coexisting neighbors; their urban existence is symbiotic.

Name your passion: food, theater, sailing, golf, fashion, music. Lifestyle attracts talent, and talent supports lifestyle. Where culture, restaurants, nightlife, and artistic production are present, talent will come. A team of researchers led by the sociologist Richard Florida, a protégé of Jacobs, has studied the characteristics of places with high levels of innovation. Florida provocatively suggests that a lot can be learned from keeping our eye on a city's "bohemian index." According to dictionary definitions, bohemians are people with artistic or literary interests who disregard conventional standards of behavior. When the researchers looked at the numbers of artists—musicians, performers, writers—in a city, they found that a high concentration of them is associated with high concentration of human capital and innovation in seemingly unrelated industries, including high-tech, finance, and high-level manufacturing. The same team also devised a "gay index." Again, the study found positive association between gay households and regional growth and development. Openness to diversity, in other words, is important to the drawing of talent.

Beyond the bohemian and gay indexes, the study observed correlations between a place's openness to immigrants, artists, and racial diversity and its economic success. When the original research team was expanded and the same studies were conducted in Canada and Australia the results were similar. The researchers concluded that cities high on the bohemian index share "a common ethos that values creativity, individuality, difference, and merit."

Florida's bohemian index is not dissimilar to the talent flow index I am developing here as I compare mentalities of control and openness in the talent wars. As we shall soon see, a region with a human capital regime that is supportive of talent and innovation is far more likely than other regions to lure new talent and keep its existing talent. The more open a place is to ideas and people, the more tolerant and accepting of new talent it is, the more human capital it will capture.

Even without knowing in advance the detailed indexes of each city, each of us intuitively holds ideas about the kinds of futures that can be found in different places. The *Wall Street Journal* recently surveyed four thousand recent college graduates, three-quarters of whom said they care more about location than about the availability of a job. At least when we are young and carefree, we first choose the kind of place where we want to live and then search for a job.[28] Florida, who has studied the location choices people make between cities for over two decades, concludes that jobs versus people is a false dichotomy: "The two come together at the nexus of place. Real places provide the thick labor markets that match people to jobs, the mating markets that enable people to find life partners, the social markets that beget friendships, the amenities that allow people to pursue the lifestyles they wish, and the smorgasbord of daily choices that encourage people to construct and validate their identities holistically."[29] Most important, the more a place lends itself to the entrance of new people and facilitates their vocation, interactions, and the nurturing of their talent, the more benefits to the place will follow.

THE ORIGINAL SOCIAL MEDIA: PERSONAL INTERACTION

Knowledge is embedded in people. Geographical clusters of inventors are not a new phenomenon. The historians Naomi Lamoureaux and Kenneth Sokoloff data mined patent data from the late nineteenth and early twentieth centuries and found that even back then inventors were clustered in regions with high invention rates. In such highly dense innovation localities, inventors tended to be more specialized and have high invention rates per inventor.[30] Today, even as communication costs have become dramatically lower and knowledge has become more accessible and searchable, inventors continue to draw upon nearby knowledge far more frequently.

In the information age, as we are able to transfer information instantly and freely and have immediate access to information digitally, isn't the world just one global hub of ideas? The answer is, in fact, no. No matter what the latest technology is, no matter how flat our globalized world gets, the evidence shows there is no substitute for in-person communication and relationships. In geographically dense areas people are able to attend professional meetings and form social connections with like-minded innovators in their field. Knowledge transmission often requires face-to-face interactions and lengthy exchanges rather than just written correspondence and scientific publications. The digital revolution and primarily the Internet have allowed us to be in one place while learning about new science and innovation from far away. Yet knowledge is bound by physical space.

We might have expected the effect of locality to diminish now that so much of our work, research, and communication are online, but the importance of place remains as strong as it has always been. Consider the distinction between general information and embedded knowledge. Knowledge that is embedded comes from experience, from learning by doing or observing; this kind of knowledge is difficult to codify and write down. Embedded knowledge (also known as tacit knowledge) is learned informally through direct and repeated contacts. People who work in the same industry and interact professionally form epistemic communities, or networks of people tied together by knowledge and expertise, that share the same vocabulary and dynamic language. Professional terms and know-how change constantly, long after people complete their formal education. Social bonds and face-to-face meetings foster professional networks and better, faster, more accurate information diffusion.

As you can imagine by now, the way tacit knowledge spreads depends on the shape of the network and the complexity of the information being diffused.[31] When knowledge is transmitted, it usually does not diffuse accurately and flawlessly across companies. Geographical distance matters. Gaps open between the original information and the way this information is received and interpreted. Highly complex knowledge resists diffusion, and the greater the distance between the source and the receiver, the more likely it is that high-fidelity transmission will fail. Imagine teaching your grandmother how to use a computer: how much more difficult would that task be over the phone than if you could sit with her and walk her through the steps? Even in an extremely high-tech world, even for the most tech-savvy generations, there are only weak substitutes for face-to-face interaction. The result is that the more complex the knowledge, the more localized its diffusion.[32] For example, despite patent filings being available to anyone anywhere in the world, innovative companies are more likely to quote research from a local university than from a more distant university (box 3).[33]

Calling to mind the significance of small worlds, studies of high-tech industries reveal that even in the absence of patents and trade secrets, success is determined by tacit knowledge and the people who embody that knowledge. In the laser industry, for example, scientific journals specified all the knowledge that was necessary to enable a company to compete. Nothing was secret or hidden. Still, when researchers looked at the likelihood of successful ventures occurring in the laser industry, the results were striking. Even with such readily available industry informa-tion, the only successful companies were those that had employees who formerly worked for competitors.[34] Similarly, the biotech industry devel-oped around a few key players who had firsthand knowledge of the newly found science. Biotech firms initially started with a few university

---

BOX 3

Space bounds the way information flows, and such flows are crucial to the growth and success of industry.

scientists who established relationships with firms while keeping their university positions. These professors, with their university's permission to engage in private commercial ventures, successfully sought early ownership stakes in the companies. In those first fifteen years the location of the star innovators in the biotech field determined the location and growth of the industry itself. The existence of star scientists played the single most important role in determining the pattern of knowledge flow and geography of the first successful ventures.

The effect of geographically bounded knowledge flows is even more significant to smaller and newer businesses, which cannot invest in large-scale internal R&D to overcome their isolation.[35] These companies must rely on new talent and professional interactions to advance knowledge.

Even with all the advantages to having competitors nearby, we naturally still fear the risk that our secret processes, our brilliant talent recruits, or our soon-to-be-launched inventions will be stolen. Would it not be better to flee competition and find an isolated region where no one is likely to poach your talent or steal your secrets? Is it not wise to seek out new frontiers and evade contact with direct competitors? Even with the continuous risks, the answer for the most part is no. Businesses can't realistically hide from competition in the modern paradigm. They can, however, let competition push them to new heights. This is the essence of our new frontier: smartly approaching the talent wars. Successful entrepreneurs know that proximity to other innovative companies drives innovation.[36] Frequent inventions coupled with rapid and efficient knowledge diffusion stimulate economic development. Talent mobility is the vehicle of all the wonders that follow.

We have reached some consensus on the ingredients necessary to a thriving high-technology district: infrastructures and capital, quality of life that can draw talent, the presence of first-rate research institutions, and a supportive environment for continuous professional interaction. It is this last bit that businesses have the hardest time grappling with, but the bottom line is that weaker noncompetes and greater mobility enrich our economy. The next step is figuring out, beyond the personal ties, what knowledge and ideas are worth sharing and which should remain secret and owned. We need to know when to loosen the reins and when to keep control.

CHAPTER FIVE

Top Secret—Not Secret!

THE LAW OF THE JUNGLE

TRADE SECRETS ARE VITAL to any business that competes in our fast-paced markets. They've been called "the workhorse of technology transfer."[1] More than ever before, we need to keep plans and ideas confidential to maintain a competitive edge. Yet trade secrets have also been called the "neglected orphan" of economic analysis.[2] Despite a consensus about their centrality, the scope and logic of trade secret protection are puzzle-ridden. Imagine you are the head of a successful production plant of a large electronics company. Your company has developed a highly secret and still unpatented process for producing methanol, giving you an important competitive advantage over your competitors. On a bright sunny day, just around noon, you notice a small plane circling low above the plant. The plane is gliding over your territory so steadily and deliberately that it cannot be random. Have your competitors hired aviators to take aerial photographs to discover your secret process? Are these spying aviators breaking any laws? Legally, the plane is not trespassing because the sky above is part of the public airspace. Still, when this exact scenario happened in the airspace of a DuPont plant, the court proclaimed that the conduct was illegal economic espionage: "Industrial espionage of the sort here perpetrated has become a popular sport in some segments of our industrial community. However, our devotion to freewheeling industrial competition must *not force us into accepting the law of the jungle* as the standard of morality expected in our commercial relations. Our tolerance of the espionage game must cease when the protections required to prevent another's spying cost so much that the spirit of inventiveness is dampened."

If indeed the law of the jungle cannot be the standard ethic of our commercial relations, how do we delineate between ethical and unethical competition? The DuPont case clarified that not all information obtained by optical extension is forbidden: "For our industrial competition to remain healthy there must be breathing room for observing a competing industrialist. A competitor can and must shop his competition for pricing and examine his products for quality, components, and methods of manufacture. Perhaps ordinary fences and roofs must be built to shut out incursive eyes, but we need not require the discoverer of a trade secret to guard against the unanticipated, the undetectable, or the unpreventable methods of espionage now available."

Realistically, how do we draw the physical boundaries between fair and unfair competition practices? And beyond the physical line drawing is the even more challenging question of how to draw the boundaries between fair and unfair use of information when employees and ex-employees are involved. Will there always be tension between owned intellectual property and free human capital?

Trade secrets are almost universally defined as confidential information vital enough to afford economic advantage. The U.S. Supreme Court summarized the principle of protecting trade secrets as "the maintenance of commercial ethics."[3] International conventions such as the General Agreement on Tariffs and Trade (GATT) similarly protect trade secrets under the rubric of "honest commercial practices."[4] Employees, the people most likely to be exposed to company secrets, have a legal duty under almost any legal system to keep their employers' secrets even after they leave. Corporate talent wars are thus deeply invested in keeping talent from disclosing secrets. At the same time, and perhaps precisely because of the moralistic tone embedded in its definition, trade secret law presents unusual challenges beyond that of any other area of intellectual property, and the field is still not very well understood, even by those who are regularly engaged in trade secret disputes.

TO HIDE OR TO PATENT?

As the owner of an invention, whether you are an individual inventor or a company, you have options in safeguarding your intellectual property. Typically, the choice is between patenting your invention and protecting it as a secret. Let's look for a moment at the comparative advantages of each protection. For several decades the pharmaceutical company Wyeth produced a hormone replacement therapy drug using a secret process, the Brandon process, named after its inventor, who worked at Wyeth. The Brandon process extracts estrogen from pregnant mare urine (PMU) and transforms it into a purified, dry powder known as Preserved Condensed Urine Desiccated (PCUD). During the 1990s Wyeth's main competitor, Natural Biologics, attempted to copy the drug but failed repeatedly until an ex-chemist of Wyeth handed over the secret information. Even though the hormone replacement therapy drug was patented years before and the patent had since expired, as had other related patents on the manufacturing process, the court found that the unpatented Brandon process was a trade secret.[5] The court issued a permanent injunction enjoining Natural Biologics from ever producing the hormone replacement therapy. The secrecy and value of the process were enough to secure legal protection.

Here lies the obvious advantage of trade secrets over patenting. Filing a patent is a long, formal, complicated process, and the issuance of a patent involves high costs and high uncertainty. As a result, many businesses and small companies in particular may be reluctant to spend the money and time to patent their innovation because, once granted, a patent is only temporary. Complicating the issue, in certain industries, such as the semiconductor industry, the life cycle of innovation may be shorter than the time it takes to patent an invention. While patent protection has a definite time cap, trade secret protection lasts as long as the secret remains secret. Another advantage of trade secrets over patents is that control of the information remains within the company. Often, even though legally you may own a patent, detection of its infringement is incredibly difficult. In particular when the information pertains to processes that occur within the firm, for example, in a pharmaceutical line of production, detecting infringement is nearly impossible. In these instances, secrecy may be the better route.

Because of these advantages, in many instances trade secrets are even more important to businesses than their patented intellectual assets.

In a recent survey, nine out of ten industries rated secrecy as more effective than patenting for protecting confidential information. Robert Sherwood, a top international intellectual property consultant, explains that even in industries such as biotech, where patenting rates are high, the large majority of technology is unpatented, and trade secrets cover over 90 percent of all new technology. Over 80 percent of all license and technology transfer agreements involve trade secret protections, either alone or together with patents. Patents themselves are very often surrounded by ancillary trade secrets that enhance the value of the innovation. Trade secrets are indeed the workhorse of the new economy!

Notwithstanding the advantages of unlimited time and strong control that trade secrets have, consider their disadvantages. Trade secrets cannot protect against independent discovery, reverse engineering, or reckless leakage. In this way, patent law and trade secret law point in opposite directions: with patent law, an inherent feature is inventor disclosure, but trade secret law requires concealment to receive legal protection. Accordingly, one court ascribes the rising role of patents to the rise in openness and transparency: "The patent system is of ever-increasing importance, due to the dependence of industry on technology, the reduced opportunity to rely on trade secrecy because of today's enlarged analytical capability, the ease and speed of imitation and modification once the innovator has shown the way, the harshness of modern competition, and the ever-present need for industrial incentives."[6]

By definition, a trade secret must be kept secret. Once revealed, trade secrets are no longer secret. When the broadcast company Fox faced a lawsuit alleging that it stole the idea for its hit show *American Idol*, the court dismissed the case. Fox's defense? The inventor had advertised his ideas on the Internet and sent out unsolicited letters detailing the specifics of his idea to several production companies. Because the creator himself indiscriminately shared his ideas, the ideas could not be legally viewed as trade secrets.[7] Quite simply, he couldn't keep his secret.

Some are better at keeping secrets than others. Although Fox was free to create *American Idol* because of the creator's inability to keep a secret, the reality of reality shows demands top secrecy. The mother of all reality shows, *Survivor,* has managed to achieve top secrecy by requiring its contestants to sign a nondisclosure agreement forbidding them to disclose the winner, the ultimate survivor. A breach of contract carries a $5 million penalty to be paid by any contestant who divulges the secret.

Every enterprise has its secrets—from showbiz and politics to industry and finance. Recently, the Walt Disney Corporation was ordered to pay $240 million to two businessmen for stealing architectural models of their Sports Island ride that they had submitted to Disney. Unlike in the *American Idol* dispute, the understanding between the architects and the Disney Corporation was that a submission of the proposal and business plan would be kept confidential. Instead, Disney used the plan, leading to the determination that the animation giant misappropriated the information.[8] Toshiba similarly lost $465.5 million when Lexar proved it misappropriated secrets about its controller technology.[9] Even at the top, people can be sloppy in keeping their secrets secret. When President Richard Nixon held a press conference following the North Korean downing of a U.S. Navy aircraft, he committed what came to be known as the worst public intelligence gaffe of his career. Nixon unwittingly disclosed the National Security Agency's read of the encryption codes used by the Soviet, Chinese, and North Korean radar systems, with disastrous consequences to U.S. intelligence operations. One analyst exclaimed following the gaffe, "I died when I heard it . . . the Soviet Union and other countries changed every frequency, every net structure—all at once. It took months to work it out."[10] If the president of the United States had trouble keeping the crown jewels of the country secret, then it is understandable that all of us, in whatever role and capacity, are fallible and can occasionally slip.

Although trade secrets are the new workhorse of our economy, they are as old as ancient Rome. In early times anyone who induced another's employee (or slave) to divulge secrets of their master's commercial affairs would suffer severe consequences.[11] In the thirteenth and fourteenth centuries, when Portugal ruled the spice and silk trade routes all the way from Africa to India and the Far East, they were able to maintain a monopoly by keeping their trade routes secret. To protect the secret maps the Portuguese kings decreed the death penalty for anyone who leaked them. Perhaps the earliest American trade secret case is *Peabody v. Norfolk,* in 1886, where the Supreme Judicial Court of Massachusetts held that a secret manufacturing process is the intellectual property of the company. In this case Francis Peabody had invented a new process for producing hemp sacks, founded a business, and hired Norfolk as his machinist. Quickly thereafter, Norfolk quit and went to work for a competitor, James Cook. The court explained that the obligation of an employee to refrain from disclosing company secrets extends beyond the term of employment. That same year Coca-Cola created what is now the world's most famous trade secret: its classic formula. Insiders know it as Merchandise 7X. No single contractor has the full recipe; each is tasked with preparing only parts of the blend. The company has kept the secret for over a century by purportedly storing it in a vault in downtown Atlanta and restricting access to only a handful of executives.

THE RISE OF ECONOMIC ESPIONAGE

The term *espionage* brings to mind pictures of the Cold War, men in trench coats passing codes, and nighttime break-ins. Economic espionage, in which employees and competitors engage in intelligence operations to reveal each other's secrets, seems like the stuff of crime novels and action movies. It is in fact very real. As a crime, it is actively prosecuted in both the international and domestic arenas. As President Obama spoke about our new Sputnik moment being about innovation, the FBI official website states clearly, "The Cold War is not over, it has merely moved into a new arena: the global marketplace." The FBI estimates that every year billions of dollars are lost to foreign and domestic competitors through the targeting and recruiting of insiders working for U.S. companies, bribery, cyber intrusions, theft, dumpster diving for intellectual property or prototypes, wiretapping, and countless other methods that give governmental spying a run for its money, literally.

The Federal Economic Espionage Act of 1996 made the theft of trade secrets a federal crime. The act was passed largely in response to an outcry in the 1990s regarding massive losses incurred by American companies from economic espionage. At the passage of the act, Senator Arlen Specter stated that for years foreign nations and their corporations had been seeking competitive advantage by stealing secrets from American companies: "The Intelligence Committee has been aware that since the end of the Cold War, foreign nations have increasingly put their espionage resources to work trying to steal American economic secrets. Estimates of the loss to U.S. business from the theft of intangible intellectual property exceed $100 billion. The loss in U.S. jobs is incalculable."[12]

The number of prosecutions under the act was just over a dozen in the first years of its enactment, but currently hundreds of investigations are pending.[13] The feeling that companies around the world were employing underhanded tactics to steal intellectual property, in other words "playing dirty," led businesses and the federal authorities to take a more aggressive stance. For example, when General Motors saw eight of its key executives abruptly leave to work at Volkswagen it alerted German authorities. The German authorities found evidence that the employees had taken large quantities of sensitive documents, including plans for a new GM car, leading to criminal charges in the United States. The penalties for such trade secret crimes are harsh, including imprisonment for up to ten years, individual fines, and organizational fines of up to $5 million. And the penalties extend not only to those who misappropriate the information, but also to those who knowingly purchase or make use of the stolen information.

Many high-profile companies have been involved in serious allegations of trade secret theft, but for the most part these companies are not implicated in the crime itself. More commonly they unknowingly receive competitor trade secrets from overzealous employees tempted by the crown jewels of big-name corporations. Espionage crimes have involved such rivals as Hewlett-Packard (HP) and IBM, Intel and AMD, and, naturally, Coca-Cola and Pepsi. A former sales manager at IBM once attempted to gain an edge in his new position as vice president at HP by bringing over documents containing IBM production costs and marketing strategies.[14] The employee e-mailed the documents to other HP executives under the heading "For Your Eyes Only." Upon receiving these documents, the HP executives notified both federal officials and IBM of the theft, and the employee was indicted. Pepsi executives reacted with similar integrity when offered stolen Coca-Cola secrets.[15] Pepsi executives received a letter on official Coca-Cola letterhead offering classified documents and a sample of a new Coke product. A secretary at Coca-Cola and two co-conspirators had collected confidential materials on new Coke products and attempted to sell the information to Pepsi. The stolen materials included marketing strategies and product samples of new drinks. Pepsi immediately notified both Coca-Cola officials and the FBI. The sting operation that followed was as classic as Coca-Cola: through cooperative operations the executives recorded the secretary stealing the Coke materials. All three conspirators were arrested on the Fourth of July (really!) after FBI agents arranged a meeting to purchase the secrets.

America's most celebrated trade secrets remained secret thanks to the FBI, the wheels of the criminal justice system, and the integrity of Coca-Cola's biggest competitor.

Whether you attribute it to ethics or the risk of harsh penalties and public indignity, most businesses prefer to play it straight. Even if new employees are the ones who misappropriated information, their new companies are not immune as mere beneficiaries. Criminal and civil liability may extend to third parties when the person or company knew or had reason to know that the information was acquired by improper means and nonetheless consented to its use. In finding a competitor guilty for its employee's actions, one court explained, "They encouraged the sowing and reaped the benefit. They cannot now disclaim the burden."[16] Every once in a while, companies engage in coordinated espionage against their competitors, and the directions come from the top. For example, executives of the software company Business Engine Software (BES) were criminally convicted and forced to pay a $5 million settlement to BES's rival Niku Corporation after it became evident that BES remotely hacked into the Niku database and stole product designs and customer data over the course of several years, downloading over one thousand confidential documents with false user names.[17]

BUT WHAT IS A SECRET?

Economic espionage and trade secret theft are serious, illegal activities. But surely not everything learned on the job is to be kept secret for years to come. As one intellectual property expert put it, "Stripped of the ability to use knowledge, seasoned employees become nothing more than freshly-minted (and far cheaper) M.B.A. graduates."[18] The morality infused into the law means that the lines of trade secret protection are incredibly difficult to draw. Most states, forty-five in fact, have enacted trade secret statutes adopting some variation of the Uniform Trade Secrets Act (UTSA), defining trade secrets broadly as "any information, including a formula, pattern, compilation, program, device, method, technique, or process." Traditionally, trade secrets were focused on product-related information: formulas, recipes, design plans, production techniques, and so on. However, over the years the scope of protection gradually expanded to include information about research methods, marketing strategies, advertising campaigns, business plans, payroll and profit data, and pricing schemes.[19] Businesses litigate trade secret cases pertaining to company flowcharts, blueprints, forecasts, customer satisfaction surveys, quality control data, customer and supplier lists, and contract expiration dates. The result is that today much of the information companies view as secret is related to information about market competition itself, and we must ask ourselves whether this expansion has gone too far. For example, even a pattern of underpricing an ex-employer's company has served as an indication of misappropriation of trade secrets, namely, the competitor's pricing lists.[20] As such, the contested use of information is the anticipation of other companies' moves. It's the kind of information that does not exist independent of competition; instead, the claimed secrets are constituted by the very existence of a market. It is also the type of information that most likely will continue to be produced whether or not it is strongly protected. If you want to sell something, you must have a pricing scheme.

The expansion of trade secrets has been evident not only in the broadened scope of subjects that are deemed secret, but also in the ways businesses claim secrecy. In theory, anything we can ascertain through observation is public information and cannot be deemed a secret. Yet, particularly when it comes to ex-employees, controls have tightened. This is not surprising given the control mentality that pervades our talent wars. In theory, trade secret protections, like noncompete agreements, are not supposed to prevent competition. They cannot be designed simply to impede the professional career of a talented worker who wishes to leave. In theory, talented professionals own anything that is a general skill no matter where they go. Only company-specific skills can be deemed secret. But perhaps more than other forms of intellectual property, trade secrets are riddled with indeterminacy. Courts attempt to distinguish between general skills training, which belong to the employee, and proprietary information of companies, which a nondisclosure clause in the employment contract can protect. As one commentator explains, "Outside the fuzzy line delineating protectable trade secrets are categories of unprotectable information, personal or professional skills."[21]

The courts are certainly aware of the problematic implications of the expansion of trade secret litigation. For talented workers to be free to pursue their careers, they must be able to learn on the job and employ their skills and experience as they move. As one court put it, "The freedom of employees to sell their expertise to the highest and most congenial bidder is an important facet of individual liberty."[22] Another court explained, "No restrictions should fetter an employee's right to apply to his own best advantage the skills and knowledge acquired by the overall experience of previous employment, including those techniques which are but skillful variations of general processes known to the particular trade."[23] At the same time, drawing the line between general and special training has proven incredibly challenging. The Stanford University intellectual property expert Robert Merges describes the blurry line between general skill and specific information as "one of the most litigated issues in the pantheon of intellectual property disputes."

As in the case of noncompetes, states vary in how strongly and expansively they define and enforce trade secrets. Employers have been going after employees for using what many courts have defined as general problem-solving abilities.[24] In response, courts repeatedly struggle with separating trade secrets from employees' aptitude, mental and physical abilities, and skills. Some courts require that the protected training or education be extraordinary in order for a business to claim it, defining *extraordinary* as "that which goes beyond what is usual, regular, common, or customary in the industry in which the employee is employed."[25] But, alarmingly, a number of recent cases have allowed employers to claim ownership over employee skills regardless of the type of training.[26]

Thomas Edison once protested, "I haven't failed. I've simply found 10,000 ways that do not work." In the world of trade secrets, a remarkable example of the controversial expansion of the types of information and knowledge that can be deemed secret in the battles of our talent wars is negative know-how—the knowledge of what *not* to do. An example of negative know-how is when an ex-employee will not undertake a series of failed ways to get to a certain chemical result, but tests other unknown ways until she strikes success. Claiming theft of negative know-how is one of the strangest developments in trade secret law.[27] When courts protect negative know-how as the property of an ex-employer, the consequence for inventors who move to a new firm can be liability for not repeating past mistakes and failures.

The debate over negative know-how is one of the many battles over where to draw the line between company secrets and knowledge that talented employees carry on with them to their next job. Another example of the uncertain line between protected and unprotected company secrets

concerns the relevance of who developed the information. In a few jurisdictions, information an employee has developed on his own belongs to
him, and he is free to use it elsewhere later. However, in most jurisdictions the answer is different: the secret belongs to the business, regardless of the contribution of the employee in developing it.

Even more challenging is predicting when a court will find information that could generally be compiled from public sources to be a secret.
The same piece of information can be deemed a protected secret or not
depending on the degree of investment in its development and the efforts
put into keeping its secrecy. That is to say, the courts undertake an inquiry
into how data were assembled. For example, a court may find that even if
the customers' names can be found in telephone or trade directories, the
company's list of clients can still be deemed confidential. If the company
can show it invested a lot of research and development time and substantial effort and costs, the information is more likely to be protected.

Similarly, courts are split over the question of whether information that
has been memorized and internalized in the mind of an employee can also
be deemed the property of her ex-employer. In other words, are secrets
taken only when copied or physically removed from a plant? Or is it enough
that they are memorized by the departing employee? Should we distinguish
unconscious internalization of information from conscious or intentional
memorization? Again, the legal responses vary. Some courts, like the one in
a recent British case, believe that if a former employee carried the information "in his head, no one can prevent his doing that and making use of it."
But nowadays, and rightly so, most courts will not limit trade secret protection to the physical theft of data or documents and will include instances in
which the employee is able to reproduce the information from memory.[28]
Whether the employee removed physical materials from the office is imma-
terial: intellectual property is intellectual. Even the ability to "dredge up this
information from the recesses of memory" can be enough.[29] Thus, the
prevailing rule is that confidential information that is merely in memory
can still be misappropriated by the person who memorized it.[30]

STRICTLY CONFIDENTIAL

Although trade secrets, unlike noncompetes, are always protected,
even without a formal agreement, because of their rising significance
companies increasingly use contracts to expand the scope of protected

information beyond trade secrets. Trade secrets are statutorily defined, but confidentiality agreements (or nondisclosure agreements, also known as NDAs) attempt to broaden the scope of what can be protected as company proprietary information. As a result, some businesses attempt to use confidentiality agreements to protect nearly everything the employee learns in the workplace. Many courts, however, will find a confidentiality agreement to be unreasonably broad if it defines confidential information "as essentially all the information provided by [the plaintiff] to [the defendant] 'concerning or in any way relating' to the services offered by [the defendant]."[31] Defining confidential information as all information "concerning or in any way relating" to one's job turns the confidentiality agreement into a de facto noncompete, unrestricted in duration or geography. In other words, as in the case of noncompetes, the breadth or vagueness of an NDA can call into question its reasonableness. Courts may refuse to enforce a confidentiality agreement when the employer does not articulate the actual information that must be kept confidential. Conversely, the more specific and highly specialized the information listed as confidential in the NDA is, the more likely it will be enforced in court.

The battles over the enforcement of NDAs are fierce. Can a contract expand company-owned information to include any information that is not widely held common knowledge? Some courts show great deference to employers' definitions of proprietary information as listed in a nondisclosure contract, while others are concerned about promoting competition and the free flow of information and protecting employee mobility and the right to work.

Once again, as it did in the case of noncompetes, California has taken a more cautious approach to the use of restrictions. California courts have explicitly refused to recognize a category of confidential information distinct from trade secrets.[32] Because California prohibits restraints of trade, confidentiality agreements that protect more than trade secrets are rendered void. California courts worry that if broader protections are allowed, "employers could insert broad, facially illegal covenants . . . and many, perhaps most, employees would honor these clauses without consulting counsel or challenging the clause in court." The New York Court of Appeals has similarly stated in the past that "where the knowledge does not qualify for protection as a trade secret and there has been no commercial piracy, we see no reason to inhibit the employee's ability to realize his potential both professionally and financially by availing himself of opportunity."[33] More recently, however, the New York courts have broadened the definition of protected employer information to allow the listing of information that would not, absent a confidentiality contract, be considered secret.[34] In short, courts vary on their treatment of confidentiality agreements, just as they do with regard to noncompetes: some will enforce them outright without questioning scope or validity, while others will question their necessity with the same rigor they employ for noncompetes. A middle ground, quite common in most jurisdictions, is to apply some reasonableness inquiry but in a looser way than with noncompetes, such as allowing longer duration and wider geographical scope.

Illinois courts, for example, have recently invalidated several NDAs because of their overbreadth and unlimited duration. In one case an Illinois judge found that the description of the protected secrets, including strategic planning, policies, and marketing plans, was too vague and would entirely prevent the employee from working in the same industry. The court deemed it disingenuous for the employer to claim that it only sought to prevent a former employee from using confidential information, not to prevent other companies from hiring the employee altogether. It reasoned that the new company obviously hired the talented executive for his expertise, skill, and experience as a director of marketing in the industry, and if he was restricted from using any of his past experience, skills, and knowledge, then in effect he would be prevented from continuing his career altogether.[35]

Indeed, the most controversial of all trade secret disputes is the attempt of one company to prevent other companies from hiring their employees entirely by claiming that the mere move itself will inevitably result in the moving employee revealing secrets at some point in the future. These heated controversies are attempts to create de facto noncompetes out of trade secret claims.

INEVITABLE DISCLOSURE: MUFFIN MAN, BAGEL BOY, AND SOFT DRINK KING

In 2010 a federal judge granted an injunction against a former senior vice president, let's call him Muffin Man, at Bimbo Bakeries, which prevented him from working at a competing bakery, Hostess, because of his extensive knowledge of trade secrets. The famous Thomas's English muffins prompted the dispute. The tasty breakfast muffins generate $500 million in annual sales for Bimbo Bakeries. There are three secrets for making the muffins: the ingredients for its "nooks and crannies" texture, the engineering of the bakery, and the baking process. Most Bimbo employees know only one of the three secrets, but Muffin Man knew all three. All the facts pointed to an ominous threat to the bakery; Muffin Man had accepted a competing job several months before disclosing his plans to leave. He also surreptitiously accessed confidential information on his last day of work at Bimbo, leading the judge to find that Muffin Man was "simply not credible." Ultimately, the court used the most severe weapon at its disposal: it completely barred Muffin Man from obtaining the new job even though he had not signed a noncompete. The judge explained, "We seriously doubt that Defendant will somehow clear his mind of Bimbo's trade secret information when working on related tasks at Hostess."

The food industry has seen some of the fiercest wars over secrets and talent. Take Del Monte and Dole, the two leading canned fruit companies. When one of Del Monte's senior scientists left after sixteen years to join Dole, the court considered whether the inevitable disclosure of trade secrets or just the mere threat of disclosure should justify barring the employee from taking the position in the absence of a noncompete. The court found that the employee had not taken documents with him upon his departure and did not appear to have memorized important trade secrets. The court was also convinced that Dole had taken adequate steps to ensure that there would be no misappropriation of secrets in his new position, such that there was no justification to prohibit the move simply because of Del Monte's fear of Dole's recruitment of their talent.

Similar to the food industry, the high-tech industry has been another intense battleground for trade secret disputes. Recently, Procter & Gamble attempted to enjoin a former vice president from accepting a similar position with its main competitor, Clorox; IBM attempted to prevent a senior engineer from taking a position with Seagate; Dow Chemical requested an injunction against former engineers and sales executive from taking jobs with General Electric. In all of these cases, even though there had not been a noncompete agreement, the companies sought to bar the new employment. Some states allow this; even absent a noncompete, a talented employee can find herself jobless and completely barred from working for a competitor upon departing if a court concludes that there is no realistic way to perform the competing job without disclosing the trade secrets the former employee possesses. This is the highly controversial doctrine of inevitable disclosure, in which an after-the-fact de facto noncompete is created. The doctrine prevents an employee from assuming a new position even when the company never asked the employee to sign a noncompete agreement. States that adopt the doctrine of inevitable disclosure give a very harsh tool of control to businesses fighting the talent wars. The courts look for direct competition between the former employer and the new employer and whether the new position is highly similar to the prior position held by the employee. Under such conditions, those who subscribe to the doctrine view the nature of the employee's knowledge and pending work as such that the imminent and eventual disclosure of confidential information is a virtual certainty.

Notably, character plays a central role in these cases. Evidence of dishonesty serves to convince courts of an employee's likelihood to misappropriate trade secrets. One court reasoned that if the former employee "would misrepresent the truth in order to gain more money through a severance package, he might also find that the temptation to succeed in his career would be too much for him to ignore the confidential information he has about plaintiffs' operations."[36] For example, when two software employees were found to have a "cavalier attitude" toward their former employer's secrets, they were enjoined not only from working for any competitors but also from starting up their own company.[37]

The story of Pepsi battling the departure of one of its marketing executives to Quaker is telling of how dramatic trade secrets disputes can be and why the doctrine of inevitable disclosure is so controversial. The Pepsi battle pitted one of the world's largest drink companies against a relative newcomer to the soft drink wars. William Redmond, a senior marketing executive, had worked for Pepsi for ten years. When he left Pepsi he was the general manager of the company's California region, which had revenues of over $500 million and represented 20 percent of Pepsi's North American profits. Pepsi alleged that owing to Redmond's senior position, he had gained access to sensitive information and secrets regarding Pepsi's strategic plan, annual operating plan, attack plans, and planned innovations in its selling and delivering systems. The district court of Illinois enjoined Redmond from working for Quaker for six months in addition to enjoining him from ever using or disclosing any of Pepsi's confidential information. The court reasoned that because Redmond's new position at Quaker was so closely related to his former position at Pepsi, "unless Redmond possessed an uncanny ability to compartmentalize information, he would necessarily be making decisions about Gatorade and Snapple by relying on his knowledge of Pepsi's trade secrets." This would, in the eyes of the court, allow Quaker to be unfairly armed with Pepsi's plans, able to anticipate distribution, packaging, pricing, and marketing moves. "In other words, Pepsi finds itself in the position of a coach, one of whose players has left, playbook in hand, to join the opposing team before the big game." The court further found that Redmond could not be trusted because of his lack of forthrightness during the period when he accepted the position with Quaker without informing Pepsi of his decision. Even though Redmond never signed a noncompete he was prevented from working at Quaker for six critical months.

One year after the Pepsi case was decided in Illinois, a New York court took a similar approach when faced with a war over fresh bagels. Uncle B's Bakery, a maker and seller of fresh, never-frozen bagels, sought to enjoin his former manager from taking a job as a manager at Brooklyn Bagel Boys. The ex-manager had never signed a noncompete agreement. The record showed that Brooklyn Bagels asked their new hire to be careful not to reveal any trade secrets. Still, the court found a significant danger of inadvertent disclosure, enough to prevent the hire. The court acknowledged that employees are entitled to use the general knowledge they accumulate in the course of employment, but the court viewed the lines between general knowledge and trade secrets as "sufficiently uncertain," leading to a realistic threat of inevitable disclosure. In other words, the fact that general knowledge and special knowledge are hard to separate led to the prevention, rather than the allowance, of all related postemployment work. The court defaulted to control instead of flow.

This is precisely the kind of alarming expansion of the control mentality in our talent wars that we should be questioning. The implications of these battles, whether over the talent that runs our soft drink world or battles in the bagel wars, are dramatic. Key talent is prevented from putting to use its knowledge and skills, and in addition it can be altogether prevented from working for a competitor. The inevitable disclosure doctrine alters the employment relationship without advance consent or compensation and changes the ways human capital is valued in the market.

CIRCLES OF EXPANSION

To summarize, we've seen the incremental broadening of control over company information through the expansion of what is deemed a trade secret, through the use of confidentiality agreements that extend beyond trade secret definitions, and through the adoption of the doctrine of inevitable disclosure, which creates a de facto prohibition on competition due to the existence of trade secrets (fig. 5.1).

As in the case of noncompetes, the ambiguity in delineating reasonable corporate interests with regard to secrecy has meant that both employers and employees frequently misinterpret their rights and obligations. Even without intending to take any company information, employees are exposed to the risk of trade secret suits. If employees are at risk for using any sort of information and knowledge, whether it be positive or negative know-how, memorized or copied, secret or public, disclosed or just likely to be disclosed, will they not be deterred from using their acquired skills, including their general skills?

My longtime collaborator Yuval Feldman has interviewed Silicon Valley executives about their understanding of trade secrets. Researching the interactions between psychology, social perceptions, and legal realities, Feldman surveyed several hundred high-tech employees to identify their psychological perception regarding confidential information. He wanted to know if the fact that an employee personally developed information made a difference in the employee's mind as to whether she were legally bound to keep it a secret from the next employer. He also studied how employees perceive information stored in their heads as different from information stored externally, say, on a hard drive. His interviews revealed a clear consensus among high-tech workers: they believed that the information and skills they developed themselves could (and should) move with them. They also thought that companies did not own information that they had memorized. Rather, they believed that they and other high-tech talent working in the Silicon Valley should be able to use the information since it was stored in their minds. The ambiguity in the legal

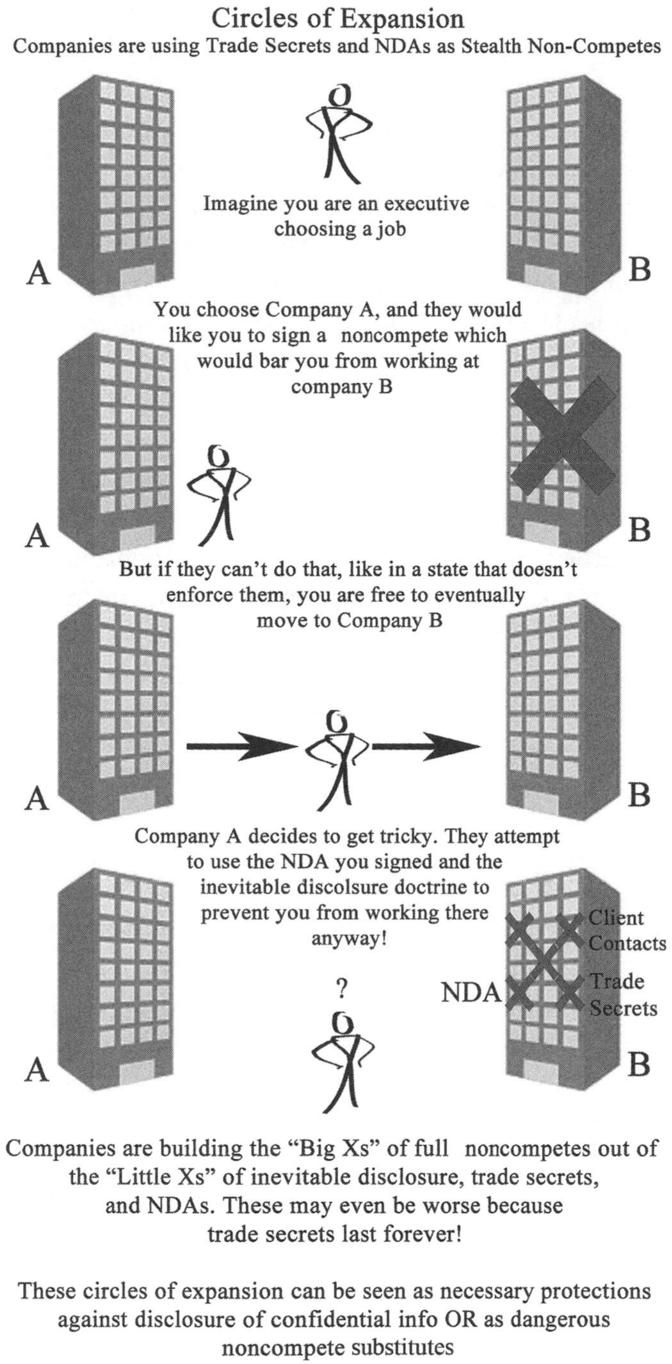

Circles of Expansion
Companies are using Trade Secrets and NDAs as Stealth Non-Competes

Imagine you are an executive
choosing a job

A · B

You choose Company A, and they would
like you to sign a noncompete which
would bar you from working at
company B

A · B

But if they can't do that, like in a state that doesn't
enforce them, you are free to eventually
move to Company B

A · B

Company A decides to get tricky. They attempt
to use the NDA you signed and the
inevitable discolsure doctrine to
prevent you from working there
anyway!

?   NDA   Client
Contacts
Trade
Secrets

A · B

Companies are building the "Big Xs" of full noncompetes out of
the "Little Xs" of inevitable disclosure, trade secrets,
and NDAs. These may even be worse because
trade secrets last forever!

These circles of expansion can be seen as necessary protections
against disclosure of confidential info OR as dangerous
noncompete substitutes

Fig 5.1. Nondisclosure agreements as stealth noncompetes.

definition and reach of trade secrets and their uneven enforcement across various industries exacerbate misperceptions among employees about their possible liabilities. Beyond the ambiguity in defining trade secrets, Feldman's research demonstrates the significance of work culture and industry norms. As we shall continue to explore, even when the law says otherwise, professional networks will establish their own practices on what is kept secret and what is revealed, what is owned and what is shared, and what is controlled and what is free.

As is true of all the strategies of the talent wars and the mechanisms to control human capital and intellectual property, the struggle here is to balance the legitimate interests of competitors, talented individuals, and the public good of free-flowing information and people. As in other intellectual property debates and talent war disputes, trade secrets are traditionally debated in terms of a tradeoff: the benefits of investment in research and development versus the costs of monopolizing information. Richard Posner, known for his pioneering economic analysis of the law, warns, "If trade secrets are protected only if their owners take extravagant, productivity-impairing measures to maintain their secrecy, the incentive to invest resources in discovering more efficient methods of productions will be reduced, and with it the amount of invention."[38] Along with his collaborator William Landes, Posner warns against the counterproductive consequences of allowing employees to run off with their employer's secrets:

> If the law refused to enforce contracts in which employees promise not to spill their employer's trade secrets (or not to compete with their employer), employers might be led to reorganize their businesses in a manner that might be grossly inefficient were it not for the imperative of secrecy. They might move their operations to jurisdictions that protect trade secrecy, pay much higher wages so that employees would be reluctant to quit (taking the employer's trade secrets with them), split up tasks among more employees so that each knows less, or employ family members even though they may be less competent.[39]

Here, as in the case of noncompetes, we can see the orthodox economic analysis of trade secrets which views protections as necessary to encourage investment in training, research, and development. Employees are not expected to pay for the information themselves, as they surely would not be able to afford such training. Instead, employees offer their secrecy. While the risks are very real and Posner's concerns are acute, you can imagine that with our new outlook on the world of competitive innovation, the tradeoff between secrecy and investment points to a counterconcern: overly strong trade secret protection not only harms employees in their pursuit of future work but also hurts the economy and the ways in which knowledge and talent pools are nourished.

The standard and most basic justification for protection of intellectual property, whether patent or copyright, is that it encourages innovation. In every nation, in constitutions and statutes, the vision of offering intellectual property protections rests on the goal of promoting investment in ideas and allowing inventors to recoup the rewards of such investment. The rationale for trade secrets would appear to follow a similar route: the ability to control the information and knowledge created by a company will offer the right incentives for their development in the first place. There is one major difference, however, between trade secrets and other types of intellectual property. Trade secrets do not require disclosure. In fact, while other types of intellectual property need to be disclosed, registered, and made available for public view, a trade secret's very secrecy defines it. To receive patent protection, you have to file your invention at the patent office, publicly disclosing the entire process of its reverse engineering. Indeed, to use our terminology about the benefits of spreading information, we can think of patent documents themselves as creating positive knowledge spillovers.[40] By contrast, to receive trade secret protection, you must hide your ideas from the public. Given this inherent characteristic of trade secret, the tradeoffs between investment in new ideas and the flow of knowledge are tipped; the costs of monopolizing knowledge are even more dramatic than with other intellectual property controls.

And precisely because the knowledge is stored and hidden, pulsing in brain cells and otherwise locked up in a vault, trade secret protection battles potential within its carrier: the person who, as we've seen, can hardly be conceived of as separate from the knowledge he or she embodies.

NO MORE SECRETS IN THE SILICON VALLEY

Trade secrets and noncompete clauses have a circular relationship. We have seen that employers often justify their claim for an enforceable noncompete by showing that it is designed to protect trade secrets. At the same time, the very existence of contractual agreements not to compete and not to disclose information demonstrates a business's efforts to maintain its secrets. Consequently, trade secrets come to define the scope of the contractual postemployment restrictions, while the same contractual restrictions support the scope of trade secrecy. Moreover, noncompetes can prevent trade secrets from being leaked (hence the attempts of some competitors to create de facto noncompetes by claiming inevitable disclosure), while trade secret protection can be viewed as an alternative to noncompete restrictions. For example, we might think that in California, where noncompetes are not a viable option, companies rely more vigorously on trade secret protection to prevent leaks and raids of their talent. Indeed, do the talent wars in California rely more than in other places on trade secret protections because of the absence of the absolute controls of noncompetes?

Unlike the case of noncompetes, where California has formally taken an exceptional route via their prohibition, the black letter law on trade secrets in California is similar to that of most other states. California courts have officially stated that by enacting the California Uniform Trade Secret Act in 1984, "the state legislature added California to the long list of states which have determined that the right of free competition does not include the right to use confidential work products of others."[41]

At the same time, California courts have been hesitant to allow unlimited expansion of trade secret controls. For example, one court explained that its decision to limit the claims for trade secrecy of a business against its ex-employee reflects "a policy choice by California in which the interest in promoting the free use of ideas is elevated over the interests in rewarding holders of economically significant secrets."[42] As we've seen, California courts have refused to define information that would not be deemed secret under its trade secret act as confidential simply because an employer has listed the information as confidential in an NDA. Recall also Feldman's findings that the high-tech talent of the Silicon Valley had a narrower definition of trade secrets than the one inscribed in the law.

California's approach has been to balance an employer's right to proprietary information against an employee's right to use his knowledge, training, and experience to advance his career and livelihood.[43] Over the years, with the rising prominence of the Silicon Valley as an exemplary high-tech regional economy, California courts as well as business leaders in the industry have somewhat informally developed an exceptional stance toward underenforcement of trade secrets. In practice, the number of trade secret disputes in the Valley has been relatively low in comparison to other competitive regions. While NDAs are commonly signed in the Silicon Valley, many believe that they don't really matter and will not be enforced.[44] And they are right; competing firms and ex-employers have not pursued many potential claims of infringement of trade secrets against prior employees.

Economic geographers have pointed to the geographic proximity between companies in the Silicon Valley as a contributing force to a culture of information sharing. The economic geographer AnnaLee Saxenian has claimed that in fact this physical proximity has led talented programmers to feel that they were "working for the Valley" rather than for any one particular company. Strikingly, lawyers themselves, the foot soldiers in the litigation battles between competitors, are also repeat players in the Valley who move between multiple firms. Defying the typical image of lawyers, they have undertaken the roles of dealmakers and counselors instead of encouraging costly litigation battles.[45] These Silicon Valley lawyers, like modern bosses, reinvented themselves in the Valley as facilitators rather than litigators.

The companies of the Silicon Valley seem to have consciously understood their general interest in developing the semiconductor and high-tech industry as a whole and also understood that firms cannot learn all they need to know internally.[46] Businesses around the Valley are not perceived as the enemy, moving between companies is not thought of as betrayal, and entrepreneurs are not labeled thieves. In fact, the firms that have been militant in pursuing ex-employees for using their company's confidential information have damaged their reputation as responsible corporate players in the Valley, the internal morale among their best employees, and their ability to recruit new talent.[47]

The considerable employee mobility in California that we've explored in the previous chapters has created many opportunities for talent to use trade secrets in their new firms. What we see here is that letting go of the mentality of control embedded in zealous use of noncompete restrictions does not necessarily entail channeling the control mentality through other strategies. On the contrary, competitors may learn the many benefits that derive from the flow of talent and knowledge.

CHAPTER SIX

Sharing and the Miracle of Cognitive Freedoms

MY FATHER LIKES TO SAY, "If you want something, give it away." That quote chimed in my head when I learned that Ben Franklin, one of the most talented and prolific inventors of all time, did not patent a single one of his inventions. Franklin believed that "as we benefit from the inventions of others, we should be glad to share our own . . . freely and gladly." The world is not *quite* so simple for companies, but they could stand to learn a thing or two from Ben.

Intuitively, we know that secrecy and innovation are often at odds. It's a fine balancing act between controlling ideas in which we're greatly invested and allowing knowledge to be shared and built upon. The two ends of the spectrum of secrecy and sharing are captured in these two opposing voices. On one side, a government security officer states, "An ounce of loyalty is worth a pound of brains." On another, a research physicist asserts, "Unfortunately, secrecy and progress are mutually incompatible. This is always true of science."[1]

We've known that trade secrets have always been important to competitors, but we've also seen that some businesses are fighting to expand their scope and reach. Courts have recognized that in many instances employers seek "not to protect a trade secret, but rather, to prevent competition."[2] One court explicitly describes this tension between secrets and market competition as a sword and a shield: "The protection given to trade secrets is a shield, sanctioned by the courts, for the preservation of trust in confidential relationships; it is not a sword to be used by employers to retain employees by the threat of rendering them substantially unemployable in the field of their experience should they decide to resign."[3]

Those who advocate strong protections warn against the detrimental effects of leaks. The American Society for Industrial Security, which basically consists of businesses who make a profit from securing information, treats the exposure of trade secrets as a pure economic loss, estimating the loss at the dramatic cost of $2 billion per month.[4] But these estimates are misleading. They conceal the ways in which businesses, often the same businesses that lose from the revelation of some secrets, also gain from overall industry progress. Others warn that without legal protection for all types of information important to the firm, the firm would need to invest in monitoring access to the unregulated information.[5] Yet, as we shall see, not all industries and businesses operate within this framework. And the question is not whether or not companies should be allowed to control some of their secrets, both technically and legally, but whether the control mentality that has pervaded our talent wars has harmfully tipped the balance between secrecy and sharing.

The control mentality of individual corporations continues to overshadow the gains that could come from loosening controls. As business strategists, we've come to realize the negative results that stem from excessive control in other aspects of our management styles, but many companies are still trapped in their tunnel vision when it comes to controlling information and maintaining secrecy. The overprotection of trade secrets by industries and markets at large restricts their talent pool and retards the potential progress that talented inventors, creators, and innovators would otherwise have set in motion. Endless expansion of the safeguarding of secrecy has limited the ability of ex-employees to use their skills and knowledge in their future endeavors, whether as employees or as independent entrepreneurs. Not less damaging, it has also prevented firms, both rivals and nonrivals, from mutually benefiting from the flow of knowledge. Perhaps most disturbingly, businesses that default to a control mentality of their information and knowledge become internally trapped in pathologies that disrupt their innovative processes.

Mentalities of secrecy and control have side effects. Employee morale, creativity, and information exchange all suffer under watchful eyes.

UNDER THE CLOTH OF SECRECY

Trade secret law may inadvertently cause an inflation of secrecy measures. Information leaks are nothing new, but today they happen in fast-forward. Nowadays, if production secrets are leaked, they are likely to be published on the Internet immediately, making the loss permanent. At the same time, the rapid pace of technological advancement also means that the value of secrets is only temporary and products remain attractive for shorter periods. First movers enjoy an important advantage. The first to innovate must quickly reap the benefits of their invention before the next big thing hits the market and before copycats devalue its competitive advantage. As we've seen, according to some estimates companies lose hundreds of billions of dollars annually from the misappropriation of their secret information. Secrecy may seem to managers more important than ever.

But companies are naturally caught in an internal tug-of-war between secrecy and information sharing. How do companies react? Some opt to isolate their employees and fragment their production processes to increase secrecy. Some establish rules, procedures, and practices to protect their trade secrets. Some even resort to old school techniques and physically restrict access to secrets, regulate and monitor computer use, and use old-fashioned intimidation and concealment. But at what cost? Beyond the billions of dollars companies already spend annually on computer security and other protective measures, the costs of overmonitoring are paid in different currencies: morale, productivity, creativity, and happiness.

In her book *Soap Opera: The Inside Story of Procter & Gamble* (P&G), the Wall Street journalist Patricia Swasy concludes that P&G's security practices during the 1990s reveal "simple paranoia":

> One brand group discovered just how paranoid P&G is when
> they went to lunch at a Cincinnati restaurant and discussed a
> commercial that was already on the air. Late that day the brand
> manager got a call from his boss to discuss a "security
> violation." He was scolded for talking about the advertisement

at a public restaurant. "Security people go to restaurants because P&G is convinced that corporate spies sit around to hear our conversations," he said. "They hope that by harassing you enough, you'll comply with the rules." Some security officers do little besides ride airplanes between Cincinnati, New York, and Chicago to make sure that P&G and its advertising agency representatives do not talk shop in flight. Internal phone calls are monitored too. One former officer recalls how he was interrogated by his bosses because the phone records showed that he had returned a phone call to a Wall Street analyst. . . . Others pegged as troublemakers believe their home and office calls were monitored. Some officials claimed that security helps managers obtain employees' medical and police records if they want to check out somebody a bit more closely.

Swasy herself was followed, bugged, and spied on while she was writing the series of articles on P&G. P&G even subpoenaed her telephone records. Revealing its dark side, the Ivory soap and Tide manufacturer that had thrived since 1837 became too paranoid and controlling for its own good, and by the end of the twentieth century was making totalitarian demands for worker loyalty. At one point P&G persuaded local police officials to secretly search the private phone records of hundreds of P&G employees looking for calls to Swasy's phone after her first stories began to appear in the *Wall Street Journal*. Swasy determined that these intimidation practices resulted in many talented P&G employees leaving the company to seek work elsewhere. The excessive monitoring also led to the imposition of rules that choked off potentially great synergies: "Technical people are told not to join trade organizations out of fear they'll give away secrets. . . . After P&G took over Richardson-Vicks, managers were banned from attending trade shows. 'Too much visibility' their employer declared. When P&G bought the Charmin paper mills, it ended workers' longtime habit of sharing spare parts and supplies with a neighboring paper plant. . . . 'They were told never to talk to those people again,' said one engineer. Vital knowledge was not shared. Memories and experience were lost from one generation of employees to the next. P&G engaged in security overkill."

The feeling of constantly being watched can decrease a sense of privacy and depress motivation. One employee of the defense contractor

Lockheed Martin describes the experience of being monitored unceasingly: "Toward the end of the stealth project I had nearly forty auditors living with me inside our plant, watching every move we made on all security and contract matters." He concludes that "for better or worse, we were living in a Kafkaesque bureaucracy."[6] An IBM employee describes the waste in oversecrecy in the company's internal communications mail system, which required an envelope hierarchy ranging from Internal Use, Confidential, Confidential Restricted, to Registered, the highest secrecy category: "IBM bought about four million envelopes a year . . . but IBM'ers ended up branding hundreds of mundane documents IBM confidential, even though they weren't."[7]

Overblown secrecy is often a marketing device. We've seen this with Coca-Cola's secret formula, which marketers view as more of a public relations tool than a secrecy concern. In the twenty-first-century landscape, no company is more known for its clandestine product development than Apple. Apple's secrecy tantalizes consumers. Apple schedules press releases as company events, keeping any announcement under wraps until the iconic moment when, until his untimely death, Steve Jobs would dramatically pull out the new product. The marketing hype is extraordinary. *Wired* magazine describes it as "the moment every Apple Computer nut lives for. CEO Steve Jobs is working through a presentation filled with recaps, market-share updates and some minor product announcements—and then he makes everyone hold their breath. 'One more thing,' Jobs says, and a new object of technological lust ascends into the pantheon."[8]

Apple employs extreme measures to maintain secrecy. The company provides no roadmaps whereby its customers and suppliers might foresee and plan for future products. Internally, employees working on top secret prototypes may be instructed to work under a black cloak. Guy Kawasaki, a former Apple marketing advisor, insists that secrecy is more than a marketing stunt: "It's not solely good marketing, it's good inventory management. The reality is that if everyone knew that a new iPod or Mac was coming out, then they would stop buying the existing ones. Sales would go down. Inventory would pile up."[9] For consumers, the buzz around Apple's revelation of each new product is exciting, but for Apple's employees, manufacturers, and even reporters, exposure to company secrets can be ominous. Apple adamantly pursues anyone, employees, journalists, suppliers, or bloggers, who leak future products. Recently, stories have appeared regarding Apple manufacturing suppliers brutally interrogating their employees, when, for example, employees misplaced prototypes of the next generation iPhone. Apple employees have been fired for leaking even minor pieces of information or previewing upcoming software to a business client.[10] To keep employees in line and monitor their silence, Apple employees are at times provided with incorrect information about a product's price or features. Apple then tracks down the source of news reports with the incorrect details and links it back to the defiant employee. Apple will also purposely leak false information to test the reliability of its contractors and to detect security breaches. The company deliberately misinforms the press, routinely "jamming the frequencies."[11]

Apple's lead Chinese manufacturer is Hon Hai Precision Electronics, also known as Foxconn. Foxconn produces approximately twenty-five million units of Apple's iPhone and is now contracted to produce the iPad, so its interest in keeping Apple happy is obvious. At the Chinese compound, a thick wall surrounds the production facilities. In the past few years, reports of employee suicide have been raising concerns about whether secrecy practices have reached dangerous levels. Security at the Foxconn compounds is tighter than in many public offices. There are metal detectors and physical searches. The police are alerted frequently for any suspicious activity. Employees are often investigated and questioned at length. Reports have been leaked about a Foxconn employee committing suicide after being aggressively interrogated by Foxconn security for leaking secrets. A few months later, the same month of the launch of the iPad, there were four more suicides by Foxconn factory workers and one more attempted suicide.[12] After the tenth suicide in a year, Foxconn announced plans to raise the average wages of its workers and to request that workers sign no-suicide pledges. When secrecy spreads fear and misery, it may be time to rethink its reach. We may have gone too far and are losing sight of the costs of secrecy. If this is the dark side, what is the alternative?

SHIFTING MENTALITY INSIDE AND OUT

While the benefits of openness and fluid communication have been demonstrated in research studies and in real world implementation, companies inevitably struggle with balancing openness and secrecy, both internally and with the outside world. As the story of P&G's excessive secrecy reveals, in the not-so-distant past and throughout the 1990s companies had strict rules governing conversations outside of the workplace and interactions with employees of competitors. P&G was paradigmatic in discouraging its employees from professionally networking, and, unsurprisingly, it also had a reputation for suing its ex-employees for competing with it postemployment.

Sure enough, P&G suffered a decline in productive innovation, and the market was unforgiving. By 2000 the company had lost more than half of its market capitalization while its stock slid from $118 to $52 per share. The market fall led P&G to finally recognize its organizational errors. It reacted forcefully and changed its ways. Today, as a reflection of its new attitude, the company that once prevented its employees from engaging in any outside communications now finds almost half of its new products coming from that same outside. The corporate outsourcing of new product ideas ballooned from 10 percent in 2000 to over 35 percent by the mid-2000s and has led to a dramatic increase in product hit rates and a simultaneous decrease in R&D costs. A few years ago P&G introduced its Connect & Develop program, focusing on intra- and intercompany cross-pollination. The program has quickly proved vital to P&G's growth in the twenty-first century. Even more recently P&G has publicly stated that about 50 percent of its ideas come from outside sources, emphasizing, "We don't care where the ideas come from."[13] In fact, it was an individual entrepreneur who invented one of the company's most successful products, the P&G's Crest Spinbrush, a low-cost electrical toothbrush. The company bought the technology and idea as a Ready-to-Go product.

By externalizing R&D processes P&G enjoys a rapid, cost-effective means of improving existing products and drawing in new technologies.[14] Encouraged by the success of its new approach to innovation, P&G encourages continuous technical consultation with experts and the acquisition of fully developed ideas from outside entrepreneurs. The company has also fostered relationships with academics focusing on "highly leveraged nodes," that is, members of the scientific community who are at the center of many creative scientific ventures. Commercializing a product requires extensive business plans and resources, skills very different from those needed to invent. P&G's new approach is serving as a bridge between the two worlds and bringing successful products to the market as a result.

P&G is following in the footsteps of successfully open companies like Syntex, which allows outsiders, including competitors, to visit their facilities and interact with their staff. Syntex recognized early on that a company that is open to outside ideas is likely to benefit from the movement of its creative talent. During the 1990s Syntex ran a postdoctoral program that brought young engineers to intern at the company for a few years, even if they later chose to return to competing companies. The return that Syntex received from inviting outside engineers to engage with intrafirm development teams—in the form of a priceless flow of ideas and fresh energy—has outweighed the perceived loss of confidential information.

NEW BLOOD AND THE NOT-INVENTED-HERE SYNDROME

> Given enough eyeballs, all bugs are shallow.
>
> —*Linus's Law*[15]

For P&G to make the shift from a controlling, autarkic company to a collaborative, networked organization a serious mentality shift had to occur. Companies frequently suffer from myopia. Asking people to receive ideas from the outside is no small feat and often entails a psychological shift. Not Invented Here (NIH, purposely using the same acronym as the National Institutes of Health) is an institutional pathology. P&G functioned this way for years, appreciating only ideas that came from within. Early on NIH was linked to nationalism—American companies and consumers often refused to adopt innovation developed outside national borders. There are dozens of examples throughout the twentieth century of advanced technologies that were slow to be adopted because the technologies were produced elsewhere. For example, Japanese and American markets largely ignored home computers produced by British companies. Japanese cars, now among the most popular automobiles in the world, were at first slow to reach beyond the domestic market because dealers and consumers preferred national products.

However, in the globalized market that exists today nationalism in innovation is almost nonexistent. Fast-paced markets require companies to adopt external innovations and to purchase and exchange valuable research, knowledge, and ideas from everyone everywhere. And yet, even in the face of successful advancement by other companies, old habits die hard. Evidence still suggests that firms, often to their detriment, overlook outside ideas and solutions simply because of their not-invented-here quality.

Not surprisingly, NIH syndrome happens more often in settings where there is little employee turnover. Pathologies of groupthink—whereby cohesive groups overlook important alternatives because of their desire for consensus and conformity—and NIH mentalities are exaggerated when companies are overly stable. In one study, teams with little turnover became progressively less productive.[16] Another study, which data-mined almost one million patents (and controlled for other positive effects of being in a diverse place), shows that NIH mentalities are more pronounced in small towns. In remote locations where one firm is dominant in the local economy (in other words, the company town), that company is more likely to draw on its own inventions and on the same set of prior inventions year after year compared to firms in a more diverse location.[17] Perhaps most surprising is that the same research finds that this behavior is exhibited only among the employees of the largest company in the company town, not among the smaller firms in the same location, who are just as willing as their small-firm counterparts in more diverse locations to build upon external sources of innovation.

Good ideas are out there, but only companies with a structure of openness will be able to increase their absorptive capacities for innovation. Companies who close themselves off, sinking into the depths of secrecy measures, are limiting their capacity to recognize and make use of external valuable information. The ability of companies to open themselves up to external progress is analogous to how supposedly being lucky is not really a matter of luck. One of my favorite behavioral experiments is one that demonstrates that people get lucky when they perceive themselves as lucky. In the study, researchers place random dollar bills in the path of their subjects. Those who had identified themselves prior to the walk down the path as lucky people were far more likely to find the money. Metaphorically, organizational leaders have to encourage their teams to look for that dollar bill lying on the ground. Openness means that it does not matter much where ideas come from as long as they are useful.

REUSE: PROUDLY FOUND ELSEWHERE

> If you wish to make an apple pie from scratch, you must first invent the universe.
>
> —Carl Sagan, American astronomer, 1934–96

Why not outsource innovation? The clock is ticking. Innovations today have a much shorter life span than in the past, which makes broadening the field from which we mine ideas even more critical. Companies like P&G that were traditionally leaders in introducing new products on the market have had to rethink their practices, redesign their organizational structure, and reinvigorate their research and development arm. Companies have outsourced physical production for a while. The day of the vertically integrated company has come to a close, while horizontal formation, that is, the use of subsidiaries and long chains of production, has emerged as the dominant form of competitive business. Companies that were once domestically self-contained have evolved into multilayered global firms. Functions once accomplished in-house are now split and shared by subsidiaries and subcontractors. Much work is off-shored to other countries, where labor and other costs of production are cheaper.

Like physical production, the production of ideas can often be cheaper on the outside. Vertically integrated firms traditionally focused on innovation coming from within their own research arms.[18] In twenty-first-century competitive environments, however, in-house innovation is not always a sustainable approach. The rise in both venture capital financing and employee mobility has increased competition from start-ups. Outsourcing innovation is not a far leap from outsourcing all other aspects of production: "Just as best-in-class companies manage increasingly extended supply chains, superior innovators are learning to outsource segments of the innovation value chain."[19]

Several new companies have leveraged the growing market of outsourcing innovation. InnoCentive, a network of external contract researchers, takes on problems submitted to the company via its website. The company is headquartered in Waltham, Massachusetts, but many of its researchers reside abroad in countries like China, Russia, and India. The company draws on the idea of crowd sourcing, expanding a company's sources to millions of potential problem solvers around the world. Diverse businesses and organizations, including Eli Lilly, Life Technologies, the National Aeronautics and Space Administration (NASA), Nature.com, *Popular Science,* Procter & Gamble, Roche, Rockefeller Foundation, and the *Economist* have partnered with InnoCentive to solve some of their most immediate challenges. InnoCentive calls these companies seekers, and those they rein in for help are called solvers. Yet2.com is another example. The website is an online intellectual property marketplace, hosting inventors and companies who can post descriptions of innovative ideas or problems in search of a solution. The site serves as a matching place for technology transfer and collaboration. The company and its online marketplace were founded in 1999 with the capital investments of leading companies, including Siemens, Bayer, Honeywell, DuPont, Procter & Gamble, Caterpillar, and NTT Leasing. Yet2.com now has offices in the United States, Europe, and Japan. Recently, the company announced a partnership with another online innovation platform, ideaken.com, which operates mainly in India and Singapore. A group of my MBA students in San Diego launched a company called Tech-Seeds, which helps universities connect to venture capitalists and industry to commercialize innovative products coming from academic research.

It may seem surprising that even NASA has been experimenting with decentralized, amateur science outsourcing. But even beyond using such networks as InnoCentive, in 2000 NASA launched its own program, Einstein@Home, asking individuals for help in mapping Mars. The concerns over NIH and stagnated groupthink were sadly illustrated by the recent debate concerning whether bureaucracy played a role in the oversights that preceded the tragedy of the space shuttle *Columbia*. On February 1, 2003, as a result of damage sustained during launch when a suitcase-sized piece of foam insulation broke off under the aerodynamic forces of the launch, *Columbia* burned up and broke apart upon reentry over Texas. The question was whether NASA's anachronistic organizational structure was partly to blame. Following strong criticism that NASA's mammoth operations hindered individual critical thinking and accountability, Congress appropriated for NASA a $12 million contest budget to encourage competitions organized and run by private nonprofits. The winner, who must be a solo inventor operating out of his or her garage, retains the rights to the winning invention.

A cultural counterweight to NIH is emerging: Proudly Found Elsewhere (PFE). Looking at the quickly-evolving world of computer programming, where innovation and modification are essential to success, the rejection of the NIH syndrome stems from the clear realization that most, if not all, innovations of the twenty-first century will be based on previous knowledge. The second of the nineteen guidelines of software development, as purported by Eric Raymond, reads as follows: "Good programmers know what to write. Great ones know what to rewrite (and reuse)."

The wheel has already been invented. Inventions today are build-ons or spinoffs from previous inventions. Starting anew with every task is inefficient and counterproductive. Smart teams reach out and utilize other eyeballs and minds that are working on similar problems around the world. In the open source community, advocates believe that "given a large enough beta-tester and co-developer base, almost every problem will be characterized quickly and the fix will be obvious to someone."[20]

There is, as often is the case, another side to the story. Bugs may disappear when enough eyeballs are on it, or they may multiply. The mindset, "I'm sure somebody else will catch that" can be a recipe for disaster. It's the age-old dilemma managers must face: how much control and how much freedom will achieve the best outcome? Here is how one strategist describes it: "When you're working on a really, really good team with great programmers, everybody else's code, frankly, is bug-infested garbage, and nobody else knows how to ship on time. When you're a cordon bleu chef and you need fresh lavender, you grow it yourself instead of buying it in the farmers' market, because sometimes they don't have fresh lavender or they have old lavender which they pass off as fresh."[21]

The refusal of teams to use innovation that they did not directly create might occasionally be justified by a need to oversee and gain thorough knowledge of all aspects of your product. At times there may be financial benefits to vertical integration. But the fact remains that in most instances, reusing innovation saves energy, time, money, and resources. To capture these benefits, managers must have faith in the product and faith in the legal regime that sustains such reuse.

The concepts reuse and recycle travel beyond environmentalism to the challenges of innovation and the replenishing of our talent pools.

These concepts tell us a cautionary tale about organizations that become too controlled and closed to the outer world. This tale becomes all the more ominous when we look inside the organization and begin to understand the costs of monitoring and oversecrecy imposed on the creativity of individuals and teams.

BIG BROTHER AND CREATIVITY

> *Esprit de corps:* the common spirit existing in the members of a group and inspiring enthusiasm, devotion, and strong regard for the honor of the group.
>
> —*Merriam Webster*

Too much supervision can smother creative sparks. The management guru Peter Drucker warned that much of what we call management consists of making it difficult for people to do work. A new era of innovation is here, and Drucker's warning is being taken seriously. Contemporary organizational psychologists caution against too much supervision, which can curtail self-motivation. Excessive surveillance can have counterproductive boomerang effects of mistrust and suppressed motivation.[22] In turn, embedded mistrust, signaled by tight controls and commands, creates an expectation of slacking and failure, hindering self-initiative.[23] Just as reminding women of their gender or minorities of their race can cause them to perform worse than their counterparts who were not reminded, the signaling of distrust in an organization can be a self-fulfilling prophecy. As the social psychologist Robert Cialdini explains, "When people perceive of themselves performing the desirable monitored behavior, they tend to attribute the behavior not to their own natural preference for it but to the coercive presence of the controls. As a consequence, they come to view themselves as less interested in the desirable conduct for its own sake . . . and they are more likely to engage in the undesirable action whenever the controls cannot register the conduct."[24] The heavy controls rob an individual of his or her intrinsic drive to engage in an activity for the simple pleasure of engaging in it.

Atlassian, an innovative software company based in Australia and with offices in San Francisco and Amsterdam, demands hard work from its employees in building new software tools, but it also takes time to involve them in scavenger hunts, training as acrobats, and sail-cart racing. Atlassian also allows its employees free time to explore new ideas and gives its employees a fully paid leave of five days per year in which to volunteer at their community cause of choice. You might wonder how they get any work done considering that every office of the company is equipped with video and board games. But Atlassian's unique methods have proven incredibly successful, and the company has thrived in a highly competitive market.

Other companies take a more traditional route to building esprit de corps, focusing on days or weekends of adventure retreats designed to "bind participants to each other and instill greater unity once they return to the workplace." Executives play games like the classic trust fall, in which a worker stands on a tree stump with coworkers behind, falls backward, and is caught by his coworkers, hopefully before hitting the ground.

No one disputes that the way we organize work has changed dramatically in the past few decades. Paralleling these changes, our understandings of teamwork and collaboration have also evolved. During earlier periods in American history industrial workplaces also tried to foster a corporate esprit de corps. Henry Ford, the visionary of industrial work, cared greatly about instilling values in his workers, so much so that he created a body called the Sociology Department, which consisted of social workers and researchers who were in charge of eliminating the supposed immoral behavior of company workers. Moral issues ranged from the cleanliness of workers and of their homes to smoking cigarettes to gambling. Controls included supervision regarding church attendance, personal savings, and even whether workers made their beds every morning. Ford instituted serious consequences for immoral behavior in the form of such disciplinary sanctions as payroll deductions. Oddly enough "no one discerned anything improper in investigators [of the Sociology Department] knocking on the door of workers' homes to check that the beds were made up, in demanding to see savings account passbooks, or in requiring an itemization of household debts. Fellow workers, neighbors, wives, children, and even the doctors of workers were interviewed."

The most invasive of the Sociology Department practices were eventually ended by Ford, who in retrospect felt they were overly controlling. In his memoirs of 1922 Ford opined that "paternalism has no place in industry." Still, Ford's overall vision of a unified cadre of workers persisted largely unaltered despite this specific excision, and it continued to inspire organizational theorists even beyond the industrial era.

As team innovation becomes the golden standard of our economy, organizational culture looks very different from Ford's Sociology Department. Companies are attempting to actively shape interpersonal skills by hiring group dynamics consultants, facilitating collective "think sessions," setting up extracurricular activities, and sending their employees to leadership workshops and executive retreats.

But we also know now that, unlike the Fordist era of Big Brother, less control can in fact breed more loyalty and dedication among employees and improve group dynamics. Organizational Citizenship Behavior (OCB) is the formal term developed by organizational theorists to describe a set of actions in the workplace whereby individuals voluntarily behave in ways that are beneficial to the organization, without direct or explicit commands or reward systems. To further enhance the environment needed for OCB to flourish, taking steps such as decentralizing decisions and allowing lower-level employees to exercise discretion in their work is essential.[25] Closely monitored and regulated workdays have been replaced in companies like Google and Atlassian with a culture of transparency, independence, and free time to invent. These successful companies solicit the expression of employee concerns and implement participatory structures. They have open-door policies and inclusive meetings at which discussions are coordinated on topics as diverse as improving work and client relations to designing and marketing new products. The research is conclusive: organizational commitment and shared identity increase productivity.[26]

A BEAUTIFUL (INTERACTIVE) MIND

Share everything you can!

—*Marissa Mayer, Google (now CEO of Yahoo!)*

Open Company, No Bullshit. Atlassian embraces transparency wherever at all practical, and sometimes where impractical. All information, both internal and external, is public by default. We are not afraid of being honest with ourselves, our staff and our customers.

—*Atlassian's Value Statement*

> BOX 4
>
> ## THE SHIFT FROM INDUSTRIAL TO KNOWLEDGE WORK
>
> Application of human force on commodities → Interaction between human beings

Trade secret law may inadvertently cause an inflation of secrecy measures. Twenty-first-century production is interactive. The mega consulting firm McKinsey calculates that the fastest growing jobs in the past decade have been those involving complex interactions, high levels of discretion, and independent judgment. In fact, these jobs have rocketed off the charts, growing three times faster than other positions and accounting for 70 percent of all newly created jobs. In the twenty-first century almost half of the jobs in the American labor market require such discretion. But this is not just an American phenomenon. A similar pattern exists all around the world as countries continue to develop and compete globally. The MIT economist Michael Piore succinctly contrasts industrial era and contemporary work by describing the former as the *application of human force on commodities* and the latter as an *interaction between human beings.* Unlike yesteryear's controlled and partitioned work, that of the new economy requires employees to both exercise independent judgment and be team players (box 4).

The evolution from single inventors to teams, from individual to coordinated work, and from defined hierarchies to discretion isn't simply a personnel shift. It also demands a shift in organizational mentality. In 2008 Marissa Mayer, then one of Google's youngest vice presidents (and now CEO of Google's direct competitor Yahoo!), mused about Google's principles of innovation. She described innovation as being an ongoing learning process and warned against trying to control the innovative process from above or aiming for instant perfection. At Google, ideas are organic, coming from anyone and everyone: the engineers, managers, users, and financial advisors. Mayer's philosophy is, therefore, to encourage Google's workers to share everything that can be shared. Mayer herself practiced sharing by putting every piece of information on Google's ongoing projects on the company's intranet so that all employees have access to current projects and knowledge about whatever is in the works. Mayer aims as a leader to foster a culture of sharing, brainstorming, and team efforts, and, along the way, everyone becomes committed to the company's success. Everyone has ideas on how to make the company better. Successful organizations like Google that implement this philosophy develop the coveted esprit de corps of shared norms and beliefs, with a tremendous impact on the behavior of their creative workforce.

Thomas Edison instructed his fellow inventors to take the following steps when launching an innovative project: "Ask for all past experiences . . . study and read everything you can on the subject."[27] The best ideas of research come primarily from interactive settings. We've seen how more populated settings and more dense social networks produce more innovation. When we build something, we are building on past experience and all that has come before. To do so, we need to have the right connections. Companies need to have the physical capital and investment to pursue ideas, but, just as important, they need talented people with the right ties and the right mindset to collaborate, share, and exchange ideas. If we are changing our organizational culture to reflect a collaborative spirit, how do we revise our attitudes about openness and closeness more broadly?

In contrast to the assembly line's emphasis on individuated, routine work, today's prevailing consensus, backed by research and the best practices of leading firms, is that groups outperform individuals in decision making and innovative problem solving.[28] For example, in comparisons of teams of scientists to individual scientists in arriving at patents and scholarly breakthroughs, teams consistently come out ahead. In almost every field teams are outperforming individuals. A recent study published in *Science* examined twenty million academic papers and two million patents over five decades to demonstrate the relative impact of teams. The results were even more surprising than the researchers expected. Strikingly, teams didn't just dominate solo authors in one or two areas; they proved stronger in the production of knowledge across nearly all fields.[29] The analysis of these vast data reveals that the patents and articles produced by teams are more frequently cited than those of individuals. In other words, comparing well-placed, single-authored articles with the same number of coauthored articles shows that in the long run the coauthored articles are better received, more frequently cited, and ultimately more central to the scholarly community. Research of patent filings also reveals that at present more coauthored patents are filed than individually authored patents.[30] Teams today are contributing exceptionally high-impact knowledge.

Prolific inventors tend to be part of larger teams; notably, the same is true of foreign inventors, which resonates with our findings on the effects of geography and mobility.[31] Equally revealing is that the more collaborators an individual has, the higher the likelihood that she will participate again in a collaborative venture. This suggests that collaboration is a learning process that is reinforced with experience and time.[32] More generally, these findings show that the modes of production of knowledge have changed. Collaboration is more common than it was in the past. Nonetheless, fields of research and creativity vary when it comes to the size of collaboration. A particularly interesting study compared collaborations in two very different creative environments. Indeed, it's hard to think of two less similar laboratories than dramatic, brash, cacophonic writers' rooms compared to the calculated, carefully measured, tidy labs of astrophysicists, biologists, and chemists. Comparing data of creative collaborations of Broadway musical writing with scientific collaborations in astrophysics, biology and chemistry, the study finds differences in the average size of successful collaborations. In Broadway, the chronological changes are noticeable: team sizes increased until the 1930s and then leveled off and remained set with an average of seven contributors for the past seventy years. In scientific ventures an entirely different picture emerged. There, the number of contributors continues to increase, averaging in some fields above ten collaborators per research project.

Competition is the creator and the destroyer. Healthy contests motivate and capture the attention and imagination of their participants. Intense competition between teams, on the other hand, can hinder the sharing of information, even when all the teams are working for the same corporation. When a company gets too large, it can be the victim of its own success. The vastness not just of the physical space between departments, but also between layers of personnel causes exactly what we would imagine: separation, separation of ideas and separation of people. Separation between R&D departments and the rest of a company can create innovation barriers. Departments become compartmentalized, and the groups are less likely to know one another and to interact regularly. Hewlett-Packard's response to the unwieldy size that the company had become (swelling to over 150 divisions) was its Strategic Planning and Modeling (SPaM) group, described as "politically neutral" among the HP groups.[33] Spammers are charged with knowing what other groups are doing, so that they can coordinate information, prevent repetition of mistakes and failures, and help maximize the potential for innovation across the company. Some degree of healthy rivalry between teams and coworkers is desirable, but a coordinating function like SPaM has proved invaluable in ensuring that teams do not spiral into unhealthy enmity and remain in sync.

WHAT HAPPENS IN VEGAS DOESN'T STAY IN VEGAS

Innovation never happens in a vacuum. The need for mutual learning goes beyond the walls of the corporation. David Neeleman, founder of JetBlue, came up with some of the most remarkable innovations of the airline—satellite TV at every seat, at-home reservations, and self-selected seat assignments—by attending conferences and networking with people in the industry. Even in the most market-driven industries, the exchange of information happens through direct connections and friendships. In fact, demonstrating the power of friendship, inventors are more likely to approach a friend for reference than read a scientific journal.[34] An executive at National Semiconductor describes the climate of familiarity in the field: "We all know each other. It's an industry where everybody knows everybody because at one time or another everyone worked together."[35] In some industries allegiances among professionals across companies are stronger than to any one particular firm. It is the norm for scientists and engineers to help members of their network solve technical problems, even when the request comes from someone working for a rival company.[36]

During times of stress and uncertainty, when the need to succeed is perhaps the greatest, social ties are particularly valuable. Companies face questions like, how do we know whether a risk is worth taking? how can we assess the potential of a new product when there is nothing like it yet on the market? How do we value rare and incomparable assets such as intellectual property? We rely heavily on the signals of experts and cues from our friends for the answers to these questions. The thicker the ties, the more monitoring and feedback we receive while we grapple with uncertain paths.

Given the value of friendships and network connections, it is especially troubling that many of us are finding ourselves working in fear and solitude. The political scientist Robert Putnam warned against societies in which people are "bowling alone." He is worried that people are engaging less and less in the interactive activities that enrich their social networks. If we have an overcontrol mentality, we must also worry that we are innovating alone. Recounting the necessity of direct contact and social networking, the researchers Robert Lang and Mark Muro of the Brookings Institution admire the convention centers and tourist capacity of Las Vegas, extolling the benefits of enabling entire industries to gather in a common space to interact and make deals. Ironically, despite the slogan that what happens in Vegas stays in Vegas, what happens in Las Vegas makes a difference for business activities all around the world. The social ties that form in Sin City do not stay there, they spread and bloom, supporting markets well beyond the city's borders. Paradoxically, Las Vegas's reputation for discretion in personal matters actually supports the ability of businesses to use it as a unique public space that enhances their long-term professional connections. Lang and Muro explain that the fun and frivolous nature of Vegas, "an adult Disneyland," draws businesses to it for their conventions and professional meetings: "To all the killjoys who now want to shame people out of a Las Vegas convention visit, we say that a major stimulus for the country remains the social lubricant that Sin City provides business contacts."

The metaphor of "an adult Disneyland" is a potent one for strategies that seek to connect individuals and teams, and, within a networked industry, networks and organizations. While some strategic advances, such as using ideas from outside sources, have slowly been gaining steam, the introduction of these insights has proved extremely challenging for some firms. A better understanding of the full costs and benefits of both secrecy and sharing better equips us to make smarter choices, allowing us to make full use of the talent, knowledge, and ties of our innovative environment.

CHAPTER SEVEN

Mine—Yours (or Ours)

The difference between a mad scientist and a famous inventor is the difference between failure and success.

—*Brian Turner, Kansas City Space Pirates*

WHO OWNS EVAN BROWN'S BRAIN?

A KILLER INSTINCT MAY jump-start our brainpower, upping our skills to the next level. In one of my favorite scenes from Stieg Larsson's *The Girl Who Played with Fire* the gifted but troubled protagonist Lisbeth Salander sets out to kill her murderous father. For months she has been wrestling with the solution to one of the thorniest of all algebraic problems: a problem that has fascinated mathematicians for centuries. Larsson goes to great lengths to tell his readers that the solution would not be found until the invention of powerful computers, yet through her use of sheer brainpower, in the moment preceding the attack everything settles in the heroine's mind, so much so that she stops, sits down, and bursts into silent giggles. In the vicinity of her treacherous father, Lisbeth Salander reaches the eureka moment of discovery, the coveted flash of genius.

Evan Brown, a computer programmer from Texas, claims to have experienced one such eureka moment while driving his Mercedes one sunny weekend in 1996. What had become clear to him was "the

Solution," as court holdings later repeatedly referred to it, using a capital *S*. For twenty years he had been contemplating a computer program that would convert software written for obsolete systems into usable programs for newer computers. Then suddenly, in one brief moment, everything came together in Brown's mind. The Solution that crystallized was a groundbreaking algorithm that would allow for the easy upgrading of computers and make old software compatible with new hardware.

One major hurdle loomed in front of Brown's eureka discovery. At the time the Solution became clear to him Brown was working in the technical support department of the mega telecom company DSC/Alcatel USA. Even though Brown claims that the eureka moment happened during the weekend on his day off, he had signed a contract granting his employer "full legal right, title and interest" in all of his inventions. Brown's contract required disclosure and transfer of all inventions made or conceived from his first day of employment with the company until his departure. When Brown refused to reveal his solution to Alcatel he was fired and then sued. Five and a half years of litigation ensued. Eventually, a Texas court ruled in favor of Alcatel, holding that the algorithms Brown developed were his former employer's property. Following the court order, Brown was forced to travel to Alcatel's offices, where, for three months, he wrote down hundreds of pages of computer code without pay. Outraged, he has documented his woes on his website. In his own words, here is how Brown describes those troubled years of litigation:

> Now DSC/Alcatel has legal right and title to thoughts that existed only in my brain when they filed the lawsuit. DSC/Alcatel used their corporate influence with the court system to deny me my rights and steal my thoughts. I am extremely discouraged. . . . I had an idea that I had developed on my own time over many years. My idea had not been written down or recorded in any way. DSC/Alcatel claimed that since I was their employee at the time I solved the last portion of the problem, they owned my idea even though they had never paid me to work on it. DSC/Alcatel told the court that I stole their "invention" and misappropriated their Intellectual Property. . . . In the end there were no winners, everybody lost. Now that the case is over, I'm going back to what I enjoy, computer programming.

Fig 7.1. Dilbert—Billion-Dollar Idea (Dilbert ©2009 Scott Adams, used by permission of UNIVERSAL UCLICK. All rights reserved).

Brown's story, although not particularly unique in its legal history, has become something of a symbol of the moral outrage felt by inventors who are required to hand over their ingenuity to their former corporate employers. Brown's battle attracted a great deal of publicity around the world. Intrigued by accounts in *Forbes* and *Playboy,* the media have latched on to the story, fascinated by its implications for modern inventors and producing articles with titles like "Not a Penny for Your Thoughts" (*Wired*), "Calling Mr. Orwell" (*Time*), and "Another Case for the Thought Police" (*London Times*). Scott Adams was also inspired to create a Dilbert strip about the Brown experience (fig. 7.1).

Why has Brown's battle struck such a chord with inventors all over the world? Perhaps because the Solution seems to be the product of Brown's lifework, spanning a career that bookends his decade at Alcatel. Brown began translating computer programs from one system to another while he was an undergraduate student at Texas A&M, almost two decades before starting to work at Alcatel (then DSC). He claims to have conceived of the basic idea for the conversion algorithm almost ten years earlier. During those early years Brown worked for several companies, writing computer conversion programs for them. He doesn't deny that he perfected his brain-child while working at Alcatel. When he felt that his basic idea was nearly complete, after having worked at Alcatel for almost ten years performing other software development, Brown requested that he be released from his invention disclosure agreement. Alcatel refused but offered him up to $2 million as profit from internal money savings in addition to 50 percent from sales to third parties. Brown turned down the offer, and when it became clear that neither of the sides would accept the other's compromise,

Alcatel fired Brown and sued him for breach of contract. The Texas court agreed with Alcatel; it viewed the case as a simple breach of contract and ordered Brown to hand over his idea.

The court was unabashed in its ruling. It ordered complete disclosure of the Solution to Brown's ex-employer and refused to apply a noncompete analysis of reasonableness to the contract Brown had signed early in his career at Alcatel. Instead, the court viewed the invention assignment clause as a different and more powerful stick in the hands of employers. The media attention, public controversy, and scholarly commentary of the case reveal, however, the complexities of such cases. Are there no limits to the scope of control over individual inventions? And at what point can a broad concept developed in the mind of one person be considered a material invention owned by another?

Brown claimed that his job had nothing to do with the Solution. But perhaps even more acute, the Solution at the heart of the dispute had remained in its incubation stages throughout the dispute. The idea, while valuable, was incomplete and still abstract. Brown had not worked out the details of its operation, and he had not put it in writing. The Solution never left his mind. For all of these reasons, coercing disclosure at such an early stage of innovation appears technically premature and ethically harsh. Pragmatically and, indeed, cynically, the legal result leads to the conclusion that Brown would have been better off never revealing the fact that he had an idea, but rather quitting and going off on his own to develop it. Consequently, transferring ownership of fledgling and individually conceived innovation may impede the move from conception to a full blueprint by disincentivizing the very person who possesses the foundational ingredients.

IRONCLAD INVENTION ASSIGNMENT (OR, IF I SIGN, IT'LL NEVER BE MINE)

Abraham Lincoln famously stated that we grant exclusive patent protection to add the "fuel of interest to the fire of genius."[1] The American Constitution provides that inventors shall have "the exclusive right to their discoveries." On the basis of this principle, federal patent law requires individual inventors to file their own patents. Corporations themselves cannot author a patent, but they can nonetheless become patent owners. These days, in practice, they almost always own the patent. Because most inventions today occur in the context of the work-place, corporations, not hired inventors, own the vast majority of inventions.

Corporations obtain ownership in several ways. In the United States, in contrast to most other nations that patent at high rates, there is no federal law governing the ownership of employee inventions. Instead, the regulation is left to state contract law and common law rules. At first glance, the rules seem rather simple. The basic principle is that if an employee is hired for specific inventive purposes, the employer is the rightful owner of the accomplished work, such that both the physical and intellectual fruits of the inventive job for which one was employed belong to the employer.[2] For example, even in the absence of a contract requiring the handing over invention rights, an employee who had made original sketches of an invention at his home can still lose ownership rights to his invention because the company had tasked him with inventing the process at issue.[3] Recently, courts have expanded the definition of what it means to be "hired to invent" and have held that, even if hired for a general purpose, an employee charged with the specific task of invention as one of many work responsibilities implicitly cedes ownership of all related inventions to the employer.

At the same time, courts have long held that, in the absence of a specific duty to invent, ownership lies with the inventor unless otherwise agreed. For years the law has attempted to strike a balance in these situations—that is, when the employee invents without being asked to do so by her employer—between the employee's ownership and the employer's interest in having a partial stake in the invention. The solution has been the *shop right,* or an implied license granted by the inventor to his or her employer. The shop right gives employers a nonexclusive right to use an invention related to the company and to which the work environment contributed even when the invention was not within the scope of the employee's duties.[4]

In theory, then, the ownership rights of all other inventions outside the specific duty to invent remain exclusively with the employee. But in reality, just as businesses have sought to expand their control over postemployment competition by noncompetes and over trade secrets by confidentiality agreements, so they have demanded more and more invention assignment contracts. Typically today, the employee-inventor

BOX 5

The tiered system of invention ownership rules:

1. Hired for inventing → invention is "work-for-hire" and company owned.
2. Hired not specifically for inventing → employee ownership.
   Employer may have shop right.
3. *But* (the exception that in practice swallows all the other rules): Contract can preassign all inventions (including postemployment) to firm regardless of employment purpose.

agrees in advance to assign her rights to any future invention to the employer. In other words, even though the legal default is one that leaves most inventions employee-owned, the default can be changed by contract. In practice, businesses routinely demand such contracts, which involve ceding all rights to future inventions. Many companies demand that all of their employees, from the low-level manufacturing employees to design engineers and creative workers, sign an invention assignment clause upon being hired. In turn, employee inventors receive only a token payment, if that, in exchange for the transfer of all property rights of past and future innovation (box 5).[5]

As was the fate of Evan Brown, in most states courts interpret preassignment contracts broadly and favorably for the employer. Some courts will allow preassignment even via oral or implied agreements in the absence of a signed contract.[6] Although other countries with high patent rates limit the ability to demand such preassignment, in the United States only a minority of states, including California, restrict the scope of these agreements by prohibiting employers from demanding preassignment of patent ownership of inventions wholly unrelated to one's job.[7]

California's labor code states that an employment agreement requiring an employee to transfer his rights to an invention is not enforceable if the invention was developed entirely on his own time and without using the employer's resources or trade secrets, unless the invention was anticipated as part of the job for which he was hired.[8] It is a narrow exception, but, for example, if I invent a new pedometer for cycling, the California-based university that employs me cannot demand ownership over it because my job as a law professor does not cover athletic inventions. Beyond the few states that have similar limitations inscribed in their written laws, several

other states, such as Massachusetts (but not, as we know from the Brown/
Alcatel battle, Texas), limit the scope of assignment by applying a court-
developed standard of reasonableness. A Massachusetts court observed,
"For over one hundred years, courts have looked skeptically upon employment contracts that require an employee to assign his inventions to his
employer." Nevertheless, the reasonableness inquiry is rather limited, and
even the statutory limitations, where they exist, are usually drawn quite
narrowly. Even in California, which, by most other state standards, is
generous to the inventor, the aggregate result of law and contract is that
most employees do not have property rights in their inventions.

TRAILING INNOVATION TRANSFER

How far into the future can an employer demand that an employee
hand over his ideas? Does it extend only during the term of employment
or beyond? What if Brown had had his eureka moment after leaving
Alcatel? What if he had agreed to assign all of his future inventions over
the next few years after his employment back to his ex-employer? This is
the question of the trailer clause. A trailer clause, or patent holdover as it
is sometimes termed, is designed to ensure a company's right to future
inventions, even after the employee quits or is fired. A typical trailer
clause states that after the employee leaves her job, her former employer
owns any patent she files within a specified period.

Like other human capital controls, trailer clauses raise questions
concerning their wisdom, legitimacy, enforceability, and scope. The
dilemma traces the familiar concerns I have uncovered in previous chapters. Economists fear that granting employees too much freedom to leave
their employer and independently engage in inventions based on what
they've learned would lower a company's investments in human capital.
Conversely, we intuitively understand that permitting overly restrictive
holdover clauses will stifle competition and prevent talented inventors
from fully practicing their trade and developing their ideas, thus harming
the interests of the general public. The bottom line of the dilemma is, you
can tell opposite stories in which important ideas are never born because
of either too much control or too much freedom. To manage this dilemma,
most states apply the logic of balance. We are already well-familiar with
this balancing act from other human capital controls. Courts require that
holdover clauses be "fair, reasonable, and just." As with noncompetes and

NDAs, the reasonableness test applied to invention assignment contracts attempts to weigh the legitimate needs of businesses against the burden placed on the employee and the public. To determine if a holdover clause is reasonable, courts apply a three-prong test (recalling the three prongs of noncompetes), finding a holdover clause reasonable if it (1) protects the legitimate business interests of the employer, (2) imposes no undue hardship on the employee, and (3) is not injurious to the public.

The story of Armand Ciavatta, a born inventor, illustrates the force of the trailer clause. During his years of work as an engineer at Ingersoll Rand, Ciavatta submitted ideas to the company's Idea Box dozens of times, but the company never pursued them. After thirteen years at the firm he was fired over a manufacturing disagreement with his boss. In his spare time, unemployed and searching for a new job, he came up with an idea for a roof stabilizer. Ciavatta tested his idea, built a prototype, and filed for a patent. He also prepared a business plan and used his life savings and a loan from his brother to manufacture his invention. Though his invention did not use any trade secrets or confidential information belonging to his former employer, it was related to the industry in which Ingersoll Rand was engaged, so the company demanded ownership of it.[9]

Like Brown, Ciavatta lost his case at trial. But he fought the matter all the way up to the New Jersey Supreme Court. There, the justices unanimously ruled that the "interest of fostering ingenuity and innovation of the inventor and maintaining adequate protection and incentives to corporations to undertake long-range and extremely costly research and development projects" pointed to an unreasonable and unenforceable demand by an ex-employer. In other words, Ciavatta was free to invent and own, regardless of the restrictive contract he had signed. Ciavatta had not been hired to invent, was not involved during his employment in the company's research and development arm, had not divulged any trade secrets in producing the invention, and had exhibited no bad faith. Additionally, the court refused to enforce the holdover clause because it would leave Ciavatta unemployable within his field of expertise and would unduly restrict competitive products from entering the market.

The New Jersey Supreme Court's ruling was a victory for the employee-inventor. But Ciavatta's ultimate success in the legal battle reveals the limitations and flaws of the legal system. Years after the victory Ciavatta bitterly thought the court system had failed to protect him against the zealous big guns of his ex-employer. As a sole inventor, Ciavatta had a better product on the market and a Supreme Court verdict stating that he owned the patent to his invention. And yet he was driven out of the market by the cost of litigation and the marketing efforts of Ingersoll Rand, which convinced most customers to reject Ciavatta's new product. Twenty-five years after he had invented the stabilizer and seventeen years after winning his case, Ciavatta stated in a letter, "Unfortunately for me and others the law is used to punish the creative and productive elements in our society . . . [as] the sole purpose of the litigation was to put me out of business. I won the verdict. I lost my business with a better product. This will not stop until the financial penalties for this kind of litigation are significant."[10]

Beyond the personal story, Ciavatta's legal win is even more limited in its principled scope when we consider most inventors. The very reasons that led a sympathetic court to draw limits on corporate holdover delimit the scope of such sympathy. The counterfactual scenarios, more realistic for the majority of talented and creative professionals in today's markets, would likely fail in court. Most of the time today, ex-employees had been generally tasked with invention and innovation or had been part of an R&D team or had quit, perhaps strategically, to pursue their own ideas— all of these factors weigh heavily against inventors attempting to challenge a trailer clause. Ciavatta's victory appears to posit trailer clauses as a small block of ice floating on the ocean's surface. Unfortunately, the reality is that the block is an iceberg, and thousands of inventors beneath the surface never dare to run the legal gauntlet Ciavatta did, preferring instead to let their potentially life-changing inventions gather dust.

When Brown, the man who was forced to hand over to his former employer a computer algorithm that existed only in his brain, was interviewed years after the dust settled on his legal battle, he attributed his difficulty in finding a new job after being fired by Alcatel to the then-pending lawsuit. I see this recurring burden in many cases in which inventors seek to switch gears and jobs. The burdens of the lawsuits, whether they eventually end in a win or a loss, are disproportionately heavy for these inventors because they float jobless during their battle, trying to convince not only the courts but also the market of potential employers of their freedom and their ownership of the human capital they possess.

Alcatel, the company that pursued Brown for the Solution, has a practice of going after former employees and alleging theft of trade secrets and IP infringement, leading the *Wall Street Journal* to call it the most litigious company in the Telecom Corridor of Dallas. Like noncompetes and NDAs, invention assignment agreements become forceful restrictions on talent mobility and the dissemination of ideas.

A PENNY FOR YOUR THOUGHTS?

One of the more salient features of the American system of intellectual property (IP), and one of the primary bases for comparison with its high-rate-of-patent counterparts, is the complete absence of any required compensation for private employee inventors. Unless contractual arrangements state otherwise, private employers are under no affirmative duty to compensate employees for profits derived from their inventions. In contrast to the American way, other countries with high patent competitiveness legally require businesses to pay fair compensation to the inventor who assigns an invention to them. Germany, for example, requires that the employee-inventor be fairly compensated for any assigned invention. Under German law, inventions cannot be subject to carte blanche preassignment agreements. Rather, during the term of their employment, employees are obligated to report any invention connected to their employment, after which the employer has four months to claim the invention and file for a patent. If it chooses to do so, it is obligated to compensate the employee with an initial lump sum and a fair share of the patent value. Compensation will be lower if the employee's job duties include inventing or if the employee significantly relied on company resources and knowledge.[11] Similar mandatory fair compensation requirements exist in France, Finland, and Sweden.

China, now a high-rate patent nation soon to surpass most of its Western competitors, grants employers full rights to "service inventions." A service invention is any invention made during the course of employment while using the employer's materials and technical resources. A striking feature of the Chinese invention assignment law of service inventions is that it includes inventions produced within one year of an employee's resignation, retirement, or change of job as long as the invention relates to the former employee's duties. In other words, China has an encompassing built-in trailer requirement tracing inventions back to ex-employers. Yet, at the same time, in stark contrast to the United States, Chinese employers are required to reward the employee-inventor with reasonable compensation, including at least 2 percent of any profits from the invention and at least 10 percent of licensing profits.

The Japanese system also guarantees employee-inventors a reward for assigned work.[12] Japanese employers must provide their employees with reasonable compensation, proportionate to the employee's relative contribution to the invention. So, like Germany and China and unlike the United States, Japan gives every employee the right to reasonable remuneration for her patentable inventions, well above their regular salary and bearing a certain connection to the profits from the invention.

Recently, the Japanese Supreme Court breathed new life into these compensation standards. When an inventor named Shumpei Tanaka, a former employee of the Japanese company Olympus Optical, developed a key videodisc-reading component that is commonly used in CD and DVD players, Olympus claimed the rights to the patent. Tanaka, as the employee-inventor, was compensated according to Olympus's usual internal policies. While Olympus made millions from the invention, the company awarded Tanaka about $1,800. After leaving Olympus, Tanaka filed suit, claiming that the compensation he received was not the reasonable remuneration required by the Japanese Patent Act. The Japanese court agreed and found that Tanaka was entitled to 5 percent of the total licensing profits.

This landmark decision has since sparked a wave of claims against Japanese employers, several of which have yielded multimillion-dollar settlements for employee-inventors. Shuji Nakamura sued his previous employer, Nichia Chemical, for compensation for his contributions to a commercial blue-light-emitting diode. Initially the company had awarded Nakamura $200 for his invention, but a Tokyo District Court awarded him $190 million. In other recent cases the Tokyo High Court awarded $1.7 million to a former Hitachi employee and supported a similar settlement between the employee-inventor of Flash memory and Toshiba. As a result of this surge in litigation claims by employee-inventors, Japanese companies are sitting up and taking notice. A number of them have revised their inventor compensation schemes, guaranteeing higher levels of compensation for patented products.

So while other major patent-producing nations legally guarantee that inventors receive some share of their invention even if ownership is transferred to their employer, American companies are under no similar obligation. Smart companies, however, have, on their own initiative, put into place reward systems for their inventive workforce. Qualcomm, the San Diego–based wireless telecommunications company and the largest chip supplier in the world, gives its employees a significant reward for any patent filed in their name. The reward system is laddered on the basis of the stages of patent use. As a result, Qualcomm employees regularly receive large annual bonuses for patents they have contributed to in the past. Hewlett-Packard's "right of first refusal" program is another example. When an HP employee develops an idea on his own time and volition, HP requires disclosure and the right to market the invention but grants the employee a cut of the profits.

THE COMMERCIALIZATION OF SCIENCE

As long as I have any choice in the matter, I will live only in a country where civil liberty, tolerance, and equality of all citizens before the law are the rule.

—*Albert Einstein, 1933*

When you think about going to jail, it's so terrifying I couldn't get out of bed in the morning. But at some point I made the decision I wasn't going to let them use the criminal court to get something they weren't entitled to.

—*Petr Táborský, scientist imprisoned for not handing over his research notes to his university, 1997*

In an ideal world, university-based scientists would gain recognition for their discoveries, not property rights. Still, in the twenty-first century the annual income of American universities from patents well exceeds a billion dollars. Do scientists profit from the commercial fruit of their findings? Do they receive a share of the commercialization of their science? Petr Táborský, once a talented science student at the University of South Florida and now a professor in his home country, the Czech

Republic, preferred going to prison to abandoning the rights to his research.

While still an undergraduate lab assistant Táborský discovered a way to turn kitty litter into a reusable human waste–cleaning device. The project began with a small grant from a Florida utility company, Florida Progress Corp. The project as initially scheduled had ended before Táborský made his discovery, but the young researcher received permission to continue to pursue the research path under the supervision of his professors and as part of his master's thesis. When he made the breakthrough, both the university and the utility company claimed the invention as their own because it was made in the department laboratory. Táborský was convinced that the discovery was his to keep. He filed for a patent for his idea and held on to his handwritten lab notebooks. These notebooks became the heart of the litigation that eventually led to his imprisonment. When he refused to hand them over, the university brought criminal charges against Táborský, for the theft (self-theft, if you will) of his handwritten notebooks. Táborský readily admitted that he possessed these four notebooks that he had purchased and always kept in his possession on and off campus.

Although Táborský had not signed a confidentiality agreement or any other employment agreement, the court deemed that he stole his own research because it was, by virtue of university policy, the property of the university. But the fight did not end there. Táborský, who was young, bullheaded, and fueled by his conviction of the injustice of the verdict, refused to comply with the judge's order to transfer ownership of his patent and to return the notebooks. With his refusal came a prison verdict, and Táborský was incarcerated in a maximum-security state prison. The price of his moral convictions included not only Táborský's loss of freedom, but also a divorce, which he considers the result of his decision back then to give his battle for justice priority over his marriage. When offered clemency by the governor of Florida, Lawton Chiles, Táborský declined and stated that accepting would be tantamount to admitting guilt.

While Táborský's tragic saga is unique because of the severity of its consequences, the conflict that started it is by no means rare. Faculty–university disputes have surged in the past two decades. In 2005 a U.S. District Court ordered the Nobel Prize winner and former Yale University professor, the eighty-seven-year-old John Fenn, to pay Yale over $1 million in royalties, penalties, and legal bills. The renowned chemist had developed a method for mass spectrometric analysis of chemical compounds. In more simple terms, he invented a way to quickly evaluate new drugs, including the development of new AIDS medication in the mid-1990s. Yale sued Fenn for licensing the rights to his patent to a company that he partly owned. The court sided with the university, calling Fenn's failure to hand over part of the patent rights to Yale "fraud and civil theft."

Yale ultimately prevailed because of the university's written policies requiring the transfer of inventions by its employees to the university. But only a few decades ago such disputes over ownership between researchers and their institutions were rare. In a case from 1933 on determining ownership of employee-generated inventions, two researchers at the National Bureau of Standards developed several inventions for which patents were later issued.[13] These inventions were not substantially related to the employees' work at the bureau, which the court found to consist primarily of basic research rather than invention. Nonetheless, the researchers used their employer's resources while developing the patents, a fact which the government used as the basis for its claim of ownership. In deciding the case, the court drew a critical distinction between basic research and invention. The court explained that the investigation of natural laws, which was what the men were employed to do, is distinct from the application of natural laws to concrete practices. The separation between these two distinct processes means that inventions developed in the course of basic research, outside the scope of the employee's specific duties, belong to the employee. For years government and university researchers were quite free to capitalize on practical inventions that came out of their basic research. Only recently, trailing the for-profit market world, universities have come to demand, by contract and by written policies, the assignment of research findings and any invention that can be patented and commercialized. The incentive to mandate such assignment came from a law passed in 1980, the Bayh-Dole Act.

THE VIAGRA OF UNIVERSITY INNOVATION

In academia, as in private industry, the push for precise methods of assigning patent rights has been driven by the large financial rewards available. The sea of change in university invention was the passage of the Patent and Trademark Law Amendment Act, known as the Bayh-Dole

Act, in 1980.[14] Before the 1980s universities were largely unable to claim ownership of government-sponsored inventions; government agencies rather than the research institutions owned the inventions, even though not much was done to patent them and profit from them. The Bayh-Dole Act changed this limitation by granting universities the right to own and pursue patent licensing on government-funded inventions.

In a campaign led by the University of Wisconsin–Madison, universities lobbied to pass the Bayh-Dole Act so they could retain title to the inventions that were made in their labs and workshops. Senator Birch Bayh supported the campaign, viewing the previous arrangement as nonsensical because the government was simultaneously spending billions of dollars each year to support research and preventing the commercialization of the fruits of this research. He warned, "A wealth of scientific talent at American colleges and universities—talent responsible for the development of numerous innovative scientific breakthroughs each year—is going to waste as a result of bureaucratic red tape and illogical government regulations." Since its passage, the Bayh-Dole Act has been described as "the most inspired piece of legislation to be enacted in America over the past half-century"[15] and "the Viagra for campus innovation."[16] While that may be a bit hyperbolic, the act has changed the ways research institutions as well as researchers themselves perceive the commercialization of basic research.

Vast amounts of money and basic research are at stake. Not long ago universities largely took their nonprofit status to mean they should discourage patenting and encourage the free flow of ideas by rejecting involvement in the commercialization of the sciences. At the same time, this meant that researchers were free to venture into the business world and patent their own inventions. Faculty describe the time when universities receiving government funding could not capitalize on inventions as the good old days. Many companies were founded during those years by university professors: some started trends, others started entire fields. One such company founded by a university professor before universities could commercialize on the employee invention is Genentech, the biotechnology corporation credited with founding the biotech industry. Genentech was founded in 1976 by the biochemist Herbert Boyer, a University of California San Francisco professor and a pioneer in the field of recombinant DNA technology.

Once the Bayh-Dole Act gave incentives to universities to patent and capitalize on their researchers' inventions, they began to file patents at unprecedented rates and to rethink the freedom they allowed their researchers to pursue private ventures. Technology Transfer Offices (TTOs) were born. TTO is the university department dedicated to the licensing of university IP, and it has sprouted at almost every research institute. The recent figures on university patenting provide a striking context to understand these developments. Whereas only 250 patents were issued to American universities in 1980, thousands of patents are now issued to universities every year. The revenue generated by the University of California, which currently holds the most patents among American universities, is a particularly telling example. Over the past five years the university has generated an average of over \$100 million per year from its patents, including multimillion-dollar settlements with Genentech, Monsanto, and Microsoft.[17] As in the private market, such gigantic profits underscore the need for equitable means of resolving potential disputes between the institutions and their scientists.

As the winds have changed in the ivory tower since the passage of Bayh-Dole, the university setting opens a window onto the practice of shared ownership. In the United States the only statutes imposing mandatory compensation to the actual inventor pertain to federal employees and government-funded projects. In the government world all workplace inventions by government employees are owned fully by the government, but the employee inventor receives a lump sum for the first profits and a minimum of 15 percent of any royalties.[18] Similarly, the Bayh-Dole Act requires that university faculty be rewarded with a share of the royalties generated from transferred inventions. To find the right balance, universities are continuously redefining and refining their invention ownership policies.

University faculty members are typically hired to conduct general research rather than research related to specific inventions or profit-oriented tasks. Therefore, the law requires an explicit transfer agreement before the university can pursue patent licensing on an employee's invention. The vast amounts of money and academic prestige at stake have led most research centers to turn to employment agreements as a way to resolve potential disputes before they ignite. The current approach to tech-transfer polices, however, varies widely between universities.[19] Some universities have adopted more faculty-friendly standards. For example, Harvard, MIT, and Johns Hopkins University require transfer only when the academic inventor has made extensive use of the university's resources and facilities.[20] Under this type of agreement, in which the invention is not the product of a specific inventive task, the patent rights remain with the inventor unless they were developed with significant use of university resources, although, as you can imagine the term *significant use* is often vaguely defined and receives conflicting interpretation.

At the other end of the spectrum are universities that have adopted all-encompassing policies that grant the research institution ownership of all potential patents developed by their employees. The University of Pittsburgh's patent policy states simply but very broadly that "the University claims ownership of patent and intellectual property rights which result from the activity of its faculty, staff, and students." Like many private industry employment contracts, such a policy attempts to capture any profitable invention by mere association. At one point in time, the University of California's policy similarly required associates to assign all inventions to the university.[21] It has since moved away from such absolute requirements, opting for a more balanced middle ground. Recall that California delimits such broad preassignments by law.

In the middle of the spectrum sit universities that take ownership of all potentially patentable ideas developed with "more than incidental use" of university resources (Stanford's policy) or "during the course of employment" (Yale's and Columbia's policy).[22] As in any employment relationship, defining the actual scope of employment is an area of contestation, but the contracts and policies usually define the scope broadly, including teaching, research, and other intellectual activity conducted under university auspices.[23] Notably, Stanford's policy explicitly provides that inventors "are free to place their inventions in the public domain if they believe that would be in the best interest of technology transfer."

If universities are still in a trial-and-error period concerning the scope of invention assignment they require from their researchers, they have also been testing various compensation schemes for such assignment, recognizing that these variances impact the number and quality of inventions. Many universities designate roughly 30 percent of the royalties to the inventor. Some also allocate an additional 10–20 percent to the inventor's department.[24] The University of Chicago's royalty-sharing scheme grants, for example, faculty inventors 25 percent of the gross licensing royalties and 25 percent of the stock of new companies that are based on their inventions.

As in other debates about the wisdom of human capital controls, variations provide fertile grounds for comparisons of the most effective incentives and structures for invention at the university. The University of Wisconsin is an example of a highly successful research institution, ranking in the top five universities nationwide in federal research grants. Historically, however, the Wisconsin legislature prevented faculty from starting a business while tenured at the university. But this limitation was removed, and Wisconsin consequently experienced a surge in its high-tech start-up economy. The balancing of the missions of research and growth with their nonprofit and for-profit ambitions and their roles in regional and global development is a tricky one for universities. Compared to the private market, there is still relatively little litigation between universities and their faculty on ownership, perhaps because of the relatively generous arrangements granted to the employee-inventor vis-à-vis the private market.[25] Nevertheless, disputes over faculty inventions, such as the battle between Yale and Fenn, are becoming more common as inventors and research institutions alike join the race for commercial innovation.

WHO OWNS BARBIE'S BODY?

> For 40 years Barbie was the only doll in town. And then Bratz came in and knocked her off her pedestal.
>
> —*Tom Nolan, closing argument for MGA*

Barbie's reign over the dreams and playtime of little girls everywhere is loosening. New tastes and new dolls on the block are threatening her empire. Many of us are probably not too sorry to witness these developments. I would like to believe that as a child I had already developed a sense of the distorted realities of Barbie's world. My mother is a clinical psychologist and professor of child development who studies gender differences in children. In middle school my friends and I posed for short videos for her research experiments. The experiments asked children what they thought of girls who played with "boy toys"—trucks, a soccer ball, transformers—and boys who played with "girly toys"—Barbie, tiaras, and jump ropes. Overwhelmingly, my mother and her collaborators showed that at every age and around the world kids think highly of girls who play with boy toys but lowly of boys who cross over. I grew up knowing that we all had a choice but that choices had consequences.

Feminist jurisprudential studies I read in law school put into words what I intuitively sensed was problematic with Barbie dolls: they fed everybody who played with them unrealistic images of physical perfection and passive dreams about marrying Ken and living happily ever after. A recent study in the United Kingdom confirms that girls playing with Barbie tend to have "heightened body dissatisfaction after exposure to Barbie doll images." It is said that if Barbie were a real adult woman, she would literally tip over due to the disproportionate weight of her breasts compared to the slenderness of her waist and limbs. Regardless of her impossible ratio, for decades Barbie has cemented gender roles and proscribed women's aspirations.

Barbie, maturing and transitioning to the twenty-first century, has been toiling with her own image. After numerous image makeovers and new roles for Barbie as an ambitious career woman, Mattel announced in 2004 that after forty-three years of marital bliss Barbie was divorcing Ken. Nonetheless, as the new century advanced it became clear that Barbie had lost her edge. New dolls called Bratz appeared on the shelves. Bratz were different from the start. Instead of presenting a museum model woman, they were independent and sassy and sought to empower girls. Notably, the Bratzy persona did not escape feminist scrutiny and psychological critique. According to a report issued in 2007 by the American Psychological Association Task Force on the Sexualization of Girls, Bratz's miniskirts, fishnet stockings, and feather boas are overly sexualized, and the dolls' "objectified sexuality . . . is limiting for adolescent girls, and even more so for the very young girls who represent the market for these dolls." A loud reminder that competition over innovation and market taste does not always get it right or produce worthy results.

The Barbie-Bratz legal saga began in 2004, the same year Barbie split from Ken (which Mattel no doubt announced as a publicity stunt and others interpreted as an inevitable end given lingering rumors about Ken's sexuality), when Mattel launched its attack against Bratz, claiming that one of its employees, Carter Bryant, had secretly created the competing doll.

Bryant, who worked at Mattel for seven years, was a fashion and hair-style designer for high-end Barbie dolls. But he had an idea for a set of multiethnic, trendier girls—Zoe, Lupe, Halide, and Jade, who eventually made it to market as Cloe, Yasmin, Sasha, and Jade: the first generation of Bratz dolls. While still at Mattel, Bryant made the initial doll designs out of pieces he found in the Mattel recycling bin: a Barbie body and Ken (Barbie's ex) boots. He pitched the idea of Bratz to MGA Entertainment. In 2000 Bryant left Mattel to work full time on the development of Bratz, and a year later MGA introduced Bratz to the toy market.

In Mattel's internal memos, executives described the Bratz competition as a "rival-led Barbie genocide." The internal memo explained, "This is war and sides must be taken: Barbie stands for good. All others stand for evil." Launching a nearly $2 billion lawsuit, Mattel sued MGA for owner-ship over the Bratz copyright, claiming that since Bryant created the doll while still a Mattel employee all copyright for the doll and thereby all profits that followed belonged to Mattel. Bryant had signed an agreement under which he assigned all his creative ideas and inventions to his then-employer.[26] Mattel argued that the contract meant it owned the drawings and a major stake in the Bratz empire. Mattel also claimed that MGA knew of the contract and tried to cover up the true origins of the Bratz idea.

Much of the trial drama centered on whether the moment at which Bryant created his brainchild, the Bratz doll, could be pinpointed. Bryant argued that he invented the doll while on a year's leave from Mattel in 1998. Bryant's mother and his life partner both testified that he showed them the designs that year. Mattel urged the jury not to believe their testi-mony: "Mr. Bryant's mom sees him through the filter of the greatest love you can have for someone," Mattel's lawyers told the jury. As for Bryant's life partner, the lawyers made clear to the jury what was at stake: "He and Mr. Bryant share a life together. They also share $30 million," referring to the money Bryant earned in royalties from creating Bratz.

Bryant himself reached a settlement with Mattel shortly before the trial began, but the long, combative trial between the two companies continued thereafter. Mattel's lawyers insisted that "there is a right way and a wrong way to compete, and what [Bratz] did here is crossing that line." At first, a California jury agreed. It found that MGA had intentionally interfered with the contractual duties that Bryant owed to Mattel as an employee and aided and abetted his breach of loyalty. The jury ultimately awarded Mattel $100 million stemming from MGA's interference with the employment contract Bryant had signed and the copyright infringement that followed from Bryant's required assignment of the doll designs.[27]

On appeal, however, Judge Alex Kozinski of the Ninth Circuit Court of Appeals opened by musing about the connection between being fierce and fiercely competing: "Barbie was the unrivaled queen of the fashion-doll market throughout the latter half of the 20th Century. But 2001 saw the introduction of Bratz, 'The Girls With a Passion for Fashion!' Unlike the relatively demure Barbie, the urban, multi-ethnic and trendy Bratz dolls have attitude. This spunk struck a chord, and Bratz became an overnight success. Mattel, which produces Barbie, didn't relish the competition. And it was particularly unhappy when it learned that the man behind Bratz was its own former employee, Carter Bryant." Reversing the lower court's unambiguous victory for Mattel, Judge Kozinski concluded his opinion with the statement "America thrives on competition; Barbie, the all-American girl, will too."

Like Evan Brown, Carter Bryant had an idea for a different product in the industry in which he was employed. Brown's idea was patentable once it became more than an abstract idea solely in his mind, while Bryant's idea, an artistic design of a fashionable doll, was copyrightable once it was penned and drawn on paper. Who should own their ideas? Should it be the inventors or the companies that employ or used to employ them? And at what point can ideas become the subject of transfer requirements? Is it when these ideas are patentable or copyrightable, meaning that they have been translated into a tangible invention or design as the traditional IP protections require? Or is it even earlier, when still abstract and barely developed in the mind of their creator?

Both the patent assignment dispute over Brown's algorithm and the copyright dispute over Carter's concept of Bratz raise a central question of whether an abstract idea can be preassigned and exclusively owned. To square these cases with each other, we may need to draw upon what we know about the different default tendencies of different courts (think California and Texas) when it comes to human capital control. California's aversion to overcontrol comes through in the distinction between an idea and the expression of that idea, colorfully described by Judge Kozinski in the Ninth Circuit's opinion: "Degas can't prohibit other artists from painting ballerinas, and Charlaine Harris can't stop Stephenie Meyer from publishing *Twilight* just because Sookie came first. Similarly, MGA was free to look at Bryant's sketches and say, 'Good idea! We want to create bratty dolls too.' "

After seven years of litigation and after Chief Judge Kozinski reversed the first jury award in favor of Mattel, a new jury trial ended the legal battle in April 2011. In this trial MGA countered Mattel's claims for ownership over Bratz with its own claims about trade secret misappropriation. MGA accused Mattel of gaining entry to toy fairs with fake identification to steal trade secrets. Mattel denied the spying allegations, claiming these were invented to distract the jury from MGA's own wrongdoing.

In a stunning turn of events the new trial was a complete victory for MGA. The new jury ordered Mattel to pay MGA $88.5 million in damages for trade secret misappropriation—almost the same amount that the previous, overturned jury had ordered MGA to pay Mattel in the earlier stages of litigation. MGA's chief executive, Isaac Larian, wept tears of joy as the new verdict came down. He declared that the eventual victory "very well shows that in America, even huge corporations are not above the law" and that Mattel's "Kill Bratz!" anticompetitive business strategies (allegedly referred to internally by Mattel's executives as "Litigate MGA to Death") had not prevailed.

A notable feature of the Barbie/Bratz saga has been the great losses suffered by both companies. Both companies paid hundreds of millions of dollars in legal fees to pursue the deadlocked trials. Following the Ninth Circuit's decision in July 2010, Larian boldly announced that MGA would be releasing a new line of ten Bratz dolls in October to commemorate the dolls' ten-year anniversary. The development of these new dolls was a notable gamble. The new line made the new generation of Bratz more demure in an attempt to acknowledge parental complaints that previous generations were too sexy. Noteworthy, however, is Larian's commentary on retailers' lukewarm response to the new line. Commenting on the fact that sales were significantly lower than the nearly $1 billion annual sales mark the Bratz line hit at its height of popularity in 2005, Larian remarked, "Retailers don't like to get involved with competitors' disputes. I don't blame them." Like Ciavatta, the roof stabilizer inventor who won his case at the state Supreme Court but lost clients because of market aversion to unsettled human capital disputes, it seems that the litigation cost both megacompanies more than they expected. Perhaps a more sportsmanlike approach would have been for Mattel to develop its own bratty line and simply outdo the competition. Would such an approach have resulted in a copyright lawsuit from MGA? How much litigation and talent control are too much?

WHITHER THE ROMANCE OF AUTHORSHIP?

"Who is that?"

"Nobody. The author."

—*Marc Norman and Tom Stoppard, Shakespeare in Love*

The idea of the individual creator runs powerfully throughout copyright law. The principle seems simple: copyright gives the owner of an artistic expression the right to control against copying. Like patent law, copyright protections aim to induce the creation of expressive works. The Constitution vests Congress with legislative powers "to promote the Progress of Science and Useful Arts." The Supreme Court has explained that copyright law is "based on the belief that by granting authors the exclusive rights to reproduce their works, they are given an incentive to create."[28] The Court has repeatedly expressed the view that the "encouragement of individual effort by personal gain is the best way to advance public welfare through the talents of authors and inventors."[29]

Copyright law, again, like patent law, is reasonably clear in its initial allocation of ownership. The basic default of federal copyright law is that the author of a work is its owner. The author of a copyrighted work is the person who transforms an idea into a tangible expression. The exceptions, however, which practically swallow the rule, are the work-for-hire doctrine and the copyright assignment agreement. The work-for-hire doctrine, which has been embedded in the Copyright Act for a century, states, "The word 'author' shall include an employer in the case of works made for hire." When an employee is hired for creative work, the employer owns both the work and its copyright. The legal historian Catherine Fisk has documented the development of the work-for-hire principle and has called it a legal fiction that frequently renders the employer the author. Even when the employee is granted utmost creative freedom, the work-for-hire doctrine has been vigorously applied. Famous for such an extension of the doctrine is the case of the world-renowned choreographer Martha Graham.

Graham was a choreographer who created some of the most famous modern dances of our times. After she died, the beneficiaries in her will claimed ownership over the copyrighted choreographies. In Graham's case the court concluded that "the fact that Graham was extremely talented understandably explains the Center's disinclination to exercise control over the details of her work, but does not preclude the sort of employee relationship that results in a work-for-hire."[30] The court held that her employer, the Martha Graham Center of Contemporary Dance, was the true owner of her legacy, not the named parties in her will.

Beyond the expansion of what is considered work-for-hire, companies can and do require the preassignment by contract of the creative work, and possibly also ideas that have yet to become tangible work, of their workers. The Bratz/Barbie dispute, like the Brown trial before it, demonstrates the battle over contractual extensions of ownership over concepts and ideas, even before they have made their debut outside the designer's mind.

Copyright is where many of the most heated challenges to IP rights reside. Copyright law affords the copyright owner exclusive rights to reproduce and distribute his original work, to prepare derivative works, and to perform and display the work publicly. The focus is on the owner, who may or may not be the creator. In 2003 the Supreme Court upheld the constitutionality of the Sonny Bono Copyright Term Extension Act, which extends copyright terms by twenty years.[31] Prior to the extension act, the term of copyright protection was the life of the author plus 50 years or 75 years in the case of a work of corporate authorship. The act extended these terms to life of the author plus 70 years and 120 years after creation or 95 years after publication of corporate authorship.

Many have decried the extension of copyright, asking whether a successful author would really care if her book was to be copyrighted for 70 years after her death rather than a mere 50 years. Larry Lessig, the copyright scholar and activist who litigated and lost the case, refers to the loss as one of his greatest defeats and regrets.[32] At trial, leading economists filed an amicus brief explaining that since future value should always be discounted, extending copyright has very little value to the individual owner.

The cultural critic Lewis Hyde, whose writing has been hailed as a manifesto "for protecting our cultural patrimony from appropriation by commercial interests,"[33] gives as an example the poems of Emily Dickinson, which are and will continue to be owned by Harvard University Press until 2050. So while copyright has been characterized as "a tax on readers for the purpose of giving a bounty to writers,"[34] the romantic notion of a bounty to creators is eviscerated by a reality whereby most copyright is owned by corporations.[35] In creative work environments—think Hollywood screenwriters, *New York Times* journalists, Broadway playwrights, Nashville musicians—how much does the intellectual monopoly granted for artistic expressions trace back to the artist? As in the case of inventors and patents, the creative workers, writers, artists, musicians, and filmmakers typically earn only a small share of the proceeds from their copyrighted work. The cast of *Gilligan's Island,* for example, is known in the industry for the lack of rerun royalty provisions in their TV contracts. After about thirty years of reruns they haven't seen a dime. When inventors and artists regularly capture only a small portion of the value of their inventions and creations, how does it affect the world of innovation?

Outside the United States, copyright protections extend beyond a focus on financial rewards to the owner of the copyright to protections of personal and moral rights for the author, for example, the right to have work attributed to its author and the right to have work preserved and presented in ways consistent with the author's vision, even if the author assigned the copyright to another. Fisk has argued that "to most employees most of the time, what matters is not that you own your . . . copyright, but that you can truthfully claim to be the . . . author of it." The Copyright Act contains no such rights, although several more recent laws contain certain protections that attempt to address the issues. The Digital Millennium Copyright Act of 1998 includes a right of attribution, and the Visual Artists Rights Act (VARA), which was passed as a result of the United States joining the International Berne Convention for the Protection of Literary and Artistic Works, prohibits unauthorized intentional modification of visual art—paintings, drawings, prints, and sculptures—that will prejudice an artist's honor and reputation.

MYTHS AND REALITIES: THE SHOULDERS OF GIANTS

> The world owes as much to inventors as to statesmen or warriors. To
> them the United States is the greatest debtor. . . . In this century the debt
> will be piled still higher, for inventors never rest.
>
> —*Charles H. Duell, commissioner of the U.S. Patent Office, 1899.*

In 1970 the sociologist S. Colum Gilfillan announced in his book *The Sociology of Invention* that "The popular belief in individual, single, great inventors for things has been grotesquely developed by the same process as that which built all the classic mythologies to account for the origins of this and that, so that our traditional great inventors, even when really great and the doers of much of what is ascribed to them, are still, from another aspect mythic heroes in our school-propagated national epos."[36]

Gilfillan maintained that the myth of inventors as demigods stems from inventors' own desire for heroic status combined with society's need for heroes and a common cult. Gilfillan was deeply suspicious of these attitudes, and the book proceeds to debunk the myth: "The reality of the great invention . . . is a conglomeration of detail inventions so vastly numerous that no one hero, nor century, is enough to produce it." More recently, the *Harvard Business Review* repeated the sentiment and summarized the matter bluntly: "The image of the lone genius inventing from scratch is a romantic fiction."[37]

Nevertheless, the inventor continues to be a hero in many of our stories. As the philosopher and scientist Michael Polanyi noted many years ago, knowledge and discovery are both deeply collective and deeply individual endeavors. Individuals and teams both can have moments of inspiration or epiphanies—the metaphoric light bulb flashing on above their head. But at their birth most ideas do not have that singular moment or unified quality. Ideas are networked. Within firms, research and development is designed to "identify, assimilate, and exploit knowledge from the environment."[38] Innovation necessarily relies on the dual foundations of progress and existing knowledge.

Despite the traditional romantic notion of the lone inventor, relying on existing knowledge is not unique to the new century and our technology-driven society. In 1675 Sir Isaac Newton wrote in a letter to his rival Robert Hook, "If I have seen further (than you and Descartes) it is by standing upon the shoulders of Giants." Whether Newton was being sincere or cynical is still fiercely debated. Whatever the true motivation behind his words, we nevertheless know now that the greatest minds continue to stand upon the shoulders of giants. Indeed, it may be this trait, the ability to build on the work of greatness, which distinguishes our greatest minds. Many years after Newton's famous quip, Stephen Hawking titled his own book *On the Shoulders of Giants,* based on Newton's observation about the flow of ideas. Google Scholar, the massive search engine for scientific and scholarly writings, has adopted the phrase *Stand on the Shoulders of Giants* as its motto. As Albert Szent-Gyorgi, the Hungarian Nobel laureate in medicine who discovered vitamin C and the citric acid cycle, mused, "Discovery is seeing what everybody else has seen, and thinking what nobody else has thought."

Innovation is a nuanced mistress hiding beneath layers of hard work and knowledge. Asking the right questions is half the battle of finding her:

> Is innovation largely a matter of an individual endeavor? Or is it the result of a more collaborative process?
>
> Does innovation happen in flashes of brilliance and radical eruptions of eureka moments like proverbial light bulbs unexpectedly alighting overhead? Or does innovation come about regularly and predictably in the course of incremental improvements upon extant knowledge?
>
> Why create in the first place? Where does the drive to innovate come from—internal drive, passion, and curiosity or the external lures of profit and acclaim?
>
> How do the psychology of innovation and the economics of innovation matter?

Each of us holds competing ideas about the essence of innovation and conflicting views about the drive behind artistic and inventive work. The classic (no doubt romantic) image of invention is that of exogenous shocks, radical breakthroughs, and sweeping discoveries that revolutionize all that went before. The lone inventor is understood to be driven by a thirst for knowledge and a unique capacity to find what no one has seen before. But the solitude in the romantic image of the lone inventor or artist also leads to an image of the insignificance of place, environment, and ties. If the spark of genius of the mind and the fire of the heart primarily spur innovation, it can happen randomly, anywhere in the world. In fact, the new century, in its celebration of the "death of distance," supports this idea of a global boundary-less world of innovation. If knowledge exists everywhere and travels quickly and if lone inventors instigate the most important of innovations, then the landscape is universal; the world of innovation is flat, as the journalist Tom Friedman would say.

The decidedly less romantic but more realistic picture of innovation is that of an ongoing process. The search for better combinations of known elements and outputs begets innovation. A defining moment can seem like a sudden explosion, a crack of light above a single person, but the process leading up to that moment often involves years of teamwork and many types of professionals working together. While in the romantic vision of innovation the boundaries between institutions, disciplines, and people are fixed, our modern understanding reveals the many invaluable connections between inventors, firms, and industries which are necessary for continuous innovation. Human creativity that brings innovation is both patterned and stochastic:

> *Dualities of Innovation:*
> Individual/Collaborative
> Radical/Incremental
> Accidental/Deliberate
> Global/Local
> Passion/Profit
> Art/Science
> Exclusive/Shared
> Inscribed/Tacit

In the history of ideas about IP, two competing theories have become most prominent: Lockean and utilitarian. While the utilitarian theory focuses on outcomes to explain the need for IP, the Lockean theory of labor explains IP protections by the natural right one has to the fruits of one's labor. The rationale is that because people are autonomous free beings, whatever they produce with their body and mind naturally belongs to them. John Locke, one of the foremost prophets of liberal thought, famously articulated the labor theory of property when he declared, "Labour, in the Beginning, gave a Right of Property, wherever any one was pleased to employ it, upon what was common." Locke mused,

> Though the earth and all inferior creatures be common to all men, yet every man has a property in his own person. This no body has any right to but himself. The labour of his body, and the work of his hands, we may say, are properly his. Whatsoever then he removes out of the state that nature hath provided, and left it in, he hath mixed his labour with, and joined to it something that is his own, and thereby makes it his property. It being by him removed from the common state nature placed it in, it hath by this labour something annexed to it, that excludes the common right of other men.[39]

Put simply, creators who make creative work, according to Locke, should be awarded ownership of these works.[40] Creativity without a property right, or at the very least attribution, has been compared to the very act of alienation of one's self. In a memoir the ghostwriter Jennie Erdal compares ghostwriting to prostitution: "There is more than a random connection between the two; they both operate in rather murky worlds, a fee is agreed in advance and given 'for services rendered,' and those who admit to being involved, either as client or service provider, can expect negative reactions—anything from mild shock and disapproval to outright revulsion."[41]

Today, utilitarian IP theories prevail over the principle that people have a natural right to the fruit of their labor. IP is understood as a necessary means to the end of promoting innovation. But perhaps the two theories—Lockean and utilitarian—are intertwined. Perhaps ownership and the freedom to create affect motivation and progress in very real ways, suggesting an inextricable link between the means and ends of innovations.

CHAPTER EIGHT

Ownership and the Miracle of

Innovation Motivation

TO BE HUMAN IS TO INNOVATE. Human beings thrive on creativity. These aspects of our nature raise some fundamental questions. What drives us to engage in innovation in the arts and sciences? Is it innate passion? curiosity? play? the desire to learn? ambition? competition? the promise of wealth and fame? Psychology, sociology, business, and economics offer different perspectives on the motivation to innovate. Poets light the way. The American poet Henry Wadsworth Longfellow wrote the following:

> In the elder days of art
> Builders wrought with greatest care
> Each minute and unseen
> For the Gods are everywhere

When internally motivated, the Gods—our internal artistic and innovative powers—are everywhere. In those moments and for those actions, we care about every aspect of the work. Even the unseen, uncompensated, and unglamorous aspects are important because the reward is the work itself. Arthur Miller explained his need to be creative as a physical need; a need that will cause physical ailments if not pursued: "If somebody doesn't create something, however small it may be, he gets sick. An awful lot of people feel that they're treading water—that if they vanished in smoke, it wouldn't mean anything at all in this world. And that's a despairing and destructive feeling. It'll kill you."[1] Henry Miller described the best part of creative labor as being performed in a silent, dreamlike state. Others have described creative people as prisoners of their passion: "They get 'captivated,' and the only way out is to beat a path away from the point of captivity. If my attention is 'captured,' it is impossible to simply get away. The bars are not physical. They are produced by the intellectual, the emotional, or, more usually, a combination of the two. But, they are as functional as any jail cell you will ever construct in the material world."[2]

Artists describe their work as something they simply cannot help but do: it is a calling. The composer Roger Sessions described this calling as akin to a possession; the composer is "not so much conscious of his ideas as possessed by them."[3] Creativity is also commonly compared to addiction. "Forget whiskey," says one author, "forget sex, cocaine, and chocolate; writing is the best fucking drug in the universe."[4] Indeed, the association between creation and addiction is not confined to artists. Computer programmers, for example, particularly those who engage in open-source projects, have described their work as addictive and very much like any other productive activity: "Programming, at least for skilled programmers, is highly creative . . . good programmers are compelled to program to feed the addiction."[5]

At the same time, scientists, poets, philosophers, and artists reveal that their innovation motivation is often mixed. Artists are often recognized only after they die, and scientists may not see the full significance of their discovery during their lifetime, so surely something greater than fame and fortune drives devotion. And yet, fame and fortune can hold sway over even the strongest of motives. Charles Darwin, the father of evolutionary thought, admitted that his love of natural science was very much fueled by his ambition to be esteemed by his fellow scientists. The great philosopher René Descartes revealed the same competitive impulses when he expressed his concern that another great philosopher of his time, Thomas Hobbes, was intent on poaching his ideas. In a letter to a friend Descartes wrote, "I also beg you to tell him [Hobbes] as little as possible about what you know of my unpublished opinions, for if I'm not greatly mistaken, he is a man who is seeking to acquire a reputation at my expense and through shady practices."[6]

Going back even to ancient Greek thought, Plato famously portrayed the human soul as a Charioteer driving a chariot pulled by two winged horses, one white, restrained, and well behaved, the other black and wild. Plato's Chariot captures our human complexity. The Charioteer is our reason, which must balance the dualities of the Chariot: our inner workings and motivations. Each of us is both a creative *and* an economic being. We each have internal drives and external pulls, dark desires and enlightened rationale. Indeed, the coexistence of black and white impulses in our soul is rendered more complex by modern neuroscience, which teaches that our emotions and cognition are intertwined. If I am happy in what I am doing, I might be able to solve things better than when I am emotionally down. When I am internally driven, my external pulls are more easily tamed. We all experience complex motivations and wants, and each chariot has a unique driver. But despite our fieriest motivations, even the greatest of thinkers, artists, and scientists admit that inner passion alone rarely sustains a lifelong career.

EARTH, WIND, AND FIRE

As we've seen, Abraham Lincoln famously described the patent system as adding "the fuel of interest to the fire of genius."[7] Motivation has been studied intensely from an economic perspective, which focuses on incentives, and from a psychological perspective, which traditionally focuses on inner drive. Recently, both perspectives have converged in studies (including by collaborators and myself) on the interplay of internal and external stimuli of motivation.[8] This impressive body of work sheds light on how incentives and variance in regulatory regimes affect individual motivation and behavior.

The study of human motivation is a vibrant and growing field of research, but we've lagged behind in understanding the implications of these contemporary insights with regard to policy and economic growth. Moreover, experimentally, although the study of motivation has been the subject of academic inquiry and thousands of studies for over a century, few of these studies link motivation to the study of contract and strategic controls—to the very real dilemmas and battles of businesses. Particularly in the areas of intellectual property and human capital there has been a stark absence of behavioral data. This disconnect has limited the potential of existing studies to inform concrete strategy and policy.

When looking at the fundamental drivers of motivation, researchers consistently find that individual motivation depends on the goals and characteristics of the task and the work environment. The father of positive psychology, Mihály Csíkszentmihályi (pronounced me-high chick-sent-me-high-ee), was one of the first to study how we reach optimal flows at work. Looking at thousands of professionals, artists, and inventors at work, he concluded that we perform best when the task is compatible with our skill levels but hard enough to present continuous challenges. In other words, we are motivated when we are kept interested and feel capable of performing and meeting the challenges. Recent psychology research elaborates Csíkszentmihályi's lessons about a fit between challenge and skill for optimal performance. The difficulty of the task corresponds to the effort exerted in an inverse bell curve. The highest levels of effort occur when the task is reasonably difficult, and the lowest levels are when the task is either very easy or very hard. More difficult tasks require greater motivation for sustained work and completion, while an overly simple task actually suppresses motivation.

People enjoy challenges, but they also need to feel a sense of accomplishment. When you start training as a runner, experts caution the novices to find the right balance. If you start running too hard in the beginning your body will burn out and be vulnerable to injury. If you train by running too slowly and easily, then you will never improve. The key is finding balance, run hard enough that it challenges you but not so hard that you may never want to go running again. In much the same way it would be counterproductive for a manager to give an employee a task far beyond his skill set (a twenty-mile run for a beginner). The new recruit will struggle and perhaps even give up. The key is to find tasks that utilize skill sets and push employees forward.

Goals are the key to generating motivation and performance. We exert more energy when we think a goal is attainable. Indeed, we exert more effort as we get closer to attaining our goals. In experiments where people were either told to do their best or were given specific goals, the latter consistently led to higher performance.[9] Put simply, "When people are asked to do their best, they do not do so."[10] A do-your-best goal has no external reference, so people define it as they go, loosely and without focus. Specific goals such as increasing speed or profit or ratings yield more focused results. At the same time, assuming ownership over specific goals—internalizing institutional aspirations—clearly increases motivation. For example, when children participate in defining their own schooling goals or when employees participate in setting work goals, they will actually set their sights to higher goals and perform better than employees whose superiors set their goals.[11] Recall the practices of innovative companies like Google and Atlassian; these companies give their employees discretion, grant playtime, and push employees to view the company's goals as their own, resulting in enthusiastic, innovative employees who are less likely to burn out and more likely to have high commitment.

Taking an academic look at motivation, economists and psychologists agree (like Plato and his Charioteer metaphor many years ago) that motivation drivers can be roughly divided into two categories: intrinsic and extrinsic.[12] Extrinsic motivation consists of the outside driving forces— rewards and commands; carrots and sticks. Intrinsic motivation is generated when behavior is chosen from within because of inner joy, interest, or perhaps a sense of morality and destiny. An activity performed for its own sake is internally motivated, and an activity performed as a means to an end is extrinsically motivated. Although these definitions appear to draw simple lines, the interplay between intrinsic and extrinsic motivators is actually highly complex. We now know, for example, that external rewards can reduce internal motivation. Along with my collaborator Yuval Feldman, I've tested experimentally how financial incentives to behave ethically and comply with regulatory obligations might reduce internal motivation and in fact, under certain circumstances, create less compliance. When money is introduced into the equation, people may perceive it to be the main motivator and thereby perform worse than when the financial incentive is small and work appears to be internally driven.[13] Similarly, a recent study demonstrates that when extrinsic incentives are too large people may choke under pressure. Evidence of the negative interplay between intrinsic motivation and extrinsic drivers has led psychologists to argue that the introduction of monetary rewards decreases intrinsic motivation.[14]

As for creativity, experiments show that while extrinsic rewards do indeed normally serve as drivers of effort exertion, they are less compatible with stimulating creativity. For example, psychologists studying motivation of both adults and children find that when individuals receive rewards for their creativity, they often produce products of lower quality.[15] On a gut level, the research rings true. If we love gardening, we take extra care and pay great attention to our garden, and we have passion for it, probably more so than if it were just a job that a neighbor paid us to do.

Can we relate human capital controls and freedoms in similar ways to motivation and performance? What my collaborator and partner On Amir and I wanted to test, for the first time, is how freedom and control of future endeavors might impact motivation in similar ways.

OUR BEHAVIORAL EXPERIMENTS

> It is an immutable law in business that words are words, explanations are explanations, promises are promises, but only performance is reality.
>
> —Harold S. Geneen, CEO of ITT, 1959–77

Let us assume you are lucky enough to have a job you love, one you are passionate about, one whose problems you dream up solutions to in your off-time. Now, what if you have signed a noncompete agreement? Would you behave differently at your job if your postemployment choices were restricted? Are some workers more (or perhaps less) inventive and more (or less) likely to take risks because of their future options? Do they work less or more creatively if a noncompete lurks over their heads? Do they exert more energy in performing their jobs when they have a more robust career trajectory? Do they think more creatively when their time-line at their firm is projected to be longer? These questions are not easy to answer. While the success of corporations and regions can be measured by examining systematic field data, it is far more difficult to directly observe variances in the behavior of workers. Much of the research I have explored in previous chapters on the success of regions with higher mobility can be at least partly attributed to motivational effects by human capital freedoms. In other words, I hypothesized that being the subject of control can affect how one functions in productive settings. Productive employment is inadvertently tied to the motivation of employees to perform, and the ways we organize work and mobility matter. People, work environments, and relationships are symbiotic. For years, however, these indispensable questions about the interaction between the ways we organize our talent wars and motivation remained largely unanswered.

With funding from the Kauffman Foundation's Southern California Innovation Project, we were able to run experiments with over a thousand participants to try to get some answers. On Amir and I designed lab and online experiments to simulate market and organizational behavior, testing employee performance as a function of human capital restrictions. We sought to identify how controls such as noncompetes, nondisclosures, and IP ownership alter performance and motivation. Recall our dynamic model. The dynamic model challenges the orthodox assumption that control enhances innovation by suggesting not only that the flow of talent and ideas creates growth over time, but also that freedom to move and pursue one's talent positively affects motivation. The experimental approach enables investigation of this prediction by isolating the effects of human capital variations while controlling for such factors as external rewards, goals, and task environment.

We decided to test two types of tasks: one that is purely effort driven and one that relied more on creativity. The Matrix task involves finding two numbers that sum up to exactly 10. We told participants that their goal was to solve as many matrices correctly as fast as possible. The Remote Associates task involves finding connections between trios of words. We hypothesized that human capital controls would reduce motivation, leading to less completion and worse performance of given tasks. At the same time, based on the science of motivation, we expected that worse performance would be significantly more pronounced in a pure effort-based task like the Matrix task than in a task involving creativity, like the Remote Associates task, because the latter is more intensely fueled by intrinsic drivers. Our prediction was that higher internal motivation would lessen the negative impact of restrictions.

The experiments simulated market employment in the sense that the incentives were real: the longer and better participants performed, the more actual money they earned. Our participants were representative of the high-skilled marketplace: nearly all had an undergraduate degree and about half of them had graduate degrees and several years of work experience. We randomly assigned the participants to one of six conditions: half were assigned to a Matrix Search task (the effort-based task) and the other half to a Remote Associates task (the creative task).

We assigned a third of the participants to a noncompete condition, in which participants were informed that they would be prohibited from taking the same type of task in the future stages of the experiment; a third to a partial noncompete condition, in which they could buy their freedom out of the control by allocating some of their future earnings to their ex-employer; and a third group was under no such restriction.

We gave all participants across all conditions the same payment scheme: for each correctly solved set you can earn fifty cents. Moreover, if they finished the task quickly they could gain a bonus. The bonus was structured in such a way that you are better off solving correctly than guessing, but if your overall speed in the task is fast you can gain a larger reward.

The strongest measure of motivation to complete the task successfully is just that: completion. Participants who dropped out received no payment or compensation. We also tested time spent, quality of performance, and participant's reported enjoyment.

QUITTING THE TASK

As in most lab and web experiments, some participants in our experiment quit midway. While in most experiments the experimenter worries that dropouts may cause sample selection effects and therefore will make sure the departures from the experiment are not correlated with specific conditions, in our experiment dropout rate was a dependent measure. The strongest economically meaningful behavior stemming from task motivation is forgoing payment by quitting. If our assessment of postemployment restrictions was correct, the prediction was that they would increase dropout rates. We therefore compared the dropout rates across the different conditions. As we predicted, the participants working under controls were more likely to drop out than were the groups working without restriction. There was a 20 percent increase in dropout rates among participants who were told that in future assignments they would not be able to choose the same task, that is, were under a noncompete regime. Put in economic terms, people were far more likely to forgo earning opportunities when they were told that they would be restrained in the future. Or, in our terms, those bound by strong human capital controls were simply less eager to stay on task.

PERFORMANCE

Apart from the striking findings of the high quit rates, we wanted to test the quality of performance among those who completed the tasks. We

measured performance by the number of matrices or word trios participants solved correctly. The results again are remarkable. Participants who
decided not to leave the task were no more likely to skip matrices or word
trios in the restricted conditions than their control counterparts. However,
those participants who completed the easier search task (Matrix) were far
more likely to provide erroneous answers than control participants
completing the same task in both restricted conditions: in fact, participants were twice as likely to make mistakes. Participants subject to human
capital controls also spent less time completing the task. By contrast, as
we predicted, participants in the Remote Associates task (invoking more
intrinsic motivation) had similar performance levels—same error rates,
skipped answers, and time spent—whether restricted or not. These
results were also present, albeit to a lesser degree, in the condition of
partial restrictions that provided a mobility buyout for the employee.

The conclusions are dazzling: our findings suggest that human
capital controls directly suppress motivation. At the same time, our experiment also demonstrates that when intrinsic motivation is strong because
the task is more creative, performance effects are diminished but quitting
rates remain.

R&D AND HUMAN CAPITAL INVESTMENT

If we were to subscribe to the orthodox economic predictions, we
would expect to see greater investment in R&D and skill development
when companies can control the flow of the products, whether human or
intellectual, of their investment. But recall that our Dynamic Model
suggests an alternative: although businesses may fear the loss of their
investment, this fear is offset by the motivation of people to develop their
skills and perform better. Employees' motivation increases when outside
options are a reality. Supporting our model and complementing our
experimental research, new field data show that tougher human capital
controls actually reduce R&D spending and capital expenditures per
employee.[16] The field data are consistent with the assumptions of our
dual-sided model: noncompetes may initially encourage firms to invest in
their managers' human capital, yet at the same time discourage managers
from investing in their own human capital. Empirically, the effect of
noncompetes on the latter—self-investment in one's human capital—
appears greater than the investment of a company.

Let me elaborate on this. The orthodox economic model relies on the intuitive understanding that the more strictly a noncompete is enforced, the more a company can rely on their recruited talent to stay. According to this earlier model, reliance on job stability encourages the company to invest in building the skills of the employee. Otherwise, the company fears its investments will be lost. At the same time, however, we've come to understand that the talented individuals also realize (rationally and emotionally) that under a controlled regime their options are narrowed. Noncompetes, NDAs, patent and copyright transfers, and the constant threat of litigious battles diminish their ability to move to a different company. Think of yourself being in this situation. Knowing about limits and stagnation can discourage investment in one's skills and career options. Put differently, when a competitive tournament over talent is a less likely event, one may be less eager to show off one's talent. Knowing that companies will be unable to compete for her and knowing that she is essentially bound to her current employer, an employee is less likely to strengthen her professional profile.

This and more: it turns out that stronger enforceability of noncompetes lowers executive salaries and shifts compensation from bonuses and performance-based pay to a heavy reliance on a base or fixed salary. Again, this is intuitive: when, in regions like California, businesses need to actively retain their talent because they cannot control their movement by requiring a noncompete, they will offer carrots in the form of performance-based pay and incremental bonuses. This in turn will increase the commitment and incentives of creative and innovative workers to contribute to the success of their employer.

Recall Mark Garmaise's study that found that noncompetes strongly reduce mobility among executives, the most skilled and highly paid workers in the industry. Reflecting this fact, executives in jurisdictions that strongly enforce noncompetes have longer job tenures. More surprising are Garmaise's findings regarding compensation and investment in human capital. Tougher enforcement reduces compensation growth. In jurisdictions where noncompetes are broadly enforced, the compensation of their top executives is lower than in other regions. When managers do leave their jobs in states with human capital controls, they tend to go to lower-ranked positions and receive a lower pay increase relative to managers who move in low-control states. In other words, to leave employment in these highly controlled regions, workers must make painful compromises.

But it is not only the overall compensation that varies. The form of compensation differs with the ways we organize our talent wars. In jurisdictions where noncompetes are regularly enforced, compensation is lower, but it is also more salary-based, as opposed to performance-based. Garmaise concludes that "non-competition agreements do bind human capital to firms, but in doing so they change the *quality* of that capital."

To summarize, tougher noncompete enforcement strongly reduces R&D spending and capital expenditures per employee, lowers executive salaries, and shifts compensation from bonuses and performance-based pay to a heavy reliance on a base or fixed salary. These findings lead to the conclusion that one's incentives to invest in one's own training and skill development are stronger than the company's decision: "The negative incentive effects of non-competition agreements on managerial investments in their own human capital outweigh the positive incentive effects on firm investment in managerial human capital."[17] In other words, our Dynamic Model wins.

Experimental behavioral economics research happens in a lab setting, which means its strength is also its weakness: it fails to fully capture the realities that individuals face in real life, but, at the same time, it allows us to zero in on the data and connections we want to see by eliminating all the noise that complicates and clutters reality. There is a growing consensus that such experiments tend to match real life behavior quite accurately. Here, we have the advantage of empirical field data supporting our experimental findings and vice versa. The studies observing differences between states that encourage or impede talent wars support the findings of our experimental work: they all point to the same conclusion. That companies invest less in R&D when they can employ strong human capital controls is evidence of a behavioral effect. It suggests that, beyond the positive effects of mobility over time, additional benefits from freedom are in play. Our experiments show that even in the sanitized lab setting, contractual controls in the background affect people's motivation and performance. Our respondents quit and erred more frequently when they were asked to submit to controls over their own human capital. And in the realities of the market these effects are further pronounced by the expanded use of carrots—performance-based compensation—as an alternative to the sticks of confinement in places that protect the spirit of the talent wars: the freedom to move, share, and learn.

CARROTS, STICKS, AND GOLDEN HANDCUFFS

The philosophy at the famous AT&T Bell Labs was that creativity takes time. Our research demonstrates the effects of restraints on future mobility on motivation and performance. What about the reverse situation—the effects of job security and the ease with which business can fire their employees—on innovation in creative environments?

A new set of studies tests the connections between dismissal laws and innovation.[18] These studies score states on the basis of how strong or weak their legal protections against dismissal are (similar to the coding of degrees of noncompete enforcement that we've seen). The research then cross-checks this dismissal protections code with data on patent filings and patent citations. The findings suggest that stronger employee protections result in more and better patenting activity. To illustrate, if a state has more laws against random firing of employees—take, for example, protections against retaliation for blowing the whistle or antidiscrimination protections—evidence shows that these protections are positively correlated with more patents being filed. What can explain this? It may be that regulated job security provides firms with a commitment device that avoids punishing short-run failures, which in turn spurs employees to undertake riskier innovation activities. Employees who know they will not randomly be fired may be more willing to invest in long-term innovative ventures.

Most interesting about this new set of research is that it supports our intuition that the ways market relationships are framed, sustained, and nurtured affect patterns of innovation. These studies, while still in their infancy, provide additional insights about the connections between talent mobility, motivation, and innovation. When these insights are put together, a bigger, clearer picture emerges: stability can improve inventor performance when it comes from safeguards against random job loss. At the same time, restricting mobility by controlling human capital is counterproductive.

If we shift away from our control mentality, what, then, are alternative paths to retain talent? Valuable individuals will inevitably have attractive outside offers. Pay increases are an option always looming in the background. As a society, our tendency is to overcompensate management positions and undercompensate the creative and inventive workers. Despite the turn-of-the-century's disillusionment with financial markets and the leaders of corporate risk, we still carry a parochial attitude of sky-high compensation schemes for managerial executives and far less for star inventors. We tend to glorify certain types of jobs over others, creating a compensation imbalance between sectors. Responding to this imbalance, President Obama cautioned, "We don't want every single college graduate with mathematical aptitude to become a derivatives trader. We want some of them to go into engineering, and we want some of them to be going into computer design."[19] Nevertheless, the talent wars have brought with them notable exceptions to the traditional gap between extremely high executive compensation and underpaid star inventors. At eBay, for example, the lead technologist reportedly earns more than twice as much as the CEO. Apple recently paid an employee who is an expert in portable audio/video players around $8 million to secure his continued employment. Google paid an engineer $3.5 million in restricted stock to keep him from defecting to Facebook. Google also announced a 10 percent raise for every employee in January 2011 despite the economic downturn.

Not every company, however, can pay these kinds of sums to retain their inventive employees. The composition and structure of the compensation package are just as important as the raw amount of pay the company gives its employees. Although in the past compensation variance was guided more by seniority than by merit, employers today try to retain their most talented and inventive employees by offering them higher salaries based on merit. Compensation streams are diverted toward employees to encourage them to stay. To try and keep their talented recruits, businesses also focus on offering more attractive work environments and ensuring atmospheres of continual learning and professional growth.

Performance-based pay is a burgeoning feature of employment compensation. Even historically, successful companies recognized that giving their employees bonuses and a portion of the profits from their inventions incentivized them to innovate. At the height of the talent wars, if we see controls against departure (or sticks) and incentives to stay (or carrots) as alternatives, the way we organize our talent wars will change the composition of compensation. As we've just seen, Garmaise's study confirms that in states where noncompetes and other controls are strongly enforced, compensation consists more of a fixed salary. In states where noncompetes are not (or mostly not) enforced, compensation schemes are based more on performance.

Carrots, like sticks, have complex effects on innovation. Stock options, bonuses, and profit-sharing programs induce loyalty and identification with the company without the negative effects of oversurveillance or overrestriction. Performance-based rewards increase employees' stake in the company and increase their commitment to the success of the firm. These rewards (and the employee's personal investment in the firm that is generated by them) can also motivate workers to monitor their coworkers. We now have evidence that companies that use such bonus structures and pay employees stock options outperform comparable companies.[20] And yet, while stock options and bonuses reward hard work, such pay structures also present challenges. Measuring employee performance in innovative settings is a difficult task. One of the risks is that compensation schemes may inadvertently emphasize observable over unobservable outputs. Another risk is that when collaborative efforts are crucial, differential pay based on individual contribution will be counterproductive and impede teamwork, as workers will want to shine individually. Individual compensation incentives might lead employees to hoard information, divert their efforts from the team, and reduce team output. In other words, performance-based pay in some settings risks creating perverse incentives, driving individuals to spend too much time on solo inventions and not enough time collaborating. Even more worrisome is the fear that employees competing for bonus awards will have incentives to actively sabotage one another's efforts.

A related potential pitfall of providing bonuses for performance and innovative activities is the creation of jealousy and a perception of unfairness among employees. Employees, as all of us do in most aspects of our lives, tend to overestimate their own abilities and efforts. When a select few employees are rewarded unevenly in a large workplace setting, employers risk demoralizing others. Such unintended consequences will vary in corporate and industry cultures across time and place, but they may explain why many companies decide to operate under wage compression structures with relatively narrow variance in their employees' paychecks. For all of these reasons, the highly innovative software company Atlassian recently replaced individual performance bonuses with higher salaries, an organizational bonus, and stock options, believing that too much of a focus on immediate individual rewards depleted team effort.

Still, despite the risks, many businesses have effectively replaced the sticks of controls with the carrots of performance-based pay and profit-sharing schemes. But there is a catch! Sticks can be disguised as carrots. The infamous golden handcuffs—stock options and deferred compensation with a punitive early-exit trigger—can operate as de facto restrictive contracts. We could even think of the threat of economic loss as having a restraint on competition similar to that of noncompetes. Should forfeiture provisions that revoke training expenses, stock options, or deferred benefits if the employee leaves the company be subjected to a reasonableness analysis? Should courts scrutinize them in the same way they do noncompetes? Not surprisingly, given all we've seen, here again courts are split on the answer. A few jurisdictions uphold such provisions without regard to reasonableness and do not view them as restraints on trade. Other states see the provisions as restraints on trade and subject them to the same reasonableness analysis as a noncompete agreement.[21] In most states, courts subject forfeiture provisions to a similar but more relaxed reasonableness analysis. For the most part, forfeiture provisions are enforceable if an employee is made reasonably aware of them. This middle ground makes sense. Forfeiture of benefits does not prohibit employees from competing and using their skills and knowledge in the market in the same absolute ways that noncompetes or inevitable disclosure injunctions do. Notably, our lab experiment supports a more lenient approach, as our findings suggest that the partial noncompete, the payback condition, had a less dramatic effect on motivation and performance.

IN THE ZONE: HOW WE WORK AND PLAY SUCCESSFULLY

Work, art, science, sex, sports, religion: what do these activities have in common? While engaging in them, humans are able to reach a state of being in which the outer world disappears. When the world fades away and we reach a state of optimal experience, we lose our sense of time. Immersed in the experience, we lose any sense of self-consciousness and fully engage in the present act. Our awareness is as narrow as the activity itself. During those precious moments we can achieve excellence, as thinking synchronizes completely with doing. This is when we find our flow. How can we create these moments of perfect alignment? The ways we organize work, relationships, creative environments, and goals can all contribute to the likelihood of such optimal performance.

Csíkszentmihályi has studied each of these human activities in which we strive for excellence. World leaders, including Bill Clinton and Tony Blair, business tycoons, and athletic stars (the Dallas Cowboys coach Jimmy Johnson used Csíkszentmihályi's writings in preparing for the Super Bowl in 1993) all speak about Csíkszentmihályi's impact on their lives. These days he is a psychology professor teaching in the sunny, laid-back land of palm trees and candy-colored convertibles: California. But his life began in a much different time and in a much different place. The son of a Hungarian diplomat, Csíkszentmihályi was born in 1934 in Fiume, Italy, an area that is now part of Croatia. When he was a child, he and his family were taken prisoner during World War II and held in an Italian camp. Many of the family's friends and relatives were killed during the war, and the horrific suffering Csíkszentmihályi witnessed would play a crucial role in his desire to understand the human psyche. Facing the horrors of war at such a young age, he escaped into a world of play that made the treacherous and unpredictable outside world disappear. He played chess for hours, focusing on the game, which had its own rules, strategy, and order. Chess was a respite of safety and pattern when the rest of the world was in a state of chaos.

After the war, Csíkszentmihályi worked at odd jobs, at his family's restaurant, as a travel agent, and as a traveling photographer and painter. During his travels as a teenager he attended a public lecture by the renowned psychoanalyst Carl Jung. From that moment Csíkszentmihályi was hooked on studying human behavior. From then on a moment rarely passed when he was not buried in books by Jung, Freud, and other contemporary European psychologists. Inspired to find new under-standing of the human mind, he decided then that he would study psychology in the United States. He yearned to discover what motivates us and delivers us into those moments when we are our most productive selves. And so, in 1956, at the age of twenty-two, Csíkszentmihályi immi-grated to the United States.

His early experiences of war, in the labor force, in the world of art, and in the world of prison—a world full of anguish and contrasts—likely triggered his interest in the psychology of doing. Csíkszentmihályi once said he was surprised when he met Hungarians who had spent time in Soviet prisons. They seemed happier and more energized than he expected people with such difficult pasts to be. As a student and later a professor at the University of Chicago, Csíkszentmihályi was equally surprised to discover that unhappiness was a pervasive trait among the wealthiest and freest of the world. How is it that people could survive and even flourish under the worst conditions while others lead unproductive and unfulfilling lives under the best?

When Csíkszentmihályi began studying psychology, the field was focused on human dysfunction, mental illness, and pathology. Depression and neurosis were the diagnoses du jour, and treatments by medication and therapy were the conventional solutions. The mentally ill were prodded, measured, and analyzed, but regular people in their daily work and lives received very little study. There was virtually no psychology research on how one could achieve happiness and lead a productive life. Csíkszentmihályi recognized this major shortfall and decided that instead of adopting the negative or corrective focus of psychology, he would focus on the positive. The field he created is appropriately called positive psychology. He began studying what it takes to find optimal experience in what we do. He interviewed people about their creative and innovative moments. He timed and observed them during different activities throughout their day. He coded a variety of experiences and compared responses in a multitude of human behaviors. Being an artist, a researcher, and an avid mountain climber and having a garden variety of temp jobs under his belt, Csíkszentmihályi sought commonalities among the optimal experiences of every human activity. From work to leisure, from sex to meditation, his research uncovered patterns that help us find the golden zone. He discovered there were key aspects in each of the activities that proved excessively important: clear goals, feedback, and the availability of apparent points of success.

Csíkszentmihályi teaches us that, whatever the work setting, individuals need a sense of control and purpose in their careers in order to reach their full potential. In every domain of life, tasks must be challenging, but they must also maintain a good balance between one's ability level and the level of challenge. This is the principle of Fit: work should match our abilities but continue to challenge us. Otherwise we will either get frustrated and give up or get bored and give up. We also need to feel that we have a sense of control over the situation or activity. This is the principle of Control: we need a sense that we are directing our path, a sense of choosing our productive existence.

Fit and control! Think about this crucial duo as the insight we need to meet our new Sputnik challenge: the talent wars. The best combination to nurture talent is a good fit between jobs and talent and the ability to dynamically adjust this match. People are at their best when they make use of their skills in the jobs best suited for them. When the stars align and these factors are present, we find ourselves in an optimal state in which our productive activities become intrinsically rewarding.

We've all had those moments; runners call it hitting your stride, while other athletes talk about being in the zone and musicians aim to find their groove. For all of us, in those moments we are completely immersed in the task at hand and, for us, time stops. During those times, the world fades out; we ignore other needs that typically drive us—food, time, and ego. The externalities all temporarily vanish and all that matters is our current activity. Csíkszentmihályi describes this as "being completely involved in an activity for its own sake. The ego falls away. Time flies. Every action, movement, and thought follows inevitably from the previous one, like playing jazz. Your whole being is involved, and you're using your skills to the utmost." At these moments, in these environments that support our productive spirit, we experience flow, a mental state fully immersed in and focused on an activity.

THE TIGER AND THE JUNGLE: PAY FOR PLAY

Before the beginning of great brilliance, there must be chaos.

—*I Ching*

Carl Jung, the influential Swiss psychiatrist who inspired the young Csíkszentmihályi to travel to Chicago and study psychology, believed that innovation happens not through the intellect but through the basic instincts of play and necessity. Jung reflected, "The creative mind plays with the object it loves." But what is this object of love?

Environments can enhance or stifle natural ability; the best approach to thinking about managing people is creating environments that augment raw talent. Consider the analogy of linguistic environments. Compelling new research in linguistics and science suggests that the high mathematical proficiency levels of Chinese children at an early age can be explained at least in part by looking at language structure, not innate skills. In Chinese, word characters that represent numbers are shorter and simpler than those in most other languages, making it easier for kids to jump-start their math learning. Addition and subtraction, multiplication and division all become simpler because the numbers are represented in a simpler way, allowing children to focus on the tasks at hand more quickly and easily. The linguistic/math trajectory gives us a great metaphor for how organizational environment functions in the background of human innovation. Just as language serves as the background infrastructure of number representation and practical learning, organizational and contractual environments are the building blocks of an innovative path. The same way children who learn math in Chinese are a step ahead of children learning math in other languages, people working in an environment that nurtures their talent will rise above other workers. Work environments are the metaphoric language that we draw upon in the process of production.

Thomas Edison said that to invent you need a good imagination and a pile of junk. As chaos and ambiguity are transforming into virtues of modern management theory, the study of play is becoming a serious line of research. Playing with "junk" is no longer the privilege of children or mad inventors tucked away into their underground labs. There is a science of play. The National Institute for Play studies the biological, social, and physical science behind the power of play, explaining that "play is as basic and as pervasive a natural phenomenon as sleep." Serious research on play helps teach us how it creates competencies in the various aspects of our lives. Studies of play show, for example, that creative engineers who move up the ranks to management positions will lose their innovative edge if they stop using their hands and playing with the equipment and machines they oversee.

So how do we cultivate a "creative sandbox" at work? Take, for example, IDEO in the Silicon Valley. IDEO's founder, Tom Kelly, describes his firm's "secret formula" for innovation as "a blend of methodologies, work practices, culture, and infrastructure." A modern Renaissance environment of multidisciplinarity and constant innovation demands commitment, leadership, and vision. An extraordinarily innovative design company, IDEO has created a signature work environment focused on the freedom to play. Kelly muses, "New ideas come from seeing, smelling and hearing—being there. . . . If you're not in the jungle, you're not going to know the tiger." At IDEO there is no delete button, only recycle: the company retains the ideas and designs from all of its projects as a metaphorical grab bag from which its employees can extract inspiration in future projects. As other companies have recognized the unique philosophy of the company, IDEO has increasingly been lending its talents to other businesses, engaging in active consulting on management and innovation strategies.

The idea of being "in the jungle," as Kelly puts it, helps one think about environments of control and freedom, both from within and from outside the firm. For creativity to flourish you need your employees to recognize the tiger. You need to allow freedoms to explore and connect. You need to allow failure and mistakes, risks and change. Recall the behavioral study that tests the relationship between feeling lucky and being lucky (and perhaps even, as my students tell me, "getting lucky," in its salacious modern sense). In the controlled experiment, as noted earlier, the experimenters randomly planted dollar bills along a path. Those who felt lucky were far more likely to stumble on the dollar bills and discover the lost treasure. Companies like IDEO encourage their talented employees to feel lucky by granting them the freedom to play and take risks. At IDEO creative designers are encouraged to physically play, touch, and tinker with all sorts of toys: "Many designers put plastic parts, toys, prototypes, drawings, and sketches on display in their offices. One engineer, Dennis Boyle, has an amazingly eclectic assortment of items that he constantly talks about and brings to brainstorming meetings to inspire new designs. A few years ago, it included 23 battery-powered toy cars and robots, 13 plastic hotel keys collected during trips, a flashlight that goes on when the handle is squeezed, an industrial pump, 11 prototypes of a portable computer, 14 prototypes of a computer docking station, six computers in various stages of disassembly, 15 binders from past projects, a pile of disk drives, a collection of toothpaste tubes, a toy football with wings, a pair of ski goggles he designed, a Frisbee that flies underwater, and dozens of other products and parts."[22]

IDEO's work culture reflects the understanding that innovation happens through interaction, play, and proximity to other creative processes. But, as Edison mused about finding ten thousand ways that didn't work, innovation inevitably involves risks, and ways that don't work are necessary complements to success. To encourage experimentation and risk taking, Google allows its creative employees 20 percent of their work time—or an entire day each week—to play and explore. Whatever inventions and ideas the playful time yields, Google owns. Several important products have come out of this playtime, including Google News and Google+. Atlassian, the successful Australian software company, has made headlines with its pioneering approach to employee playtime linked to innovation. As part of its efforts to ignite the brilliance of its members, it allows engineers to spend 20 percent of their time to work on their innovative ideas and deliver back fresh directions. It also created intense quarterly FedEx Days, during which all employees simultaneously get twenty-four hours to work on and deliver a project they are passionate about. The science of flow similarly dovetails with the conclusion that playtime, freedom, and experimentation are key features of productive work. Csíkszentmihályi explains that "the more a job inherently resembles a game—with variety, appropriate and flexible challenges, clear goals, and immediate feedback—the more enjoyable it will be regardless of the worker's level of development."

PASSION AND THE MODERN PARADOX OF WORK

> Behold the turtle. He makes progress only when his neck is out. Let the creative employee stick out his neck.
>
> —*Gerard I. Nierenberg*[23]

Among management leaders there is a debate about how performance is affected by subjective experiences. One side of the debate believes that the more we are satisfied with our work and being at work, the better we perform. The other side counters that external pressures, deadlines, and the threat of losing your job are the best motivators. Although the debate continues, we know that in work settings as well as in controlled lab settings positive emotions are tied to higher creativity while negative moods are tied to lower creativity. A psychological study of several hundred employees working on twenty-six team projects asked the workers to write daily diary entries during the project. The study also asked the team leaders to report on the performance of team members. The conclusion was that people perform better when they have stronger intrinsic motivations, including passion and love for their work and positive perceptions of their team, their leaders, and their organization. In each of the teams, members were over 50 percent more likely to have creative ideas when they reported the most positive emotions that morning. They even found that the more someone was in a positive mood one day, the more creative they were the next day. People were also more creative when they viewed their organization as open to new ideas, able to evaluate new ideas fairly, and willing to reward creative work. More generally, they found that people performed better on all fronts, productivity, creativity, collegiality, and commitment, when they were internally motivated and perceived the organization as open and collaborative.

Resonating with our explorations of play and stochastic innovation, a growing number of copyright scholars argue that because play is inherently unpredictable, we should limit copyright protections to allow its full expression.[24] According to this view, people will create and play with existing materials even in the absence of a promise to protect their creation as legal property: "Creativity, as lived, is more than a response to incentives, working from fixed and random preferences."[25] An essay titled *Money Ruins Everything* explains that many creative people "do not have commercial interest as their primary motivating force, and so propertization of their work is irrelevant to their production of innovative material. But more than this, propertization may be inconsistent with their continued creativity and so may not just be irrelevant but actively inimical to the development of this modality of production."[26] And some further argue that that type of pure, natural innovation is different from and often better than that of people whose main driver is profit goals.

Job satisfaction, like dissatisfaction, has ripple effects. Yuval Feldman and I studied motivation and perception of roles at work. Our psychology experiments follow a tradition of research that compares monetary and intrinsic motivations of individuals within organizations. In a series of experiments, we examined the reasons people exhibited corporate ethical behavior.[27] Do people respond purely to financial calculations when deciding, for example, to report their supervisor for corporate fraud? Our research findings offer a clear no. In fact, like earlier psychological experiments, we find in our studies that in some instances compensation can lower motivation to do the right thing rather than increase it.[28] Focusing on this line of research, we investigated how employees responded to corporate misconduct: whether or not they would choose to report financial fraud, health and safety violations, environmental pollution, and various other types of wrongs. You can see how the insights connect: people are motivated in their daily job performance and in their roles as employees more broadly by factors that go beyond pure financial rewards. They care about fairness and ethics and will be happy to forgo certain monetary incentives in exchange for a better work environment. Sure, people are rationally motivated, as they should be, by economic calculations and self-interest, but as in almost all of our interactions as human beings, money doesn't define the entire enterprise.

Supporting our experimental studies on mixed drives, research on the motivations of programmers engaged in open-source projects such as Linux and Mozilla repeatedly finds that most programmers are not motivated solely or even primarily by material rewards. Open-source participants demonstrate mixed motivations, including gaining technical expertise, contributing to a common good, building reputation, and expanding professional connections. According to an MIT-based study, in most open-source projects, intrinsic motivations such as intellectual stimulation and the joy of the creative process outweigh extrinsic motivations such as pay and career advancement. Indeed, in the hacker counterculture, representing a shared identity of the free software community, hacking a lot and for pleasure is a badge of honor. In *The New Hacker's Dictionary*, we find the following definition:

> Hacker n. [originally, someone who makes furniture with an axe] 1. A person who enjoys exploring the details of programmable systems and how to stretch their capabilities, as opposed to most users, who prefer to learn only the minimum necessary. 2. One who programs enthusiastically (even obsessively) or who enjoys programming rather than just theorizing about programming. 3. A person capable of appreciating hack value. 4. A person who is good at programming quickly. . . . 8. [depreciated] A malicious meddler who tries to discover sensitive information by poking around. . . . The correct term for this sense is cracker.[29]

Hackers invest time and effort in productive work that carries little or no profit incentives for them. The desire to create and innovate is strong. Innovation and productive work are part of human flourishing. Traditionally, IP law is neutral regarding the values and aesthetics of innovation and attempts to be indifferent to the motivations, social or economic, of the creator and inventor. In copyright law, for example, "the writer who churns out formulaic potboilers for no other reason than to pay her rent is indistinguishable—qua economic actor—from the journalist who seeks through her works to enrich political debate, the scholar who advances a theory in the hope of convincing others of its explanatory power, or the poet who endeavors through words to transfigure others' imaginative horizons."[30] However, thick descriptions of the art of production matter in regard to how we regulate and incentivize individuals and institutions. When people create and work in ways that are not in their immediate financial interest, claims about incentives should be reassessed. The realities seen in open-source programs like Open Office, Wikipedia, and Mozilla and in other innovative ventures challenge the orthodox story of economic incentives as the single factor spurring creative production.

In every work setting, we know that the ingredients for optimal productive environments do not depend solely and perhaps not even primarily on material conditions such as higher pay. The Nobel laureate Daniel Kahneman was among the first to develop a grounded account of how individuals have intrinsic preferences for processes and mechanisms that go beyond the desire for particular outcomes.[31] We often care about the ways we interact and work more than about the tangible terms and conditions of our jobs. We care about our professional ties and our personal abilities to grow and dream. We care about the relative trajectories of our careers. We also care about the aspects of fairness and pride and values that the corporation embodies. A sense of progress and innovation creates excitement and motivation. A sense of futility creates frustrations and hinders productivity. Our lab experiments as well as the empirical studies indicate that future constraints affect present motivation. We also know that other features of the work environment, including a culture of openness, organizational pride, and professional growth, lead workers to engage more in work. Happiness and the joy of being playful at work create a virtuous circle with innovation: happier workers are better workers; better workers are happier. In a nutshell, when someone chooses to stay in or leave a job, money does not always buy happiness. A study of India's booming high-tech labor market describing the rise of "a global war for talent" concludes that the companies that compete best in retaining their employees have realized that no matter the environment, employees care about nontangible rewards, such as pride, satisfaction, fair treatment, and support from management.[32] Ambitious individuals with great career aspirations readily substitute some monetary compensation for work at the best companies.[33]

Motivation and performance are inextricably linked to environments. Psychologists and organizational strategists since Csíkszentmihályi have attempted to sort out the types of creative environments that will enhance moments of flow and increase the likelihood of the great payoffs hoped for in the war for talent. Up until now, few have considered the ways in which the fight for recruiting, luring, and retaining talent itself shapes the art and science of innovation and motivation. We've figured out only half of the puzzle: increasing flow in moments of complete focus at work; but we've neglected the bigger picture: optimizing the flow of talent and ideas in a sustained way.

In his study of work, Csíkszentmihályi encountered a paradox: we're happier at work, but we wish we weren't there. In order to study optimal experience in work settings, Csíkszentmihályi used a research tool called the Experience Sampling Method (ESM). In ESM studies, subjects are beeped (via a pager or handheld device) every few hours, at random intervals during the day. Subjects then write down what they are doing and how they feel: happy or frustrated, bored or challenged. When Csíkszentmihályi and his research team timed people at different times of the week and day, they found that people experienced challenge and felt skillful at work far more often than in leisure. Even so, people wished to be doing something else to a much greater extent while working than in leisure. They felt more satisfied in their moments of flow, reported more positive experiences, happiness, and feeling stronger, cheerful and more energized. Yet they still wanted to experience less work. Csíkszentmihályi attributes these findings not to an inherent preference of people to be in a relaxed, nonworking state, but in the modern worker's relation to work.

Happy workers are more likely to be productive, collaborative, and committed. They are more likely to invest more time at work and to work beyond the confines of their regular work hours. Interviews with dozens of employees working in the Silicon Valley reveal that companies are at times willing to modify software projects in order to allow a better fit with their employees' interests.[34] Talented workers are given the freedom to work on projects they enjoy. But why are most of us reporting not being too happy at work? Are our work settings conducive to enhancing satisfaction? What gives people great satisfaction is being useful, self-reliant, and understanding that work is closely tied to one's identity and personal growth. When people feel trapped in their jobs, they are, to use Csíkszentmihályi's term, in a state of apathy. For people to be in a state of challenge and to reach optimal innovation motivation, they need to believe in their ability to grow professionally. They need to know that their skills and talents, their innate passion and knowledge, are portable. They need their human capital to be part of their identity. Talent wants to be free.

Our quest to find flow, motivation, and joy at work enriches the standard economic analysis of human capital and intellectual property. Our experimental and field studies allow us to gain a better appreciation of the patterns in which ideas, people, and groups in networked, institutional, and individual settings flow. The traditional incentive model is elegant. The idea that has dominated much of intellectual property law is that people are purely economically rational. But real life is not so straightforward: motivation and performance always involve a mix of push and pull. Talent can be nourished and encouraged. It can also be crushed and suppressed. To win the talent wars, we need focus on achieving the former and resisting impulses that lead to the latter.

PART THREE THE TALENT COMMONS

NOW THAT WE'VE MAPPED the way around the strategic choices between control and freedom, we can complete the ambitious challenge of elaborating a new vision for nurturing our talent pool. Some fabulous studies in recent years have helped us peek inside the black box of innovation. Extraordinary thinkers have challenged us to question conventional wisdoms about the innovative process. Leading economists and psychologists have pointed to new directions of cooperation and shared resources in market competition. What has been missing is a blueprint for bringing together these insights to inform the logic of talent wars. Now we can restructure our vision for an era of innovation that better fits the twenty-first-century age of talent.

CHAPTER NINE

Talent Wars and the Entrepreneurial Spirit

As a matter of culture, high-tech entrepreneurs are the cowboys of our age. In the United States, as Willie Nelson has told us, our heroes have always been cowboys.

—*Joseph Bankman and Ronald J. Gilson, "Why Start-ups?"*

AN ORWELLIAN MESSAGE

IF YOU POUR a pot of gold into an infrastructure that cannot support it, the results may disappoint. To paraphrase George Orwell, in the world of talent wars all dollars are created equally, but some are more equal than others. Venture capital (VC) investments increase economic growth and entrepreneurship wherever they are injected. But the same investments yield different outcomes when background conditions vary. The lessons of innovation geographies, mobility, flow, and motivation have taught us that, far beyond raw dollar capital, the realm of human capital defines economic success. For a place to flourish it needs to nourish the entrepreneurial spirit, and entrepreneurship is determined by the ways we fight for talent.

In 2010 researchers from Yale University sought to examine the effects of VC investment across states depending on the enforcement of noncompetes. They studied a decade's worth of data on over three hundred metropolitan areas in the United States, including patent filings in each metropolitan area according to the inventor's address; the level of dollar investment per place; and the level of entrepreneurship in each of the metropolitan areas, based on the Census Bureau data on new business establishments.[1] The researchers then cross-checked this wealth of data with the variances in noncompete enforcement across the United States.

The results of this sophisticated empirical analysis are striking. The data showed very clearly that human capital controls reduce the benefits of money investment. In states where noncompetes are not enforced or weakly enforced more venture capital results in higher levels of entrepreneurship, more patenting, and better employment rates. Conversely, where noncompetes are strongly enforced, start-up activity is suppressed, fewer jobs are created, and fewer patents are filed. Put simply, the same VC amount funneled into a region will result in very different innovation rates depending on how the law shapes the fight for talent. The differences in these effects persist over time: regions with weaker enforcement of noncompete contracts continue to enjoy lasting gains. Summarizing the implications of their findings, the researchers warn, "Policies aimed at stimulating entrepreneurship through increases in the supply of venture capital may not succeed if the labor laws in the jurisdictions do not support such investments."

The findings of the study are robust, but, as in other recent studies, the researchers here sought to remove concerns about the California effect driving the observations. To avoid questions of an outlier effect (for example, questions about how California sunshine creates exceptional grounds for entrepreneurship) they replicated the results excluding the Bay Area. The significance of their results remained the same. In response to an identical influx of local VC, states that do not enforce noncompetes experience twice the increase in patents and double the birth of new companies compared to states that enforce them. Those states that have weaker enforcement of noncompetes also enjoy three times the employment growth of enforcing states. The benefits extend beyond the start-up segment of a region and span the entire regional economy. Doubling VC in an average metropolitan area with weak human capital controls results in not just several dozens more local firms but thousands of new jobs. This means that the job growth comes not only from the new start-ups but also from established firms: "Both incumbents and entrants," the researchers conclude, "benefit from the greater mobility of employees." Their overall conclusion is blunt: the enforce-ment of noncompete agreements not only limits entrepreneurship but also impedes innovation and regional growth. The success of local VCs that hope to mimic the success of regions like the Silicon Valley will depend on whether or not the area adopts the right set of supporting rules, namely, policies that enhance the free movement of talent.

Let us pause here to recapture the explanations for these striking effects. We already know that greater mobility of talent enhances informa-tion flows, enriches collaborative networks, and promises a better fit between employees and employers. It also increases the motivation and performance of productive employees. For start-ups, the ability to hire skilled talent freely increases confidence in the success of VC investment. A complementary explanation for the increased patent rates is that firms may be investing more in patentable research and development as a substitute for human controls. In other words, companies in places that do not use noncompetes may be substituting patents for noncompetes and trade secret protection. Indeed, studies find that when confronted with high turnover rates among employees companies prefer to protect their intellectual property through patent filings rather than through trade secrets and noncompetes.[2] In the chemical industry close networks and alliances increase the number of patents because of the ties among partners.[3] While this fact can explain some of the increase in patenting rates, it cannot explain the overall job and economic growth that come from higher mobility. In fact, it supports our contention that companies will find alternative ways of innovating and progressing, while benefiting from higher talent and knowledge flows.

Whatever the ultimate combination of reasons—the psychological effect on the employees themselves, richer networks from high movement and interaction, increased "biodiversity" in the business community, more entry points for new innovators and entrepreneurs—the data show without question that laws supporting mobility and exchange yield richer harvests for VC investment than job markets based on fear and control.

COWBOYS AND VULTURES

The image is familiar: young bold innovators leave companies to start their venture. The reactions vary from heroic descriptions of the "cowboys of our age" to livid derogatory characterizations of "vulture capitalists" on

202 THE TALENT COMMONS

the hunt. Either way, there can be no debate about the value of entrepreneurship as a major driver of economic growth. The entrepreneur (from the French word meaning "one who undertakes") is a natural risk taker. The smaller and newer a start-up, the more it must innovate to compete, paving the way for new markets.[4] The tiny company must quickly position itself in the land of giants. Entrepreneurship, therefore, is a distinct beneficiary of a shift in our talent war mentality.

In an early study of the biotech industry, researchers tested the effect of initial public offerings (IPOs) on founding rates of biotech firms in places that enforce noncompetes versus those that do not. The study shows that far more biotech companies were founded in states that do not enforce or weakly enforce noncompete agreements.[5] This is because stronger human capital controls and reduced mobility depress growth in general, but in particular they depress the growth of smaller, newer companies by making it difficult and far more risky to become independent and attract new talent. As a result, entrepreneurship and its innovations suffer a hard blow in states that allow severe human capital controls.

When I consult inventors on their contractual agreements I frequently come across individuals who are determined to leave their employer but prefer to mitigate the risk of a dispute by going to an established competitor that has the resources to protect and indemnify them in case of legal liability. A legal counsel of a large biotech company once described to me how his company reassures its new recruits and promises to fight their fight with their previous employers. This dynamic further contributes to an overall gain for large, established companies and curtails entrepreneurship and competition by new companies. The pull and push of going to a larger company to shield against human capital controls are strong: employees want protection, and large companies have the confidence to react to swords with swords. Small companies are faced with a much greater risk in hiring a competitor's employee. Individual employees see an even greater risk in going it alone and becoming an independent entrepreneur.

Even some of the most skilled, natural-born entrepreneurs have been forced to sit it out or go elsewhere as a result of the threat of litigation over their human capital. Known in the industry as the Lord of the Skies, the founder of JetBlue, David Neeleman, is a good example of such an entrepreneur. Neeleman was fired by Southwest Airlines years before he started his now-successful airline. While at Southwest, Neeleman signed a noncompete clause that prohibited him from competing in the airline industry for five years.[6] For those five years Neeleman's obligation, as defined by the noncompete clause, forced him to refrain from innovating in the field of his experience and passion. Some may say that this long period allowed Neeleman to perfect in his mind concepts that later revolutionized the industry. But the forced hiatus deprived the public of a creative entrepreneur who brought value and new energy to a key industry. One way to look at it is that the noncompete cost all of us five years of the broader consumer choice of JetBlue.

In 1928 Joseph Schumpeter described the challenge of innovation as "one of resistances and uncertainties of doing what has not been done before." Schumpeter believed that successful innovation is accessible and appealing to only a distinct and rare type of individual, one who takes risks, defies reason, and has the unique inclination to imagine the unimaginable.[7] More recently, we have come to understand those who engage in entrepreneurship as being especially well positioned to assume risk, deal with uncertainty, supply capital, undertake difficult decision making, and provide leadership and management.[8] But entrepreneurs find themselves at a particular disadvantage in the market. Even if an entrepreneur is pursuing an idea that is distinct from any work done for her former employer and developed independently, she may still experience the threat of the talent wars.

Many companies furiously struggle to keep their inventive employees from defecting to a start-up company. An Intel insider has described venture capitalists as the "financial equivalent of ambulance chasers." The reality is, however, that most new companies are founded by former employees. Start-ups are typically founded when an employee leaves her job hoping to launch a new company, develop her idea, and receive VC investment. In-depth studies of new companies find that over two-thirds of founders commercialize ideas developed or learned during their past employment at other companies.[9] In fact, the young, fast-growing industries see more start-ups and particularly spinoffs—start-ups emerging from past employees—as the value in these industries is mostly embedded in human capital and knowledge, not in physical capital.

That so many start-ups are founded by former employees presents a puzzle: Why are employers not developing their employees' ideas? The puzzle is even more complex than it first appears because employers have many advantages over new firms. Tax incentives and the advantage of firsthand acquaintance with their employee-turned-entrepreneur would seem to predict that employers would benefit most from pursuing their employee's innovation.[10] Since incumbent businesses know more about their employees' abilities, new firms may fear that such asymmetric information will lead to adverse selection in the recruitment of new employees trained by other firms—that only those employees who are not worth keeping leave. At the same time, despite the advantages held by employers, businesses may fear that venturing with their employees may create disincentives to collaborate internally.[11] And in view of the current trend of employers of requiring in advance that all inventions must belong to them, employees may become too obsessed with controlling their ideas and prefer to leave before disclosing their invention.

And yet, pervasive strategies of controlling human capital put entrepreneurs at a clear disadvantage. Ahead of his time, Schumpeter anticipated the contemporary excitement around entrepreneurship, or what he referred to as "wild spirits." Schumpeter worried that the in-house R&D departments were a threat to the individual entrepreneur: "The perfectly bureaucratized giant industrial unit not only ousts the small or medium sized firm and 'expropriates' its owners, but in the end it also ousts the entrepreneur and expropriates the bourgeoisie as a class which in the process stands to lose not only its income but also what is infinitely more important, its function. The true pacemakers of socialism were not the intellectuals or agitators who preached it but the Vanderbilts, Carnegies, and Rockefellers."[12]

Economic historians find support for Shumpeter's prediction of the doom of the entrepreneurial innovator with the rise of the large in-house R&D firm. Compared to the late nineteenth century, in the twentieth century patenting per capita decreased as more and more companies began to create their own research laboratories. In the heyday of the independent inventor, a division of labor emerged in which inventors would sell their property rights to companies for commercialization. This allowed the inventors the freedom to concentrate on their comparative advantage of inventing. At the time, the great majority of patent recipients were not employees. Rather, they either had no long-term attachment with any company or held ownership positions within the firms to which they assigned their invention.[13] Philo Farnsworth, the inventor of television, was one of the last of such independent inventors. In the 1930s and 1940s he fought to maintain his independence and launch the invention in the market, only to profoundly lose his battles and be outsmarted by the corporate moguls that wanted his invention.

The technological advances of the nineteenth century made it more difficult for independent innovators to pursue their inventions on their own. Individuals needed partners with capital and technological resources to apply their ideas to practice. In the early twentieth century the number of productive inventors who pursued a career as independent inventors declined.[14] The higher cost of R&D transformed the organization of innovation, and the career paths of inventors changed. Young inventors moved to regions where they could secure long-term positions at large companies. But losing their independence may have affected their creativity, and, as we've seen, that period did indeed witness a decline in patenting rates.

THE NET LOSS OF LYING LOW

Many employees who are bound by noncompetes, NDAs, or invention assignments try to escape and avoid them by either taking shelter with a competitor or taking some time away from the industry in which they have built their career (Neeleman, for one, took a professional detour before reentering the airline industry). The survival strategy of forgoing entrepreneurship opportunities and instead, if leaving one employer, opting to seek work at another, larger company because of the fear of legal battles has been confirmed in a broad study. The MIT professor Matt Marx recently studied almost one hundred thousand inventors, all of whom are listed as authors of patents in the U.S. patent registry, examining whether their career path was affected by the enforceability of noncompetes. For inventors bound by noncompetes, four types of strategies emerge:

1. Move to the shelter of a large company with the promise of indemnification in case of a lawsuit;
2. Take an occupational detour by switching to another field of work;
3. Take unpaid sabbaticals and unemployment;

4. Lie low and/or hide out at any new position to prevent former
   employers and colleagues from discovering the inventor's
   new whereabouts.

Recall the change in the State of Michigan from a free flow (like California) to a noncompete-enforcing state in the mid-1980s. This change in state law allowed Marx to research these effects in a single region under two opposite talent flow regimes. Once Michigan began to enforce noncompetes, its inventors were likely to use one of the above survival strategies. Marx's research shows that they were likely to join large companies, confirming that, even more than the suppression of mobility and flow of talent and ideas generally, entrepreneurship itself is harmed when start-ups scramble to recruit talent for their ventures.[15] Marx also found that employees in Michigan were more likely than others to change career paths and to take occupation detours once noncompetes became enforceable. Interviews with inventors reveal that these detours and other survival strategies are taken reluctantly. Inventors in the state felt that detours, sabbaticals, and professional compromises hurt their income, the continued development of their expertise, and their professional networks.

The survival strategy of lying low is especially devastating to industry growth, entrepreneurship, and networks. Woody Allen said that 80 percent of success is showing up. Sheryl Sandberg calls it leaning in. What if you knew your ex-employer could go after you for taking a new position at a related firm? Would you publicize your new job? or keep it under wraps as long as possible? Would you show up at professional meetings? or crawl below the radar until the tides of legal danger turn? The strategy of disappearing and hiding impedes collaborative networks and prevents professional development. If today's knowledge workers, much like scientists and university researchers, are to stay up to date and current, their community must consist not simply of their colleagues in the workplace but also of their network of fellow professionals. If you are hiding because you do not want your former colleagues to know you have continued pursuing your profession, the chances of success—your own success, your new company's success, and, accumulatively, the success of the region—are greatly reduced. Alexis de Tocqueville quite admiringly described how American democracy led the most talented men to industry and trade.[16]

Restrictions on talent competition lead talented men and women into a hideout and depress the entrepreneurial spirit.

DAVID AND GOLIATH IN A COMPETITIVE WORLD

As businesses struggle to retain their best workers and ideas, the courts are left to navigate the gray waters of the talent wars by using the amorphous standard of reasonableness. Perhaps because of their lack of confidence in what these controls actually achieve, courts are especially reluctant to generalize in this area and draw bright lines. "Danger of the gravest injustice lurks in the unguarded use of such potentially deceiving generalities," pronounced one judge, "it cannot be too strongly stated and restated that every case depends on its own peculiar circumstances."[17] Reasonableness is employed on a case-by-case basis.

But the danger of this amorphous design is not in "deceiving generalities," but in grave market uncertainties. With so little guidance and lack of consistency, no one, not businesses nor individual inventors nor even lawyers, can determine in advance whether or not a particular noncompete, nondisclosure, or invention/copyright assignment agreement is fully enforceable. The lack of a bright-line rule increases the likelihood of over-reaching and underchallenging of human capital controls. If inventors were willing to litigate every noncompete contract consistently, the costs of contracting would increase but restrictive lines would be tested. But most employees are too reluctant to litigate with their employer over a contract they signed prior to being hired. When faced with a questionable restriction, few employees have the resources and tenacity to engage in litigation. As a result, they tend to submit to contractual terms that likely could have been successfully challenged in court. Simply because they have the resources to litigate, employers have the advantage when there is uncertainty.

The flip side is that this situation incentivizes employers to overreach and to draft stronger restrictions than are legally allowed. When restrictions may or may not be enforceable, businesses have an incentive to press the bounds of control. Indeed, overreaching dynamics explain why in California, despite the solid law against noncompetes, multiple companies still demand that their employees sign a noncompete. These companies assume that most employees will not be aware of their right to not be restricted from leaving their employer and will not challenge whatever agreement they signed.

Overreaching also explains the dilemma that courts face when presented with a contract that is unreasonably drawn. Courts have two options: throw out the entire contract or enforce the contract only to the extent reasonable. The latter approach requires the court to "blue pencil" some provisions and possibly even rewrite some of the contract. For example, if a contract states that an employee cannot compete in the market for four years, should the court strike down the restriction for its unreasonableness or change the restriction to, say, a one-year limit? Blue-penciling seems to balance the interests of the two sides. But it entails a problem: if businesses know that an unreasonable control provision will be modified to its reasonable limit by the court, then there would be practically no cost of overreaching—they would always attempt to define restrictions on human capital as broadly as possible. Where blue penciling is concerned, more is better for employers. It also creates a lot of work for the courts, however, and allows punitively written human capital controls to intimidate employees to the extent that they never challenge them. Understandably, courts are widely divided between the two approaches. In 1996 the Florida legislature repealed a law governing noncompetes, issuing a new law that significantly aids businesses in enforcing them. Among its new provisions the Florida law requires courts to modify overly broad geographic and temporal restrictions rather than declare the noncompete unenforceable. As a result, companies in Florida can now write highly restrictive noncompetes in confidence that, at least to some degree, they will be enforced.

The challenge of defining the standard of reasonableness further creates an imbalance between established businesses and entrepreneurs. While established businesses and employees/entrepreneurs all stand in murky waters when it comes to predicting what restraints will be enforced, the murky waters do not affect them equally. Newer businesses and aspiring entrepreneurs often lack the financial resources and stamina to litigate. While the economist Ronald Coase theorized that market actors would reach the most efficient allocation of rights regardless of their initial assignment, the Coase theorem does not hold up when rights cannot be well defined. In a world of indeterminacy, the allocation and scope of rights make a tremendous difference. In such a world, the real world, the opponent with the most resources is the one most likely to pursue a fight.

These asymmetries mean that established businesses can draw on their greater resources to engage in strategic litigation. Litigation is strategic when its purpose is not to vindicate a legal right or claim but to impose costs on the legal opponent with the aim of forcing submission or creating a strategic business advantage. Trade secret, noncompete, patent, trademark, and copyright litigations against former employees who start a new company are in fact prime examples of such strategic behavior. The practice is most salient when an employee leaves to form a start-up venture. Litigation over human capital and intellectual property, even if largely without basis, has the power to create sufficient uncertainty to kill a venture.[18] One such story of the legal victory but economic defeat of inventors is that of Armand Ciavatta (see chapter 7). A substantial body of research looking at the differences between large and small firms in their interface with legal rules consistently finds advantages for large firms in such areas as litigation, drug approval proceedings, patent filings, and financial and environmental regulations. Beyond simply having more limited resources, smaller and newer ventures are disadvantaged in the talent wars because of their smaller patent portfolios, their pressing need to establish their brand and reputation, and the simple fact that they usually do not have in-house counsel.

Unsurprisingly, small companies are more likely to consider the costs of legal liabilities before they decide on a research and development path.[19] The start-up company is often unable to defend itself or endure the costs of lengthy litigation, even if the claims against it are unsubstantiated. Indeed, some venture capitalists believe that start-up costs should include the costs of possible intellectual property and human capital litigation as items in their initial budgets.[20] At times investors, when faced with the risk of strategic litigation by competitors, will drop the venture even if they are convinced that the claims lack merit. Larger companies, having sufficient legal and financial resources, can aggressively drive out competition even when their legal claims are on weak or possibly even nonexistent grounds. Sometimes the battle becomes part of the war. Companies decide to go after one ex-employee not because of the importance of his or her departure but in order to deter future transgressors. The evidence is quite conclusive on this point: firms frequently use litigation as a reputation-building and fear-imposing strategy.[21]

Corporate reputations can indeed alter the behavior of your talent and competitors. But we also know that the smartest companies are realizing that cultivating a reputation of being nonlitigious can give them a competitive advantage. A reputation of being aggressive and controlling can eventually prove counterproductive. Overzealous companies are less able to hire the best talent. Intel has a reputation of going to extreme measures, including threatening their employees against competing on their own. Early in the high-tech boom, Intel's CEO reportedly ordered his general counsel to file two lawsuits per quarter with the distinct purpose of dissuading its engineers from "walking out the door" with company information.[22] While Intel aimed to gain a reputation for being tough and litigious toward its departing employees, such a reputation makes it difficult to recruit new employees.[23] By contrast, Cisco has a reputation for not suing its ex-employees, an attitude which is believed to help the company in retention, hiring, and even acquisitions, because executives of an acquired company know they will be able to later leave without fear.[24] Companies like Cisco find that recruiting talent is easier when they do not overwhelm the new recruit with demands to sign over her future human capital. And as we already know, even more than the initial attraction of no restrictions, permitting employees to leave freely allows a company to gain true commitment and motivation.

BRAIN GAIN AND THE CREAM OF THE CROP

In my conversations with lawyers and headhunters, one piece of advice comes up repeatedly: come to California, where courts will refuse to enforce your noncompete and generously interpret your self-ownership of your talent, skills, and knowledge!

We've seen how greater talent mobility within a state gives it an innovation edge. We also know that talent flows from high control to lower control states, furthering a regional advantage. Over time it may lead to significant local gains: brain gain and technology gain. California may be helping trade and competition within its own regions not only by having a policy that prioritizes human capital and the flow of talent and ideas, but also by its willingness to give refuge to employees who have signed noncompetes elsewhere. Its economy gains doubly. First, California gains from the positive effects of its policies and, second, from the restrictive attitude of its competitor states. When inventors bound by noncompetes or the founders of a new company choose to relocate to California, the local market benefits from the introduction of new technologies and new talent in the vicinity. We have seen in previous chapters that knowledge spillovers are localized by a shared culture, shared socialization, similar training, and informal connections and contacts. At the same time, however, and precisely because other ways of interpersonal interaction are less likely between distant regions, the amount of knowledge gained from job mobility is even more pronounced when hiring occurs across geographic regions. In other words, distant hiring forms bridges that may not otherwise exist.

Empirically, the brain gain effect is significant. Areas that enforce strong human capital controls have higher rates of departure of inventive talent to other locations. Conversely, areas that loosen controls have higher rates of newcomers. Most important, this movement is patterned. The cream of the crop is disproportionally driven to open regions. Over time a portion of the best of the best, the most inventive and energetic workers, leave regions that enforce noncompetes and move to places that prohibit their enforcement, like California. In Michigan, for example, the reversal of the law in the mid-1980s from a nonenforcing to an enforcing state led to an increase in the likelihood that the state's inventors would move to states that continued not to enforce noncompetes.[25] The Michigan study analyzed the career histories and patterns of mobility of more than a half million patenting inventors over three decades. Inventors who had the greatest human and social capital were the most likely to leave Michigan.

A broader study looked at the emigration of inventors from states across all regions. It found that inventors leave states that enforce noncompete agreements in far higher rates than they leave states that do not.[26] Once again, we may ask about a special California effect. When excluding California from the analysis, the effect is still very significant, showing a 25 percent higher emigration rate from high enforcement states. And when these inventors move, they disproportionately go to nonenforcing states. Inventors emigrate from an enforcing state to a nonenforcing state (mostly to California, but not exclusively) almost twice as often as from one enforcing state to another. The study concludes that "non-competes contribute to a 'brain drain' of the most valuable knowledge workers . . . driving away those with higher levels of human and social capital while retaining those who are less productive or connected. Over time, this process contributes to the accumulation of elite inventors in regions that prohibit enforcement."

We can understand quite intuitively the self-imposed exile of the most productive inventors. Workers who embody the most human capital are almost guaranteed to have outside offers and will be able to jump the hurdle of their noncompete by leaving the region. Others, the less valued employees at any given moment, will stay and be kept at their job by their noncompete. If alternatives are available, the more specialized one's skills are, the less willing one will be to take future jobs bound by noncompetes. To avoid these controls, the most skilled workers will seek alternative regions in pursuit of their evolving careers. Economists call it adverse selection: those willing to bind themselves from future opportunities may be the ones you least want for the job. The Nobel laureate economist George Akerlof might call this dynamic "a market for lemons"—the most talented, the "cherries," are driven out of markets that allow tight controls over human capital because such individuals know they have the most to gain from being free to learn and flow in the job market. Slowly, the remaining workers, the lemons, who feel they don't lose much by being bound to one business throughout their career, come to dominate the market. The most valuable and most skilled, the most inventive and most collaborative are the ones who emigrate. The results accumulate over time, and the analysis shows that by the end of the twentieth century nonenforcing states became home to a considerably larger-than-expected share of the most elite inventors.

Inventive people escape to places where they can continue their vocation. What about companies? Entrepreneurs and businesses consider a wide variety of factors when choosing their location, including natural and economic resources, state taxes, unionization levels, and labor and employment laws more generally as well as other regulatory differences, such as environmental regulation. In light of what we have learned, the ways in which we organize the talent wars should be a prime consideration. Businesses must consider their ability to attract talent and to operate in a region that is likely to flourish.

APPLES, ORANGES, AND SEARCH THEORY

Jobs are sticky. Like the forces of gravity, the forces of human nature make staying in one's place, whether a job, a city, or a relationship, seem easier than leaving. Psychologically, we all experience this stickiness—we have a bias toward the status quo and are, as humans, averse to loss and risk. This means we will tend to stick with what we know and are hesitant to switch from the known to the unknown. We can all relate to inertia: objects at rest tend to stay at rest. Search and switch costs and the uncertainties of the unknown add to this pattern of stickiness. The cards are stacked against job mobility and talent flow.

In 2010 the Nobel Prize for economics was granted to three labor economists who spent decades trying to understand why it takes people so long to find the right job, even in good economic times. Traditional economic analysis assumes that if there are job openings, positions will fill up immediately. In theory, supply meets demand almost automatically. Matches are made instantly in job market heaven. In reality, though, numerous jobs remain open while people languish, unemployed and searching.

The Nobel laureates of 2010 offer an explanation that may seem intuitive but does not square with classic economic analysis: people are not identical to one another. Job seekers are not cookie cutters, and neither are jobs. Matching people to jobs requires experimentation and time. Unlike cookie-cutter markets, job mobility has a built-in rigidity that curtails rapid and efficient placement, even in the absence of human capital controls.

The Nobel laureates' insight, termed search theory, confirms that the costs of searching for a good match in a heterogeneous market are far greater than in homogenous markets. Put simply, buying fruit or computers is a far simpler and faster process than hiring people. Therefore, the gold standard for assessing efficiency in these two markets needs to be different. For economists a few decades ago this notion seemed radical, but these days the analysis seems like common sense. The complexities of searching and matching further underscore why additional job market rigidity, by restricting the use of human capital, can exponentially slow job growth and entrepreneurship. Successfully matching people to positions where their talent will be best employed is an incredibly complicated undertaking, requiring an understanding of the many intricacies of person and position.

At the Nobel news conference in Sweden, one of the honorees, the London School of Economics professor Christopher Pissarides, suggested that governments should "make sure the unemployed do not stay unemployed for too long, to try to give them direct work experience," so that they don't lose their attachment to the labor force. Human capital controls, restricting people from moving among jobs, competing in the market, and using their acquired professional skills, stand in opposition to such coordinated efforts. Such controls in the talent wars are prime labor market rigidities, much like restrictions on firing during the relationship. In a controlled world, the fit between talent and jobs is significantly reduced: "In the absence of perfect information, anything that adds friction to the movement of employees across firms will obstruct the trial-and-error process and increase the odds of a poor match."[27]

Not only is the job market inherently rigid, its rigidity is organically patterned by the realities of our lives and identities. As much as we want to think that we are each unique in our paths, our careers tend to follow a rather predictable life cycle. Early in their careers, young workers will tend to forgo earning more money in order to take jobs that allow them more opportunities to acquire skill and human capital. Later on in life, as people become more bound by their financial and family obligations and less adventurous in planning future career moves, mature workers may choose to switch to jobs with higher pay but fewer training opportunities, or they may stay with the same company even if they could be better employed elsewhere. Geographically, our life cycles also develop in a way that moves from broader to narrower choice sets. There are many reasons workers will want to move locally rather than seek new employment far away, and these reasons become stronger as we mature. Families and social ties will negatively impact a decision to dislocate children and to move away from extended family, from communities, and neighbor-hoods. In terms of gender, geographical constraints prove especially prob-lematic in the way they pattern career options. Finding the balance between work and family is a challenge that every working parent faces. Still, on average, women face these challenges more intensely. More often than not, a wife will give up her position so that her husband can relocate. With the rise of dual careers and the increased participation of women in the workforce, deciding on where to locate has become more challenging. When economists observed power couples and their decisions on where to live over the past half century, they found that skilled, dual career couples are increasingly concentrated in large metropolitan areas.[28] The reasons should be obvious to us at this point: as skilled professionals are increasingly partnered with equally skilled spouses, smaller places experience reduced inflows of human capital. More than ever before, the size and vibrancy of a city, along with its openness and ability to absorb and nourish talent, significantly impacts its companies' ability to attract the best workers. Places that can accommodate the desire for job mobility and professional growth of both husband and wife are likely to experience a double brain gain.

GAINING GLOBAL EDGE: WHY THE WORLD ISN'T FLAT

Gone are walls and borders. Enter a world that is flat, networked, and connected. The image of a flat world captures our collective imagination, conjuring an image of a brave new world in which distance becomes meaningless.

In his bestseller *The World Is Flat: A Brief History of the Twenty-First Century*, the journalist Thomas Friedman concludes that early twenty-first-century globalization has leveled out commerce and competition across the world. Friedman describes the foundations of a "whole new global platform for collaboration." Several flatteners contribute to these new realities. Perhaps first and foremost, communication systems, particularly the Internet, have made ideas and new information instantly available and broadly accessible. Digitization allows information to travel rapidly, cheaply, and largely indiscriminately once it has reached open access. Search engines are used over one billion times per day, allowing people to manage their own learning and networking. In Friedman's words, "Never before in the history of the planet have so many people— on their own—had the ability to find so much information about so many things and about so many other people." In her provocatively titled book *The Death of Distance* Frances Cairncross describes a rapidly shrinking world, a world in which telephones, television, and network computers make physical distance irrelevant. The realities of globalization and the rapidly flattening world of production and information cannot be denied.

The world has become smaller, and the resulting narrowing between any two points has had a profound effect on innovation.[29] Companies send their employees to professional conferences around the world; the Internet provides easy access to trade and academic journals, even before articles are published; patent filings require disclosure of the invention to publicly accessible databases; even the job market has gone global, as headhunters search internationally.

It's not just about information. People, too, are moving and circulating among regions more than ever. AnnaLee Saxenian advises that the new economic mobility of the globe is more "brain circulation" than "brain drain." She invokes the ancient Greek image of the men who sailed with Jason in search of the Golden Fleece to describe "the new Argonauts": foreign-born, technically skilled entrepreneurs armed with Silicon Valley experience, who quickly form partnerships and manage cross-border business operations by traveling back and forth between California and their home countries. Most notable among the new, modern-day Argonauts are the high-tech employees who circulate regularly between the United States, Japan, China, Israel, and India.

But, as we've seen, although the world may be flatter, geography still matters a great deal. Place and local interaction continue to make a tremendous difference for companies. Despite the image of a globalized market, the majority of our interactions are still local. Around 90 percent of phone calls, financial investments, and even web communications are local. A *Foreign Policy* magazine article from 2007 titled "Why the World Isn't Flat" argues that "despite talk of a new, wired world where information, ideas, money, and people can move around the planet faster than ever before, just a fraction of what we consider globalization actually exists."[30] Innovation still happens locally. Place matters.

Geographic proximity fuels inventive ventures. We have explored how regions with dense networks, social capital, and a culture of openness experience growth and fruitful development. On a global scale, differences between the quality of human and social capital have become key to understanding the challenges of development. A new Carnegie Mellon University report entitled *Renewing Globalization and Economic Growth in a Post-Crisis World* warns that placing limits on worker mobility damages regions. The report includes human capital controls alongside other central examples of such limits, including immigration visa restrictions and the nonportability of health care and other benefits.[31]

An enduring puzzle in development economics has been the fact that similarly situated countries diverge so significantly in their rates of growth. The economist Paul Romer has shown that it's not only a company's raw access to capital and labor that determines success: the availability of local knowledge is at least as important to the equation.[32] In *The Competitive Advantage of Nations,* the Harvard economist Michael

Porter makes the related claim that regional industrial clusters give nations a global competitive edge. In his book *Geography and Trade,* the Nobel laureate economist Paul Krugman similarly argues that nations enjoy important economic advantages depending on their regional location. Japan exports electronics and computer-controlled equipment; the United States focuses on software, biotech, and medical equipment; Italy has positioned itself globally as a leader in shoes and haute couture. Among these three acclaimed economists, Porter most explicitly focuses on how legal regimes can limit clustering and competition. He concludes his book with recommendations about how we can better enforce antitrust laws in order to end monopolies and lessen the impediments to competitive entries.

Monopolies are not simply about goods and services. To be competitive, environments must also be evaluated by competitive talent and information flows. For knowledge to spill over, for networks to remain dense, for face-to-face interaction to succeed in transmitting tacit knowledge, mobility must be encouraged.

CHAPTER TEN

Win–Win–Win

The gift must always move.

—*Lewis Hyde, poet and cultural critic*

DO TOUCH! THE VIRTUES OF TALENT PIRACY

HUMAN CAPITAL CONTROLS are antitrust's neglected stepchild. When Twitter was a fledgling company trying to figure out up from down, it needed other companies to fill the gaps in providing its services, which were promising but still relatively unknown. At first, outsider developers filled its needs for essential features and apps, such as streaming for mobile clients, photo sharing, URL shortcuts, and search enhancers. As Twitter grew larger, it began to look for opportunities to integrate these functions within the company and to cut loose from the outside developers that had supported its virtual ecosystem. It bought up some of its former partners, and then some more, and then some companies it hadn't partnered with. As CNN reporters recently described Twitter's acquisitions, "There's a fine line between defeating rivals by building (or buying) better native functionality and defeating rivals by ordering them to stay off your turf." In 2011 the Federal Trade Commission launched an investigation into Twitter to investigate whether the company had crossed these fine lines.

Antitrust law, known also as competition law, is the body of regulation designed to promote and maintain market regulation by preventing
anticompetitive industry behavior. Antitrust law prohibits agreements
and practices that restrict free trade and competition between businesses,
including repressing free trade by monopolies and cartels. The history
of these laws goes all the way back to ancient Rome, and nowadays
the principles of competition law have spread globally and are internationally adopted. And yet human capital controls remain in the blind
spot of antitrust policy. The controls operate as quasi-monopolies over
people and knowledge.[1] The very same benefits that antitrust laws try to
encourage—new firms, new products, and more market competition—
are suppressed by excessive human capital controls. Restricting mobility
creates barriers to the entry of new firms, limits optimal matches between
jobs and people, and, most disturbingly, suppresses the flow of knowledge and the nourishment of talent.

In 2010 the Antitrust Division of the U.S. Department of Justice filed
a complaint against the tech giants Adobe Systems, Apple, IBM, Yahoo!,
Google, Intel, Intuit, and Pixar. The federal investigation focused on the
hiring practices of these companies, who had allegedly entered into agreements not to recruit or hire away each other's top talent. These practices
were investigated by the Department of Justice because they appeared to
be a collusive restraint on trade and competition.[2] Former recruiters from
the companies confirmed the existence of "do not touch" lists which were
maintained within each recruiting department. The companies under
investigation protested, contending that the agreements allowed them to
enter into alliances on key projects and initiatives with competitors
without fear that their workers would be poached. They also contended
that they had taken steps to ensure the agreements were narrowly
restricted to active cold calls only, allowing recruiters to actively pursue
another company's employee if the employee approached them first.

The Department of Justice saw things differently. The nonsolicitation
agreements covered the entire workforce of each company and were not
limited by geography, job function, product group, or time period. The
breadth of the agreements led the Department of Justice to conclude that
these agreements were per se violations of the antitrust prohibitions of the
Sherman Act and were naked restraints on trade. The multicompany case
never went to trial because the high-tech industry giants reached a quick

settlement with the Justice Department. The settlement enjoins the no-solicit agreements and, more broadly, prohibits agreements regarding solicitation and recruitment. At the same time, a class action launched against these companies by their employees and former employees for anti-competitive employment practices is currently being litigated in California. Amy Lambert, Google's associate general counsel for employment, issued a statement with regard to the settlement, declaring that while there was no evidence that these practices suppressed wages, Google was happy to abandon them. Yet commentators have criticized the settlement as not reaching far enough, calling the practices employed by Google and others "completely illegal" and remarking that, rather than bringing charges, the Department of Justice settled for friendly talks, allowing the companies to "still artificially depress the wages in the market, but not risk forcing the government to continue with an embarrassing court case that could embarrass these sterling examples of American capitalism." Insiders speculate that the nonsolicitation agreements were the companies' attempt to get around California's prohibition against noncompetes by colluding without the knowledge or consent of their employees. One blogger opined that these practices were a "reverse trade-unionism with collective agreements over staff poaching designed to keep wages down!"[3]

It took an extreme case to finally catch the attention of the Department of Justice and expose these anticompetitive practices. But here again is an iceberg reality. We see a chunk of ice the size of a car floating on the surface of the ocean, but when we go beneath the surface the truly enormous scope of the ice, the size of a high rise, is revealed. For too long the field of antitrust has been busy focusing on the restrictions of sale and pricing and has overlooked the monopolizing powers embedded in employment strategies and policy. As demonstrated by these concerted efforts of some of our biggest high-tech companies, it's not simply that the talent is managed and controlled through arrangements between businesses and the individuals they employ. The stick of noncompetes, trade secrets, and patent and copyright transfers impedes hiring by affecting the behavior of third parties as they navigate their position in the talent wars. Many states have made it a tort for a competitor to solicit an employee when it knows the employee is bound to human capital controls—the tort of intentional interference with a contract. The tort of poaching originated in English law hundreds of years ago when it was a crime to hire another's employee.4 Although noncompetes were not enforced at the time, the British medieval ordinances of Bristol cobblers in 1364 state, "Masters are forbidden to poach workers from other members of the craft."5 Still today, when a new "master" attempts to recruit someone bound by a noncompete, he can be found liable for tortious poaching and interference with contract. Though we have begun to shine the spotlight on guild and cartel practices and recognize them as impeding healthy market competition, quietly in the shadows human capital controls have exploded in size and power, creating an anticompetitive iceberg.

But not every industry and every competitor has chosen the path of control. Many businesses are forging their own path, leading the way and showing us that sometimes you need to let go to find out what is worth holding on to.

THE SURPRISING ALTRUISM OF INDUSTRY LEADERS

As a society we care deeply about education and research. American research centers receive over $30 billion in government funds annually. But basic research is performed well beyond the academy.6 At the same time universities are becoming more interested in profit making through patenting, licensing, and coventuring with the for-profit sector, the for-profit sector is recognizing that the production of knowledge is good for business. While the control mentality in our talent wars continues to pervade even the most sophisticated companies (as witnessed by the recent collusive agreements of nonrecruitment between the country's largest high-tech companies), other practices, even some exercised in these same companies, are heading in better directions. And it is here that a gap opens between the lingering mindset of controlling talent and the deeper understanding that markets must, more than ever before, play a leading role in nourishing talent. The missing link—how to continuously nourish and replenish the talent commons—becomes more salient when we turn to the best talent-nourishing practices of industry leaders.

Leading businesses are venturing into public knowledge-enhancing efforts, recognizing that knowledge, even when it cannot be immediately or directly translated into monetary gains, is the lifeblood of market growth. An early example of such a move comes from within IBM, which began a postdoctoral program called Almaden Lab in the 1980s. It was known for hiring postdoctoral graduates right out of school, mostly from nearby Stanford University. As in the case of university postgraduate fellowships, the expectation was that the research fellows would leave IBM after a year or two. IBM knew it would lose talent it had trained, but the company also knew it was playing an important part in the Valley's growth.[7] Recently, a Harvard Business School study examined the development of inventor networks in the Silicon Valley and confirmed that IBM's postdoctoral program was indeed a central contributor to the Valley's interorganizational networking.[8] But this isn't friendship—it's business! So why would IBM invest in research programs and in talented young scientists only to send them off to its competitors after only two years? It is true that the young fellows brought in new ideas at a relatively cheap price and left the company with abundant goodwill. It is also true that the program strengthened IBM's image and reputation and provided a technological network of former IBM research fellows, which enhanced the company's ability to expand and recruit. But the deeper drive behind the program was larger-scale regional growth.

Like many other ventures, the postdoctoral program fell victim to the bursting tech bubble in the 1990s, but other industry leaders, including Hewlett-Packard, Google, Intel, Microsoft, and Yahoo!, have picked up the torch and created similar high-quality research centers which offer fellowships and postdoctoral positions (IBM has returned as well). My friend Einat Minkov worked at Nokia's research arm for two years after getting her doctorate in artificial intelligence (AI) at Carnegie Mellon and before becoming a full-time faculty member at a university engineering department. In Minkov's field of AI this career path is quite common. Her colleagues call the industry position a pre-tenure-track industrial post-doc. IBM's research program in Boston is another example of a particularly rigorous academic center focused on purely theoretical computer sciences. The center has recruited some well-known figures from the best universities to become in-house researchers.

The Theory Group at Microsoft Research in Redmond, Washington, is another such example. Oded Schramm, who had been a promising candidate for the prestigious Fields Medal (awarded to a mathematician younger than forty years of age), worked at Microsoft Research after receiving his doctorate from Princeton University and holding faculty positions at the University of California, San Diego and the Weizmann Institute in Israel. Schramm was known for coinventing the

Schramm–Loewner evolution (SLE), a theory and tool that paved the way for mathematical work in the fields of statistical mechanics, conformal field theory, and probability theory. Until his tragic death in 2008 during a solo hiking trip, Schramm was sought after by the top math departments in the best academic institutes around the world, and yet he chose Microsoft. Like Microsoft, Google is known for hiring away prolific faculty members from top research institutions. The research programs of some of the most prominent firms in the world focus a great deal of their energy on highly theoretical and abstract research and fund knowledge building in much the same way as nonprofit research institutes.

The ability to publish in scientific journals and present at professional conferences motivates the work of research-oriented individuals. Those who straddle the academic and the business worlds want to continue publishing, so much so that, as studies clearly show, scientists working in the private sector will accept lower salaries in return for the ability to publish in scientific journals.[9] But even those workers who were never on the research path report that they are willing to forgo certain material benefits in return for a career that is fulfilling and full of continuous learning and doing. While industry leaders are building academic research arms for researchers to continue their work in the private market, nonacademics, the talented professionals of all industries, are pushing the boundaries between work and learning even further.

As both businesses and employees strive to mature the grounds of science and art in their field, the value placed on knowledge flow and networking beyond the company becomes even more essential. Chuck Morehouse, a director at Hewlett-Packard Laboratories, described HP's attitude toward encouraging interactions between their employees and the larger community: "One of the things that HP needs to do just to keep its own people alive and healthy is to participate in the scientific community. That helps us attract the best students and keep our own people alive and vibrant."[10] The Harvard Business School professor Lee Fleming, who has studied the sharing practices of leading businesses, concludes that "managers intent on being in the ferment of ideas must give their own professionals permission to share."[11]

Smart companies know how to teach their talent to draw the line between sharing and safeguarding. For the most part, knowledge sharing and the publication of basic research do not threaten a company's competitive advantage. For example, Google's original search algorithm, Page Rank, has been fully described in several publications, but Google nevertheless remains the lead search engine. The more a company puts out information, the more it experiences an inward flow of information and feedback.[12] And allowing shared publications and active interactions with the outside world does not beget chaos. As we've seen in previous chapters, the control mentality of our talent wars has led many companies to censor such outside activities. For many, it is simply easier to draw steadfast lines instead of taking risks. Yet, despite the urge to keep information secret, the smartest businesses understand the delicate and ever-evolving dance between control and freedom. Those who do will witness the benefits of dancing the dance well.

A PRISONER'S DILEMMA

In a situation where you and your opponent are face to face with swords drawn, being the first one to lower your sword is a risky strategy. In the business world the equivalent gesture is being the first business to share. Will other businesses reciprocate? Oddly, a lesson from backroom interrogations helps illustrate the dilemma. John sweats in an airless, windowless interrogation room in a police station, waiting. Down the hallway sits Mark, John's partner in crime, who is being interrogated by a detective. The detective methodically reveals the mounting evidence against Mark and his partner, John. When he finishes, the detective tells Mark that if he confesses and testifies against John, he goes free. Mark then is motivated to be the first to defect and testify against John and vice versa. Yet if both John and Mark remain silent, they are both likely to go free. What should Mark do? A simple schematic illustration of Mark's and John's dilemma would look like the accompanying figure (fig. 10.1).

The mathematician A. W. Tucker (one of whose students was the Nobel laureate game theorist John Nash) introduced this basic form of game theory in 1950, invoking the decision-making strategies of two criminals interrogated separately about a crime. In the now widely popularized prisoner's dilemma, each party faces choices between (1) immediate competitive defection with low returns with the risk of the other opting for the same, and (2) the best case scenario, cooperative action for the most gain. Each prisoner has an incentive to become an informant,

Fig 10.1. The prisoner's dilemma.

but both, if they could trust the other to do the same, would be best off denying everything.

The talent wars present a prisoner's dilemma: two companies know that if they could guarantee that the other won't attempt to control, prevent, and litigate the loss of their talent, they would all be better off—the industry would thrive, the talent pool would become richer, the region would grow stronger, and the chances of each competitor to succeed would increase. But given that at some point in the cooperative framework they may also lose talent and innovation battles, and given that the system allows controls which others can employ, competitors engage in a talent control arms race. Conceptualizing talent wars as a prisoner's dilemma can explain why companies can find themselves trapped in a suboptimal equilibrium that holds back the industry and offers perverse incentives to each actor.

Because of the prisoner's dilemma embedded in the business strategies of talent wars, industry practices of low controls, altruistic innovation investments, and knowledge sharing are hard to reconcile with the orthodox story of controls as the fuel of innovation. What industry giants are able to do voluntarily, most firms will resist. Even at the top, the practice of nourishing talent at scientific labs conflicts with a lingering control mentality that continues to pervade the talent wars. Even if convinced that they too would likely be better off over the long run if every player in the industry was willing to lose some of the time, how could they be assured that their competitors would behave similarly?

Here is the twist on the prisoner's game. Let's imagine two companies in the laser industry, say, Lazer Inc. and PhaserCo (fig. 10.2).

Game theory in market realities is far more complex than Tucker's simple formalized model. The tradeoff between the benefits of environments with low controls over their talent and the risks depends on a variety of factors. Not every industry, firm, or time will point to the same optimal equilibrium. Each company must find its own balance between controls and freedom. Despite the huge draw of the Silicon Valley, some firms chose to distance themselves. In the 1980s Intel decided to limit some of its workforce and relocate strategic departments to other centers. A big factor in Intel's decision to relocate its employees was the feeling that it had served too often as a training facility for other companies. Insiders described how "nothing was more frustrating than spending months helping an operator to learn how to work a sensitive and unpredictable piece of machinery, only to see the same operator take a job down the street at National or Fairchild for a dollar more per hour. . . . Each time it built a new lab outside the Valley, [Intel] could feed off a fresh labor pool with fewer competitors to lure its best people away."[13] This is the darker view of win–lose scenarios in talent wars, and no one can deny the negative consequences for a company losing its talent. Every company benefits from being able to hire away talent and enjoy the knowledge and skill that flow with each recruit. At the same time, companies want to prevent their own talent from

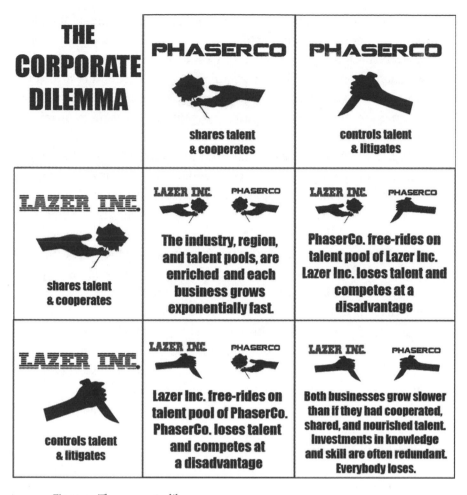

Fig 10.2. The corporate dilemma.

leaving and taking valuable intangibles: their ideas, information, and connections.

For some industries and in some situations, the departure of key people can be especially damaging. In service industries such as law and accounting firms, losing central personnel to a competitor may also mean a devastating loss of central clients. One study of law firm partners in the Silicon Valley examined the movement of partners among firms during a period of fifty years, from the mid-twentieth century until the end of the century. It found that for competing law firms, mobility can indeed be a zero-sum game. For these firms, the corollary of the benefits for the hiring firm was a corresponding increase in the likelihood that the losing firm would decline and shut down.[14] In a similar study, a group of Dutch researchers observed employee movement between accounting firms in Holland. Here again, when companies lost talent, particularly when their employees moved in groups to nearby competitors, the losing companies risked rapid decline.[15]

Still, even in the context of law and accounting firms, where the departure of key actors can be especially devastating to maintaining a steady client base, these findings should be taken with a grain of salt, and the lessons to be learned are not necessarily the kneejerk reaction of increased control. First, a caveat about the cause-and-effect connection between the departure of talent and the demise of these firms. The explanation may be found by looking in the opposite direction: "sinking ships" are the ones more likely to be abandoned, and the slow demise of these firms may have caused the departure of their key talent. This is Schumpeter's principle of creative destruction, to which I will immediately turn. Second, we already recognize the important difference between talent moves to direct competitors and to collaborators. In a different study of attorneys (in this case patent attorneys), we find again, quite intuitively, that when an attorney moves to a competitor, the former law firm suffers immediate losses. But when the lawyer departs to work for a client—for example, the attorney becomes the in-house counsel of a biotech firm that was a client of the law firm—the law firm actually gains from the move.[16] And we also know that even when a firm loses as its talent moves to competitors, the benefits from knowledge flows and social capital are frequently bidirectional.[17]

More important, as the prisoner's dilemma suggests, even with the risks of loss, firms can gain from a move to a superior equilibrium, one in which everyone is operating under risk but under a structure that makes everyone better positioned to succeed. Tradeoff varies for different industries and at different points in the development of an industry and a company.[18] At different points in the life cycle of a company, it may be more efficient to locate the company in a more specialized town or in a more diverse city.[19] Returning to the Massachusetts Route 128 and the Silicon Valley juxtaposition, the Canadian husband-and-wife researchers April Franco and Matthew Mitchell offer an explanation for the Valley's eclipse of Massachusetts's high-tech hub that takes into account this life cycle of regions. Franco and Mitchell hypothesize that, initially, noncompetes may be useful for an area. The northeastern region had an early advantage because competition was prevented and existing firms had an easier path to success. However, at a critical point, growth hit a plateau in Massachusetts because when an industry becomes relatively established, the major productivity driver is heightened competition. At that critical point, employee spin-offs, entrepreneurship, and talent flows become key to the region's success.

We have seen that despite the risks of loss, the gains from lesser controls over talent and knowledge are dazzling in their breadth. Until recently we had relatively little knowledge on how to assess the tradeoffs between gain and loss in the talent wars. But today, a fuller picture appears before us. If the positive effects of loosening controls are so robust, could there be an optimal equilibrium at which everyone agrees to eschew a particular kind of immediate advantage, such as using the sticks of noncompetes, in order for all to reap the greater benefits of mobility and flow?

REPLENISHING THE TALENT COMMONS

The prisoner's dilemma illustrates how rival firms can be caught in suboptimal equilibrium. Everyone is better off by cooperating but, in the absence of coordination of actions, each will act opportunistically. For many years the image of opportunistic behavior has prevailed as the predominant feature of market actors. In 1968 Garrett Hardin published "The Tragedy of the Commons," an influential essay in *Science* that has since strongly shaped Western thought about property, economics, and ownership. Hardin, a biologist, explained that when a group shares a resource, such as a water source or a green herding pasture, a number of problems arise: free riding, conflict, and overuse. These are all problems that are not present, according to Hardin, when the resource is privately owned. But in its shared existence, no single person has enough incentive to preserve and sustain the commons. Hardin described vividly how herdsmen sharing the common resource of a pasture would each overuse it, letting more and more cattle graze. Commons can even incentivize overuse, if, for example, herdsmen race to get as much water as possible, believing the others will use it all up. This was his tragic tale: "Ruin is the destination toward which all men rush, each pursuing his own best

interest in a society that believes in the freedom of the commons."
Hardin's parting shot sums up his philosophy: "Freedom in a commons
brings ruin to all."

The traditional commons is a finite natural resource, like cattle
pastures or fisheries. Overuse can cause its extinction—too many fish-
ermen, too few fish. Other common examples of commons include roads,
bridges, parks, and systems and infrastructures such as education
systems and communication networks. In spite of the doomsday predictions, though, the reality is that the fears of overuse have been overstated.
Many studies examining real-life cases involving commons show that
Hardin's model made a fundamental mistake. His model works on the
assumption that people act only in their immediate self-interest. In real
life, however, case after case demonstrates that it is possible, even without
law or private controls, for common resources to be wisely managed,
sustained, and made to flourish. Modern examples of what a culture of
sharing and cultivating resources has brought us include the World Wide
Web, Wikipedia, Linux and Open Source programming, and the Human
Genome Project. The real tragedy frequently turns out to be not the
potential overuse of common resources but the underuse of vital
resources—a tragedy of the anticommons through excessive private
controls and restrictions.

In 2009 Elinor Ostrom, an American political economist, became
the first woman to receive the Nobel Prize in Economics for her analysis
of economic governance. Her work, which examines the ways in which
societies advance by cooperation to benefit from common pools of
resources, has demonstrated how groups of people can successfully share
common property. For thousands of years civilizations have made
momentous advances by solving collective action problems. In the
twenty-first century, human capital is the most acute collective-action
challenge, and building the talent commons is our shared goal. In our
quest to preserve it, we must recognize its exceptional features.

Talent and the knowledge it carries are unique resources. They are at
once finite and infinite, they naturally flow without boundaries or limits,
and they are easily copied and multiplied unless the law decides otherwise.
Collectively, they construct the most cherished commons of society. The
MIT economist Daron Acemoglu describes investments and reinvestments
in workers as the key ingredients of production and growth. Acemoglu tells

us that people invest in their own human capital without knowing the type of work they will eventually do, just as companies must make investment decisions in technology and capital funds without knowing whom they will end up hiring. Acemoglu describes a magic circle in these conditions of uncertainty: When workers invest more in their human capital, businesses will invest more because of the prospects of acquiring good talent. In turn, workers will invest more in their human capital, as they may end up in one (or more) of these companies. In other words, in Acemoglu's model, the likelihood of finding good employers creates incentives for overall investments in human capital.[20] Acemoglu describes these investments as positive externalities, or benefits that go beyond any one firm; good spillovers that cannot (and should not) be contained.

In his study of the economics of labor markets, Acemoglu found that, typically, investment in human capital is too low. Our inquiry can explain why this is true: despite the potential virtuous cycle of continuous investment, the overuse of controls to prevent talent and knowledge slows down the flow and reduces the positive effects of market uncertainty. It in turn lowers the incentives to invest in human capital because the prospects of acquiring good talent are greatly reduced (fig. 10.3).

The virtuous cycle of investment under conditions of uncertainty

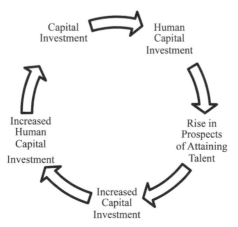

Fig 10.3. The virtuous cycle of investment under conditions of uncertainty.

GOLDILOCKS'S EMBARRASSMENT AND THE DEADWEIGHT LOSS OF HUMAN CAPITAL

> Like the size of a chair, the temperature of a porridge, or the firmness of a mattress, the provision of intellectual property rights should not vary too far to one extreme or another, but must be calibrated so that it is "just right."
>
> —*Dan Burk and Brett McDonnell, The Goldilocks Hypothesis*

> Ideas are like rabbits: You get a couple, learn how to handle them, and pretty soon you have a dozen.
>
> —*John Steinbeck*

George Bernard Shaw mused, "If you have an apple and I have an apple and we exchange it then each of us has one apple. If you have an idea and I have an idea and we exchange it then we each have two ideas." Thomas Jefferson expressed the same sentiment when he vividly wrote in a letter in 1813, "He who receives an idea from me, receives instruction himself without lessening mine; as he who lights his taper at mine, receives light without darkening me."[21] Jefferson viewed the free spread of ideas "over the globe, for the moral and mutual instruction of man, and improvement of his conditions" as "peculiarly and benevolently designed by nature, when she made them, like fire, expandable over all space, without lessening their density in any point, and like the air in which we breathe, move, and have our physical being, incapable of confinement or exclusive appropriation."[22] Information is, by its very nature, a public good. Without effort it flows freely, multiplying without running out. But ideas have commercial value, and competitive strategies are built upon commercializing unique knowledge and capitalizing on the exclusivity of new ideas. As we think of society's talent pool as shared, we must think of how knowledge, whether embodied in people or put in a tangible, expressive form, has come to be understood as property alongside its natural existence as a common resource.

From a historical standpoint the legal protection of ideas is a relatively recent development. It was not until the nineteenth century that the term *intellectual property* began to be used, and not until the late twentieth century that it became commonplace in most of the world. Though the origins of intellectual property protections can be traced to the fifteenth century, ancient times operated without formal protections. Socially the concepts of plagiarism and knowledge theft were developed, but legally information was free until not so long ago. Jefferson described the act of delineating the scope of intellectual property ownership as "drawing a line between the things which are worth to the public *the embarrassment of an exclusive patent,* and those which are not."[23] Our quest to understand the logic of the talent wars has revealed that Jefferson's notion of embarrassment extends beyond ownership over the creations of the mind. It extends in full force to the control of minds themselves: the controls exerted over human capital.

Intellectual property, the granting of ownership rights in information, has been hailed as "the foundation of the modern information economy: It fuels the software, life sciences, and computer industries, and pervades most of the products we consume."[24] This foundation, though, has a battle raging inside of it; the scope of intellectual property protection has become one of the most contested areas in academic, policy, and public debates. The past few decades have witnessed major reforms in intellectual property: patent eligibility has been expanded to new subject matters, such as computer software, business methods, and genetically modified organisms; copyright protections have been broadened and lengthened; trademark litigation has soared; trade secrets span new subject matters and modes of infringement. As a result, from file sharing to drugs for AIDS patients in developing countries, "the intellectual property wars are on."[25]

The fierce conflict around the scope of intellectual property raises questions about justice, fairness, welfare, costs, and the public interest. Most of us agree that, as a general matter, intellectual property is a necessary evil: it promotes innovation by creating a limited monopoly over information. *Against Intellectual Monopoly* is a recent book calling for the complete abolition of the system of intellectual property rights, a call to governments around the world, not to rethink the current imperfections of the system but to completely eliminate monopolistic controls. Intellectual property, the book concludes, is in fact an unnecessary evil that reduces access and slows down progress in the arts and sciences.[26]

Could we imagine a world without intellectual property? What would innovation, high-tech industries, energy consumption, health care, pharmaceuticals, music, and movies look like? The funny thing about the intellectual property debates is that, no matter which side you are on, innovation appears to be the ultimate goal. For example, in one of the most heated Supreme Court cases on the scope of copyright protection, *Metro-Goldwyn Mayer v. Grokster,* the Court was asked to decide whether peer-to-peer music file-sharing techniques were in violation of copyright law. The music and film industry claimed that the best way to encourage innovation was by allowing those who create to personally gain from its profits. The industry therefore asserted that, without strong copyright protections, "the powerful engine for creative effort and beneficial innovation is crippled." Grokster also focused on innovation, arguing that strong copyright protections "would deter investment in innovation" and "chill technological design" because innovators would face unpredictable standards, thereby risking expensive litigation. The two sides agreed that the goal was more innovation. Similarly, in one of the most eagerly awaited recent Supreme Court cases on the scope of patents, *Bilski v. Kappos,* the Court considered the question of whether relatively abstract business methods were patentable from the perspective of how to yield more innovation. In affirming the rejection of the patent application for a method of hedging losses, the Court confirmed limits on patentable subject matters. Still, the Supreme Court recognized the acute and ever-present tension between initial innovation and continual improvements: "Innovation in business methods is often a sequential and complementary process in which imitation may be a 'spur to innovation' and patents may 'become an impediment.'"

All intellectual property protections are intentionally partial. Granting intellectual property rights is a quid pro quo bargain: put in the effort to innovate and, in return, receive temporary exclusivity over your innovation. The Founders thought of granting intellectual property rights as encouraging ingenuity, but from the beginning it was clear that these rights create monopolies over knowledge and ideas that ought not to last beyond their actual utility. In addition to their monopolistic effects, intellectual property rights generate costly litigation, enforcement, uncertainty, and transaction costs during the sale and licensing of the rights. In economic terms, intellectual property constraints create costs and deadweight loss, that is, the loss of efficiency in products and markets because of suboptimal schemes.

Societal demand is not always reflected in individual deals. Markets caught in suboptimal equilibrium do not promote society's interests. As a society, we value progress in areas such as health, education, research, equality, art, and science that is not reflected solely in the dollar value of the immediate transactions that occur in the market. One of the greatest challenges of societies is to know when to collectively intervene to optimize markets and to plan for the future. In his influential book *The Code,* Larry Lessig warns against the commercial controls of cyberspace and advocates for a regulatory role to guarantee cyber freedoms. In a prophetic tone that characterizes his work, Lessig says, "It is the age of the Ostrich. We are excited by what we cannot know. We are proud to leave things to the invisible hand. We make the hand invisible by looking the other way. But it is not a great time, culturally, to come across revolutionary technologies." Lessig's words express concern about the sharp dichotomy between public regulation and the seemingly free nature of norms and market arrangements. In our talent wars, standard freedom of contract analysis envisioning an invisible hand that creates a perfect market often needs to be modified. Not all that has been deemed a legitimate business strategy in controlling human capital and restricting mobility, competition, the use of information, ideas, creativity, and science is justified in light of all that we now know and the challenges that the new era has brought.

We've come to recognize as a society—reflected in recent intellectual property cases that have reached the Supreme Court—that excessive controls threaten to become enclosures of knowledge. The concerns apply even more strongly to human capital controls. Beyond intellectual property, the control of creations and inventions, human capital controls concern the control of the mind itself. In blunt economic terms, the deadweight loss of human capital controls is the person who is prevented from using her talent and skill. The underuse of people means the worst depletion, cognitive depletion. Minds not put to good use are no doubt the greatest tragedy of all. When talent is forced to take detours, when minds are made to suppress thoughts and refrain from using skills, when knowledge is cut up into small pieces and deemed confidential, proprietary information, society as a whole loses.

FASHIONISTAS, MAGICIANS, COMEDIANS, AND FRENCH CHEFS

Ralph Waldo Emerson liked to say, "Our strength grows out of our weaknesses." Less control does not mean anarchy or decline. Sharing resources, especially human and intellectual resources, does not mean depleting them. The world of fashion turns a lot of the rationale for intellectual property restrictions on its head. The fashion world is a wrinkle in the theories of scholars of innovation because of its weak intellectual property controls and strong innovation. The high-heel pumps I wore to a cocktail party last week are sure to go out of style next week. Today's innovation is passé tomorrow. Surely there is no shortage of trends, styles, art, and innovation when it comes to our wardrobes. Yet surprisingly the fashion world consistently produces a huge variety of creative goods without strong intellectual property protection. In fact, copying in the fashion world is frequent and rampant. The legal scholars Kal Raustiala and Christopher Sprigman, who have studied the global fashion industry, conclude that "the fashion industry counter-intuitively operates within a low-IP equilibrium in which copying does not deter innovation and may actually promote it." They call it the piracy paradox: the act of copying functions as a necessary predicate to the rapid cycle of fashion innovation. Given the flourishing businesses of haute couture, it may be that designers do not actually want to protect their secrets, ideas, and innovation. Rather, the copying of their ideas increases their own hype and creates a demand for newer original designs. From the cell phone to the gaming industry, weaker controls configure as part of a central business strategy known as induced obsolescence. Schumpeter, as we shall see in a moment, would have called it creative destruction. Emerson would repeat: our strength is in our weakness.

Other industries reveal paradoxes similar to those in the fashion world: low protections for copying and high degrees of innovation. Take the world of stand-up comedy as an example. Stand-up comedians are generally neither organized nor employed by large firms. They do not use formal contracts to restrict their collaborators or secure nondisclosures. And they do not copyright their comedy lines. Still, the comedy industry flourishes and encourages the production of new, funny material. In the absence of law, the industry has established strong norms against unethical theft. A study that interviewed dozens of comedians concludes that in the world of stand-up comedy, social norms serve functions similar to those of copyright law.[27] In fact, the norms go beyond what copyright law protects. Copyright law protects expression, but not abstract ideas. The comedians' norms extend to both. The central norm among comedians is one ought not perform another's joke, including ideas of a joke. If one comedian develops a joke conceptually and another delivers the punch line, the entire joke is owned by the first comedian, not jointly, as copyright law would prescribe.

Haute cuisine and gourmet dining is another industry demonstrating that an absence of formal intellectual property regulations can be successful and still sustain high levels of creativity. Recipes and fine-dining ideas are difficult to patent or keep secret (though recipes can be trade secrets, they are often reverse engineered). Chefs are used to seeing their cooks and sous-chefs leave their kitchen only to set up in a kitchen down the street and compete against them over the palates of foodies. The management professors Emmanuelle Fauchart and Eric von Hippel studied French chefs and the ways they protect their renowned recipes. Their interviews revealed, as in the case of comedians, the development of an alternate, informal system of norms. All chefs followed certain principles (box 6).

A violation of these norms leads to consequences that may well be harsher than legal sanctions. The stealing chef will be stigmatized, deemed an imitator and a fraud, and perhaps even ostracized by the gourmet community. He or she will be exiled from the inner circle of those who share information about innovative recipes and cooking techniques.

What about the rules for magic? The pleasure of watching a magic trick is derived from not knowing how it could possibly be achieved. For

---

BOX 6

CHEF PRINCIPLES

- No chef may copy in exact form the innovative aspects of the recipe of another chef.
- If a recipe is revealed to a fellow chef, that chef may not pass on the recipe without permission.
- Chefs must give credit to the original inventor of a recipe or of any significant improvement to it.

238 THE TALENT COMMONS

magicians, therefore, the ability to maintain the secrets of their profession is what keeps the profession alive. Stage magic relies on the hope that the audience will be bewildered. And here again, without heavy-handed IP regulations, the magic community continues to thrive and innovate. In theory, magic tricks are protectable as patents and trade secrets, and a few of the most impressive tricks have been granted patents. Two of the most well-known examples are the Goldin patent of 1923 on how to saw a person in half, and the more recent levitation patent—how to make a human body rise and remain floating in thin air—which was granted to the magician John Gaughan in 1994. In practice, however, very few magical innovations are patented or would hold the legal definition of a trade secret.

The problem with having a magic trick qualify for protections is twofold. First, patents require disclosure of the mechanics of the innovation, but the value of magic derives precisely from *not* knowing. Second, trade secret law is also not very useful because rival magicians will probably figure out at some point how to reverse-engineer the trick. Equally important, magicians want to share their secrets among themselves, thereby losing the trade secrecy protection by definition, which requires a showing of serious efforts to maintain secrecy. Instead of pursuing the various potential IP protections, the magician community has developed a sharing mentality and, along with it, a guildlike set of norms. The magicians share knowledge only among the best of the best, excluding amateurs and the public. The social norms in the magician community hold that if a magician exposes even his own secrets, perhaps by performing in a tell-all TV show, he is excommunicated for betraying the profession and its standards. Recently, a magician who revealed major secrets of the trade on prime time television was lambasted by members of his community and became the community Grinch, the villain who destroyed Santa Claus and the Easter Bunny for the rest of us. In a new book appropriately titled *Law and Magic*, Jacob Loshin describes magicians as working in the "negative space" of IP. Outside the formalities of legal restrictions, magicians can benefit from the sharing of ideas and the flow of knowledge without the damage of overexposure to the lay world. At the center of this negative space operates what Loshin describes as the magician's Hippocratic oath: Never Expose a Magic Secret to a Nonmagician!

Competitive environments from fashion to magic, comedy to cuisine have managed to protect the process of innovation without resorting to the most restrictive controls. The distinction between control and freedom does not have to be a binary one, that is, one of negative spaces free of controls contrasted with formal legal systems saturated with the big sticks of protections and restrictions. An updated innovation strategy allows us to identify a spectrum of choices within the talent wars and knowledge flows. In every industry, we find practices of self-imposed confidentiality alongside practices of openness and sharing; we find places where norms substitute for law. Reputation replaces litigation. Carrots alternate with sticks. We find pockets of alternative interactions in which value comes to be understood more deeply as a repeat game and measured over time.

CONTROL WITH LESS COMMAND, COMMAND WITH LESS CONTROL

West was really not so wild.

—*Terry Anderson and Peter Hill, The Not So Wild, Wild West*

In *The Not So Wild, Wild West* the economists Terry Anderson and Peter Hill describe the emergence of property rights on the American frontier. Lacking an established legal system, farmers and cowboys, ranchers and settlers, and whites and Indians nevertheless found that cooperation was possible. Norms about property ownership, acquisition, and dispute settlement developed. This was a prelude to the creative and inventive settings we've looked at in which innovation is encouraged through shared norms and informal rules rather than be confined by formal constraints. Beyond the particular niches of fashion, food, comedy, and magic, mainstream economies are ripe with such examples. Take, for example, the steel industry. While conventional wisdom imagines that rivals always compete over information and talent, the reality of the steel industry provides us with plenty of stories to the contrary. The historian Robert Allen describes the nineteenth-century English steel industry as being engaged in "collective innovation," where competitors willingly revealed valuable information to their rivals.[28] Investigating the puzzling practices of early steel firms that released design and cost information to potential entrants that would later compete in the industry, Allen poses the following challenge: "If (as we continue to assume) the industry was competitively organized, it would appear that this action could only redound to the disadvantage of the firm. To the degree that the information release accelerated technical progress, the price of the product would decline and so would the net income of the firm that released the information."

Allen then proposes explanations for these surprising practices of information sharing among competitors. Perhaps, he asks, the companies believed they could not keep their secrets secret even if they tried? Perhaps, alternatively, they believed that publicizing their knowledge would carry prestige despite the loss in profit? Or perhaps the conditions of the industry were such that competitors believed that revealing their secrets would be profitable? If one looks back historically, the advantages appear more clearly: The entire steel industry moved together rapidly instead of one firm making sporadic leaps ahead of the others.

Other historians have recently uncovered similar dynamics of progress through sharing. Not infrequently the sharing rested on formally unlawful practices. We often have the image of the East pirating intellectual property from the West. But if one goes back just one century, nineteenth-century America was ingrained with a concerted effort to learn—for free and without anyone's permission—the secrets of British and Continental intellect. The historian Doron Ben-Atar has documented the many ways in which the economic development of the United States depended on the misappropriation of trade secrets. Entire northern magazines were dedicated to reporting on European scientific and technological advancements, and American publishers repeatedly copied European books and journals without compensating their original authors or publishers. According to Ben-Atar, this was not only inevitable, but also beneficial because "it is impossible to contain the abuse of technology without undermining the free flow of knowledge that is the prerequisite for innovation."[29]

While this history of copying from the Old World represents a fairly conscious one-sided disregard of intellectual property rights, the most exciting forms of sharing are reciprocal. The MIT professor Eric Von Hippel studies the know-how held in the minds of engineers in the steel industry. As Allen found in the early development of the industry, Von Hippel finds strong norms of sharing in the contemporary steel industry.

He has found that engineers are willing to share information with professional colleagues at rival firms, almost without exception. When they
receive calls from their colleagues requesting information, engineers
make ad hoc judgments about the tradeoffs in sharing. They consider the
type of information requested and the potential usefulness of the professional expertise of the acquaintance in the future. If they decide it is the
kind of information that is useful but not crucial, and if they believe that
the colleague may return the favor in the future, they will provide the
requested information.[30] Indeed, the sharing of information extends
beyond phone calls. Colleagues at rival companies are even willing to
come by to help set up new equipment and train their competitor's counterparts. For each act of kindness, the calculation is not explicit. And yet,
beneath the surface lies the implicit expectation of reciprocity. The
exchange must be a two-way street. In the steel industry, at least informally, "participants seemed to strive to keep a balance in value given and
received, without resorting to explicit calculation. On average over many
transactions, a reasonable balance may in fact be achieved, although
individual errors in judgment are easy to cite."[31] Von Hippel concludes
that the sharing of know-how has been essential to the development of
the industry.

The trading of informal know-how is an inexpensive, flexible form
of cross-licensing and cross-consulting services. Compared to formal
intellectual property transactions and formal recruiting, sharing has less
uncertainty and lower transaction costs. Knowledgeable professionals
rather than their lawyers (and, subsequently, judges in litigation) make
the decisions about where to draw the lines between know-how that can
be shared and secrets that must remain secret.

One of the most celebrated contexts of sharing is that of research
institutions and universities, where the collective quest for knowledge is
at the heart of the enterprise. Researchers and scientists traditionally have
exemplified a philosophy of openness with other scientists. Weak IP
protections in settings of sharing help reduce rivalry and create a circle of
reciprocity. Therefore, it is not surprising that the Bayh-Dole Act, granting
property rights to universities in products of research, may have eroded
some of these norms as scientists and university tech transfer offices race
to patent in order to halt commercial misappropriation of their discoveries. Still, sharing continues selectively and strategically.[32] A study of

research labs developing lasers concludes that, much like engineers in the steel industry, scientists regard reciprocity as the basic rule of sharing: "Nearly every laboratory expressed a preference for giving information only to those who had something to return."[33]

Beyond the laws on the books, social norms play an important role in managing intellectual property. Often, despite having the legal right to pursue litigation, organizations and individuals may choose to pursue other channels to protect their interests.[34] The lessons of industries and places that do not employ legal restrictions to protect their innovation hold a broader promise. They suggest that innovation can flourish without some of the costs of conventional human capital restrictions. They remind us that overprotection can lead to counterproductive effects; that common pools of wealth and resource can in fact lead to progress rather than tragedy. The absence of legal controls does not mean the absence of order. Social norms, ethical behavior, reciprocity, information, and reputational effects will all contribute without negating the positive effects of talent flow. Importantly, even as we let go of our default control mentality, we leave options for strategically managing our innovative edge. Abolishing the most restrictive means—first and foremost eliminating the availability of absolute noncompete restrictions and absolute preassignment of all employee ideas—still leaves companies with alternative protections, namely, the more narrowly tailored trade secret protections, confidentiality agreements, and assignment agreements. We can embrace the idea of openness and flow without giving up the idea of healthy competition and strategic choice.

THE EDGE OF CREATIVE DESTRUCTION

Schumpeter did not coin the term *creative destruction*. He borrowed it from an earlier (and rather unknown) economist, popularized the phrase, and received the glory of its splendid simple truth: knowledge flows and humanity progresses by breaking down barriers and merging separate ideas. Creative destruction—the dynamic rise and fall of winners and losers: companies, people, products, industries, and ideas—makes our world flourish. In his book *Capitalism, Socialism, and Democracy* (1942) Schumpeter argued that the essence of healthy capitalism lies in free competition and the prevention of monopolistic control of markets. Competition in products, processes, people, and prices "incessantly revolutionizes the economic structure, incessantly destroying the old one, incessantly creating a new one." Creative destruction keeps "the capitalist engine in motion." This kind of competition is not for the weak-hearted. It "strikes not at the margins of the profits and the outputs of existing firms but at their foundations and their lives."

The simple truth is that in the evolutionary process of markets, most firms eventually fail. The British economic forecaster Paul Ormerod calls it "the Iron Law of Failure." Every year a significant percentage of firms become extinct. Others are born. Better technologies replace older ones. Skills become obsolete. Secrets become known. Innovation reaches its edge. And thus the wheels of progress turn. As part of this process, the firms that are better fit for the existing environment replace weaker firms. Not all survive, but the market itself thrives exactly *because* of the fierceness of these ongoing economic battles. And in the end, we all win precisely because, some of the time, we lose.

In the end, raiding talent is a repeat game, and the losses for a firm, on average, balance out with the gains. You got raided for your best employees—move on and raid others! As some would say, "Don't get mad, get even!" New structures, new work patterns, and new technologies have altered the calculus of the costs and benefits of restrictions and controls. Evolutionary biology is a good metaphor for envisioning our new innovation ecology. Heredity, perhaps the most central aspect of biological theories of evolution, considers the patterns of reproduction and transmission of genes to offspring.[35] In our metaphor, the genes of an organization are knowledge, transmitted by the people who move from one company to form another. Ex-employees form new spin-offs, move into niche industries, and differentiate themselves from their parent companies, even as they exploit the knowledge they gained from the experience with their parent company: "Spinoffs appear to closely resemble their parents, inheriting from them their initial products and market focus. But just as organisms are not clones of any of their parents, spinoffs also differed from their parents. Perhaps similar to humans, spinoffs needed to differentiate themselves from their parents to succeed. Pushing the evolutionary metaphor further, more fit members of the species (industry) have higher rates of reproduction, which . . . bears on the fitness of the entire species."[36]

Empirics confirm that more successful companies will have more spin-offs. Statistically, the majority of patents secured by many innovative firms are shelved rather than put to commercial use because not all profitable paths can be pursued. Spin-offs regularly develop complementary products or further inventions that would otherwise be shelved. At times, the spin-off will enter a market that the parent company does not find profitable.[37] This is why corporate venture capital is on the rise. Increasingly, companies are funding their own ex-employees' efforts to start up new companies, blurring once again the lines between the abrupt image of talent departure and continuity. Under this frame, talent flow can be reconceptualized as a strength rather than a weakness. And introducing more competition, more products and related companies into a market, strengthens it. In fact, it is the lack of diversity that threatens an industry's future.[38] To further imagine the ecology of competition in terms of biology, think about how ecosystems and biodiversity survive. Conservationists agree that a high level of biodiversity is a sign of health in an ecosystem. Similarly, economists have come to agree that diversity plays a critical role in the market. At its grandest theorization, diversity has been attributed to the very success of capitalism at large.

And, as in nature, constructive destruction perfects the market by sending signals from the lifeblood of the ecosystem—the talented, creative, and inventive people who are its greatest assets—about where the best future lies. The flow of knowledge brings growth to industry and regions and keeps ineffective economies in check. Mobile talent keeps markets healthy. Unhappy talent, underutilized innovators, and people who believe they are working on a sinking ship will jump ship to accelerate the process of growth. If many of your best employees are leaving you, it serves as a warning sign to make changes. Those changes will involve, make no mistake, the hiring of new talent. But the opportunity to hire and nurture new talent is nothing to fear. Far from it—when talent is pree, everyone thrives.

NOTES

INTRODUCTION

1. "Winklevoss Syndrome," last modified February 18, 2011, http://startupblog. wordpress.com/2011/02/18/winklevoss-syndrome.
2. S. Colum Gilfillan, *Inventing the Ship* (Chicago: Follett Publishing, 1935).
3. *Rockwell Graphic Systems, Inc. v. DEV Indus.*, 925 F.2d 174, 180 (7th Cir. 1991).
4. Kenneth J. Arrow, *Collected Papers of Kenneth J. Arrow: The Economics of Information* (Cambridge: Harvard University Press, 1984).
5. Kenneth J. Arrow, "The Economic Implications of Learning by Doing," *Review of Economic Studies* 29, no. 3 (1962): 155–73.

1. THE TALENT WARS

Epigraph: Brian Walsh, "Stem Cell Central," *Time,* July 23, 2006, www.time. com/time/magazine/article.

1. Claudio Fernández-Aráoz, "Making People Decisions in the New Global Environment," *MIT Sloan Management Review* 49 (2007): 17–20 October 1, 2007.
2. John J. Kao, *Innovation Nation: How America Is Losing Its Innovation Edge, Why It Matters, And What We Can Do to Get It Back* (New York: Free Press, 2007), 121.
3. Joseph Berger, "The Pain of Layoffs for Ex-Senior IBM Workers," *New York Times,* December 7, 1993.
4. Patrick C. Flood, Thomas Ramamoorthy, Nagarajan Turner, and Jill Pearson, "Causes and Consequences of Psychological Contracts among Knowledge Workers in the High Technology and Financial Services Industries," *International J. Human Res. Mgmt.* 12 (2001): 1152; Michael B. Arthur and Denise M. Rousseau, "Introduction: The Boundaryless Career as a New

Employment Principle," in *The Boundaryless Career: A New Employment Principle for a New Organizational Era,* ed. Michael B. Arthur and Denise M. Rousseau, 3–20 (New York: Oxford University Press, 1996); Trisha Gura, "Joining a Trend, Scientists Increasingly Say, 'Call My Agent,'" *Science,* January 16, 2004.

5. Orly Lobel, "The Four Pillars of Work Law," *Michigan Law Review* 104, no. 6 (2006): 1539–57.
6. Frederick Winslow Taylor, *The Principles of Scientific Management* (New York: Harper and Brothers, 1913), 72.
7. *Independent,* 2005. http://www.independent.co.uk/news/people/profiles/riccardo-muti-the-monster-of-milan-529157.html.
8. Charles C. Heckscher, *The New Unionism: Employee Involvement in the Changing Corporation* (New York: Basic Books, 1988), 101.
9. "Google Buys Social Search Startup Angstro, Acq-Hires Co-Founder Khare," Paid Content, https://paidcontent.org/article/419-google-buys-social-search-startup-angstro-acq-hires-co-founder-khare/.
10. Erick Schonfeld, "Here Comes Apple Earth: Map Startup Poly9 Reportedly Snatched Up by Cupertino," *Tech Crunch,* July 14, 2010, http://techcrunch.com/2010/07/14/apple-earth-map-poly9.
11. "Motorola Acqu-Hires Cappuccino Developers," DZone, last modified August 26, 2010, http://mobile.dzone.com/motorola_acquires_cappuccino.
12. Fernández-Aráoz, "Making People Decisions in the New Global Environment," 18–20.
13. Ibid.
14. Rosabeth Moss Kanter, *Evolve! Surviving in the Digital Culture of Tomorrow* (Cambridge: Harvard Business School Press, 2001), 211–14.

2. INNOVATION'S EDGE

1. Salvatore Parise, Rob Cross, and Thomas Davenport, "Strategies for Preventing a Knowledge-Loss Crisis," *MIT Sloan Management Review,* July 1, 2006.
2. Eric Posner, Alexander Triantis, and George G. Triantis, "Investing in Human Capital: The Efficiency of Covenants Not to Compete," University of Chicago Law and Economics, Olin Working Paper no. 137, University of Virginia Law and Economics Research Paper no. 01–08(2004).
3. Gary S. Becker, "Investment in Human Capital: A Theoretical Analysis," *Journal of Political Economy* 70 (1962): 16.
4. Gary S. Becker, *Human Capital: A Theoretical and Empirical Analysis with Special Reference to Education,* 2d ed. (New York: Columbia University Press for the National Bureau of Economic Research, 1975), 15–37.
5. See Paul H. Rubin and Peter Shedd, "Human Capital and Covenants Not to Compete," *Journal of Legal Studies* 10 (1981): 93.
6. Mark A. Glick, Darren Bush, and Jonathan O. Hafen, "The Law and Economics of Post-Employment Covenants: A Unified Framework," *George Mason Law Review* 11 (2002): 357.
7. William M. Landes and Richard A. Posner, *The Economic Structure of Intellectual Property Law* (Cambridge: Harvard University Press, 2003), 371.

8. Michael J. Trebilcock, *The Common Law of Restraint of Trade: A Legal and Economic Analysis* (Toronto: Carswell, 1986).

9. Matt Marx, "Good Work If You Can Get It . . . Again: Non-Compete Agreements, Occupational Detours, and Attainment" (August 17, 2009). Available at SSRN: http://ssrn.com/abstract=1456748.

10. Ibid.

11. Rachel S. Arnow-Richman, "Bargaining for Loyalty in the Information Age: A Reconsideration of the Role of Substantive Fairness in Enforcing Employee Non-competes," *Oregon Law Review* 80 (2001): 2007; Cynthia L. Estlund, "Between Rights and Contract: Arbitration Agreements and Non-Compete Covenants as a Hybrid Form of Employment Law," *University of Pennsylvania Law Review* 155 (2007): 379–446.

12. George G. Triantis, "The Efficiency of Vague Contract Terms: A Response to the Schwartz-Scott Theory of U.C.C. Article 2," *La. L. Rev.* 62 (2002): 1065–79.

13. *Arthur Murray Dance Studios of Cleveland, Inc. v. Witter*, 105 N.E.2d 685, 703–4 (Ohio Ct. Com. Pl. 1952).

14. Stewart E. Sterk, "Restraints on Alienation of Human Capital," *Virginia Law Review* 79 (1993): 383–460.

15. Phillip J. Closius and Henry M. Schaffer, "Involuntary Nonservitude: The Current Judicial Enforcement of Employee Covenants Not to Compete—A Proposal for Reform," *Southern California Law Review* 57 (1984): 531–60.

16. R. C. Levin, A. K. Klevorick, R. R. Nelson, "Appropriating the Returns from Industrial Research and Development," *Brookings Papers on Economic Activity* 3 (1987): 783–820.

17. Paul Almeida, "Localization of Knowledge and the Mobility of Engineers in Regional Networks," *Management Science* 45 (1999): 905–17; Al Abowdet, "Wages, Mobility and Firm Performance: Advantages and Insights from Using Matched Worker-Firm Data," *Economic Journal* 116 (2006): F245–F285.

18. Joseph P. Ferrie, "Longitudinal Data for the Analysis of Mobility in the U.S., 1850–1910" (2004), paper, available at http://faculty.wcas.northwestern.edu.

19. Paul Almeida and Bruce Kogut, "Localization of Knowledge and the Mobility of Engineers in Regional Networks," *Management Science* 45, no. 7 (1999): 905–17; Zoltan Acs, *Innovation and the Growth of Cities* (Northampton, Mass.: Edward Elgar, 2002).

20. Margaret A. Peteraf, "The Cornerstones of Competitive Advantage: A Resource-Based View," *Strategic Management Journal* 14 (1993): 179.

21. Jaeyong Song, Paul Almeida, and Geraldine Wu, "Learning-by-Hiring: When Is Mobility More Likely to Facilitate Interfirm Knowledge Transfer?," *Management Science* 49 (2003): 351–65; J. S. Katz, "Geographical Proximity and Scientific Collaboration," *Scientometrics* 31 (1994): 31–43.

22. Jasjit Singh and Ajay Agrawal, "Recruiting for Ideas: How Firms Exploit the Prior Inventions of New Hires," *Management Science* 57 (2011): 129–50.

23. Ibid.

24. Manuel Trajtenberg, "Recombinant Ideas: The Mobility of Inventors and the Productivity of Research," paper presented at the CEPR Conference, Munich,

Germany, May 26–28, 2005; Manuel Trajtenberg, Gil Shiff, and Ran Melamed, "The Names Game: Harnessing Inventors' Patent Data for Economic Research," National Bureau of Economic Research Working Paper no. 12479 (2006).

25. Rafael Corredoira and Lori Rosenkopf, "Should Auld Acquaintance Be Forgot? The Reverse Transfer of Knowledge Through Mobility Ties," *Strategic Management Journal* 31 (2010): 159–81; Gina Dokko and Lori Rosenkopf, "Social Capital for Hire? Mobility of Technical Professionals and Firm Influence in Wireless Standards Committees," *Organization Science* 21 (2010): 677–95.

26. Ajay Agrawal, Iain Cockburn, and John McHale, "Gone But Not Forgotten: Knowledge Flows, Labor Mobility, and Enduring Social Relationships," *Journal of Economic Geography* 6 (2006): 571.

27. Deepak Somaya and Ian O. Williamson, "Rethinking the 'War for Talent,'" *MIT Sloan Management Review* 49, no. 4 (2008): 29–34, citing Michael Santoli, "Minting Money the Goldman Sachs Way," *Barron's* 86 (2006): 22.

28. Laura Rich, "Don't Be a Stranger: Alumni Programs Are a Great Way to Stay in Touch and Boost Business," *Inc.* (January 2005): 32.

29. Eilene Zimmerman, "The Boom in Boomerangs," *Workforce Management Online,* January 2006, http://www.workforce.com/section/06/feature/24/25/79/index_printer.html.

30. William Ocasio, "Towards an Attention-based View of the Firm," *Strategic Management Journal* 18 (1997): 187.

3. NONCOMPETE—COMPETE!

1. "Only the Employed Need Apply," *Wall Street Journal,* June 30, 2009, http://online.wsj.com/article.

2. Steven N. Kaplan and Per Stromberg, "Financial Contracting Theory Meets the Real World: An Empirical Analysis of Venture Capital Contracts," *Review of Economic Studies* 70 (2003): 281. Another report indicates that 88 percent of companies require the signing of noncompetes. Bill Leonard, "Recruiting from the Competition," *HR Magazine* 46 (2001): 78–83.

3. *Complete Auto Transit, Inc. v. Reis,* 451 U.S. 401 (1981).

4. Christopher T. Wonnell, "The Contractual Disempowerment of Employees," *Stanford Law Review* 46 (1993): 87–146.

5. *Woolley v. Embassy Suites, Inc.,* 278 Cal. Rptr. 719, 727 (Cal. Ct. App. 1991) (specific performance of personal services contracts contrary to Thirteenth Amendment); Restatement (Second) of Contracts § 367(1) (1981) ("A promise to render personal service will not be specifically enforced").

6. Harlan M. Blake, "Employee Agreements Not to Compete," *Harvard Law Review* 73 (1960): 625.

7. Restatement (Second) of Contracts 1981, § 188 cmt. a. Section 186(1) of the Restatement (Second) of Contracts (1981) states that a noncompete agreement will be found "unenforceable on grounds of public policy if it . . . unreasonably" restrains trade.

8. *Mathias v. Jacobs,* 167 F. Supp. 606, 606–28 (S.D.N.Y. 2001).

9. Michael A. Epstein, *Epstein on Intellectual Property* 9.01 (New York: Aspen Publishers, 2007).

10. *Arthur Murray Dance Studios v. Witter,* 105 N.E.2d 685, 687–88 (Ohio Ct. C.P. 1952).

11. *Marcam Corp. v. Orchard,* 885 F. Supp. 294, 297 (D. Mass. 1995).

12. *Neff Motivation, Inc. v. Largrou,* 2002-Ohio-2788U, at P 66 (Ct. App. June 7, 2002).

13. *Shapiro v. Regent Printing Co.,* 549 N.E.2d 793, 796 (Ill. App. Ct. 1989).

14. *Unisource Worldwide, Inc. v. Valenti,* 196 F. Supp. 2d 269, 279 (E.D.N.Y. 2002) (enforcing a noncompete because "it is clear to the court that every customer serviced by the [defendant's new employer] is a former customer of [the plaintiff] and that all of [the defendant's employer's] pricing is the same as or better than [the plaintiff's]").

15. *Lawrence v. Business Communications of Virginia, Inc.,* 53 Va. Cir. 102, 102–5 (Cir. Ct. Va., 2000).

16. *Murray Dance Studios, Inc. v. Witter,* 105 N.E.2d at 685.

17. ABA Committee on Professional Ethics, Formal Opinion 61–300 (1961).

18. ABA Model Rule 5.6(a), available at http://www.abanet.org/cpr/mrpc/rule_5_6.html.

19. See, e.g., *Dwyer v. Jung,* 336 A.2d 498, 501 (N.J. Super. Ct. App. Div. 1975); *Marshall v. Romano,* 158 A. 751, 752 (Essex County Ct. 1932); *Cohen v. Lord, Day & Lord,* 550 N.E.2d 410, 411 (N.Y. 1989).

20. Paula Berg, "Judicial Enforcement of Covenants Not to Compete Among Physicians: Protecting Doctors' Interests at Patients' Expense," *Rutgers Law Review* 45 (1992): 1, 6.

21. American Medical Association, *Proceedings of the House of Delegates* 236 (Nov. 28-Dec. 1, 1971), available at http://ama.nmtvault.com/custom/about.jsp.

22. American Medical Association, *Code of Medical Ethics,* opinion 9.02 (1998), http://www.ama-assn.org/ama/pub/physician-resources/medical-ethics/code-medical-ethics/opinion902.shtml.

23. See Colo. Rev. Stat. § 8–2–113(3) (2003); Del. Code Ann. tit.6, §2707 (1993); Mass. Gen. Laws Ann. ch. 112, § 12X (1991).

24. See, e.g., *Valley Medical Specialists v. Faber,* 982 P.2d 1277 (Ariz. 1999); *Iredell Digestive Disease Clinic v. Petrozza,* 373 S.E.2d 449, 455 (N.C. Ct. App. 1988); *Ohio Urology Inc. v. Poll,* 594 N.E.2d 1027, 1032 (Ohio Ct. App. 1991) ("These covenants should be strictly construed in favor of professional mobility and access to medical care and facilities.").

25. *Murfreesboro Medical Clinic, P.A. v. Udom,* 166 S.W.3d at 683 ("[W]e see no practical difference between the practice of law and the practice of medicine . . . [b]oth entail a duty on the part of practitioners to make their services available to the public.").

26. Ibid., at 683–84.

27. Cindy Sanders, "Tennessee Legislature Revives Physician Non-Competes," *Nashville Medical News, Inc.,* August 2007, http://nashville.medicalnewsinc.com/news.php?viewStory=1659.

28. Ibid. (stating that the "scope" requirement is limited to either [1] the greater of a ten-mile radius from the healthcare provider's primary practice site or the county in which the provider primarily practiced, or [2] any facility at which the group practice provided services while the provider was under employment).

29. See, e.g., *Oates v. Leonard*, 183 N.W. 462 (Iowa 1921); *Rowe v. Toon*, 169 N.W. 38 (Iowa 1918).

30. *Board of Regents v. Warren*, 2008 WL 5003750 (Iowa Ct. App. 2008). See also Benjamin P. Roach, *Are Physician Non-Compete Agreements Under Attack in Iowa?*, at http://www.nyemaster.com/userdocs/BPR_Physician_Non_Compete_Agreements.pdf.

31. California Business and Professions Code, § 16600.

32. *Advanced Bionics Corp. v. Medtronic, Inc.*, Cal. 4th 697, 706 (Cal. 2002).

33. Ronald J. Gilson, "The Legal Infrastructure of High Technology Industrial Districts: Silicon Valley, Route 128, and Covenants Not to Compete," *N.Y.U. Law Review* 74 (1999): 575, 613–19.

34. *Silguero v. Creteguard, Inc.* 187 Cal. App. 4th 60 (July 30, 2010).

35. *Hill Med. Corp. v. Wycoff*, 86 Cal. App. 4th 895, 900 (2001) (recognizing that "narrow restraints" on trade were allowed under old common law if in accordance with the rule of reasonableness).

36. *Edwards v. Arthur Andersen LLP*, Cal. 4th 937, 948 (2008).

37. *Bosley Medical Group v. Abramson*, 161 Cal. App. 3d 284 (1984).

38. *Application Group, Inc. v. Hunter Group, Inc.* (1998) 61 Cal. App.4th 881, 900. *Nedlloyd Lines B.V. v. Superior Court* (1992) 3 Cal. 4th 459, 465 (California courts are not bound to enforce a contractual conflict of law provision which would thus be contrary to the state's fundamental policy).

39. AnnaLee Saxenian, *Regional Advantage: Culture and Competition in Silicon Valley and Route 128* (Cambridge: Harvard University Press, 1994); Chong-Moon Le et al., *The Silicon Valley Edge: A Habitat for Entrepreneurship and Innovation* (Stanford: Stanford University Press, 2000); *Understanding Silicon Valley: The Anatomy of an Entrepreneurial Region*, Martin Kenney, ed. (Stanford: Stanford University Press, 2000); David Rosenberg, *Cloning Silicon Valley: The Next Generation High-Tech Hotspots* (London: Pearson University, 2002); David N. Pellow and Lisa Sun-Hee Park, *The Silicon Valley of Dreams* (New York: New York University Press, 2002).

40. Gilson, "The Legal Infrastructure of High Technology Industrial Districts"; Joseph Bankman and Ronald J. Gilson, "Why Start-ups?," *Stanford Law Review* 51 (1999): 289–307.

41. Lee Fleming and Koen Frenken, "The Evolution of Inventor Networks in the Silicon Valley and Boston Regions," *Advances in Complex Systems* 10 (2007): 53–71.

42. Matt Marx, Deborah Strumsky, and Lee Fleming, "Mobility, Skills, and the Michigan Non-Compete Experiment," *Management Science* 55 (2009): 875–89.

43. Lee Gesmer, "Why Has Silicon Valley Outperformed Boston/Route 128 as a High Tech Hub?" http://masslawblog.com/noncompete-agreements (December 6, 2007).

44. *Covenants Not to Compete: A State-by-State Survey,* Brian M. Malsberger, ed. (Arlington: BNA Books, 2004). Colorado, like California, is an exception in allowing noncompetes to be applied broadly. Colorado allows employment contracts to recover training costs for less than a two-year period and permits noncompetes for "executive and management personnel and officers and employees who constitute professional staff to executive and management personnel." Colo. Rev. Stat. 8–2–113(d) (2005).

45. New York recently passed legislation restricting the ability to enforce noncompetes in broadcasting, NY Labor § 202-k (Protection of Persons Employed in the Broadcast Industry). The act provides that a "broadcasting industry employer shall not require as a condition of employment, whether in an employment contract or otherwise," that a broadcast employee or prospective broadcast employee, after the conclusion of employment, refrain from obtaining subsequent employment "(a) in any specified geographic area, (b) for a specific period of time, or (c) with any particular employer or in any particular industry." The act further declares as unenforceable "any contractual provisions that would waive these prohibitions."

46. Mass. Gen. laws ann. Ch 149 section 1.

4. COMPETITION AND THE MIRACLE OF PLACE

1. Steven Pinch and Nick Henry, "Paul Krugman's Geographical Economics, Industrial Clustering and the British Motor Sport Industry," *Regional Studies* 33 (1999): 823–24.

2. Steven Pinch and Nick Henry, "Spatialising Knowledge: Placing the Knowledge Community of Motor Sport Valley," *Geoforum* 31 (2000): 198.

3. Alfred Marshall, *Principles of Economics* (London: Macmillan, 1920).

4. Edward L. Glaeser and David C. Maré, "Cities and Skills," *Journal of Labor Economics* 19, no. 2 (2001): 316–42; Edward L. Glaeser and David C. Maré, "The Complementarity Between Cities and Skills," National Bureau of Economic Research Working Paper no. 15103 (2009).

5. Kenneth J. Arrow, *Collected Papers of Kenneth J. Arrow: The Economics of Information* (Cambridge: Harvard University Press, 1984).

6. Kenneth J. Arrow, "Economic Welfare and the Allocation of Resources for Invention," in National Bureau of Economic Research, *The Rate and Direction of Inventive Activity: Economic and Social Factors* 609, 620 (Princeton: Princeton University Press, 1962).

7. Gerald Carlino, Satyajit Chatterjee, and Robert Hunt, "Matching and Learning in Cities: Urban Density and the Rate of Invention," Federal Reserve Bank of Philadelphia Working Paper no. 04–16 (2005), 17–23.

8. Lee Fleming and Matt Marx, "Managing Creativity in Small Worlds," *California Management Review* 48 (2006): 6–27.

9. Brian Uzzi, "The Sources and Consequences of Embeddedness for the Economic Performance of Organizations: The Network Effect," *American Sociological Review* 61 (1996): 674.

10. Robert K. Merton, *The Sociology of Science: Theoretical and Empirical Investigations* (Chicago: University of Chicago Press, 1973).
11. Ramana Nanda and Jesper B. Sørensen, "Workplace Peers and Entrepreneurship," *Management Science* 56 (2010): 1116–26.
12. Uzzi, "Sources and Consequences of Embeddedness," 674.
13. Jasjit Singh, "Collaboration Networks as Determinants of Knowledge Diffusion Processes," *Management Science* 51 (2005): 756–70; Robert I. Sutton and Andrew Hargadon, "Brainstorming Groups in Context: Effectiveness in a Product Design Firm," *Administrative Science Quarterly* 41 (1996): 685–718; Dorothy A. Leonard and Walter Swap, *When Sparks Fly: Igniting Creativity in Groups* (Boston: Harvard Business School Press, 1999); Paul B. Paulus and Bernard A. Nijstad, "Group Creativity: An Introduction," in *Group Creativity: Innovation Through Collaboration*, ed. Paul B. Paulus and Bernard A. Nijstad, 3–14 (New York: Oxford University Press, 2003); M. Ann McFadden and Albert Cannella, "Social Capital and Knowledge Creation: Diminishing Returns of the Number and Strength of Exchange Relationships," *Academy of Management Journal* 47 (2004): 735–46.
14. Roger Guimera et al., "Team Assembly Mechanisms Determine Collaboration Network Structure and Team Performance," *Science* 308, no. 5722 (2005): 697–702; Morton T. Hansen, "The Search-Transfer Problem: The Role of Weak Ties in Sharing Knowledge across Organization Subunits," *Administrative Science Quarterly* 44 (1999): 82–111.
15. Mendes Dorogvstev, *Evolution of Networks: From Biological to the Internet and WWW* (Oxford: Oxford University Press, 2003); Albert-László Barabási, *Linked: The New Science of Networks* (Cambridge: Perseus Publishing, 2002); *Models and Methods in Social Network Analysis*, Peter J. Carrington, John Scott, and Stanley Wasserman, eds. (New York: Cambridge University Press, 2005).
16. Ian Ayres and Katharine K. Baker, "A Separate Crime of Reckless Sex," *U. Chi. L. Rev.* 72 (2005): 599.
17. Katherine J. Strandburg et al., "Law and the Science of Networks: An Overview and an Application to the 'Patent Explosion,'" *Berkeley Tech. L.J.* 21 (2006): 1293; Lee Fleming and Koen Frenken, "The Evolution of Inventor Networks in the Silicon Valley and Boston Regions," *Advances in Complex Systems* 10, no. 1 (2007): 53–71; Bronwyn H. Hall, Adam B. Jaffe, and Manuel Trajtenberg, "The NBER Patent Citation Data File: Lessons, Insights and Methodological Tools," in *Patents, Citations and Innovations: A Window on the Knowledge Economy*, ed. Adam B. Jaffe and Manuel Trajtenberg, 403–60 (Cambridge: MIT Press, 2002).
18. Leon Battista Alberti (1404–72) developed the Renaissance ideal that "a man can do all things if he will."
19. Lee Fleming, "Perfecting Cross-Pollination," *Harvard Business Review* 82 (2004): 22–24; Lee Fleming, "Recombinant Uncertainty in Technological Search," *Management Science* 47 (2001): 117, 118–20; Lee Fleming and Olav Sorenson, "Science as a Map in Technological Search," *Strategic Management Journal* 25 (2004): 909–28; Lori Rosenkopf and Paul Almeida, "Overcoming Local Search Through Alliances and Mobility," *Management Science* 49 (2003): 751.

20. Maryann P. Feldman and David B. Audretsch, "Innovation in Cities: Science-based Diversity, Specialization and Localized Competition," *European Economic Review* 43 (1999): 409–29.

21. Lauren Weber, "The Diamond Game, Shedding Its Mystery," *New York Times*, April 8, 2001.

22. Jane Jacobs, *The Economy of Cities* (New York: Random House, 1969).

23. Alfred Marshall, *Principles of Economics* (London: Macmillan, 1920), 271.

24. Edward L. Glaeser et al., "Growth in Cities," *Journal of Political Economy* 100 (1992): 1126–52.

25. Adam B. Jaffe, "Real Effects of Academic Research," *American Economic Review* 79 (1989): 957; Zoltan J. Acs, David B. Audretsch, and Maryann P. Feldman, "Real Effects of Academic Research: Comment," *American Economic Review* 82 (1992): 363.

26. Adam B. Jaffe, Manuel Trajtenberg, and Rebecca Henderson, "Geographic Localization of Knowledge Spillovers as Evidenced by Patent Citations," *Quarterly Journal of Economics* 108 (1993): 577–98; Paul Almeida and Bruce Kogut, "The Exploration of Technological Diversity and the Geographic Localization of Innovation," *Small Business Economics* 9 (1997): 21–31; Per Botolf Maurseth and Bart Verspagen, "Europe: One or Several Systems of Innovation? An Analysis Based on Patent Citations," in *The Economic Challenge for Europe*, ed. Jan Fagerberg, Paolo Guerrieri, and Bart Verspagen, 149–74 (Northampton, Mass.: Edward Elgar 1999); Bart Verspagen and Wilfred Schoenmakers, "The Spatial Dimension of Knowledge Spillovers in Europe: Evidence from Firm Patenting Data," Eindhoven Center for Innovation Studies Working Paper 00.07 (2000); Rebecca Henderson, Adam Jaffe, and Manuel Trajtenberg, "Universities as a Source of Commercial Technology: A Detailed Analysis of University Patenting, 1965–1988," *Review of Economics and Statistics* 80 (1998): 119–27; Jaffe, "Real Effects of Academic Research," 957–70; Adam Jaffe and Manuel Trajtenberg, "Flows of Knowledge from Universities and Federal Labs: Modeling the Flow of Patent Citations over Time and across Institutional and Geographic Boundaries," *Proceedings of the National Academy of Sciences* 93 (1996): 12671–677.

27. Lynne G. Zucker, Michael R. Darby, and Marilynn B. Brewer, "Intellectual Property and the Birth of U.S. Biotechnology Enterprises," *American Economic Review* 88, no. 1 (1998): 290–360.

28. "Pick a Place to Live, Then Find a Job," *Wall Street Journal*, January 27, 2002.

29. Richard Florida, *The Flight of the Creative Class: The New Global Competition for Talent* (New York: HarperCollins, 2007), 45.

30. Naomi R. Lamoreaux and Kenneth L. Sokoloff, "Inventors, Firms and the Market for Technology in the Late Nineteenth and Early Twentieth Centuries," in *Learning by Doing in Markets, Firms and Countries*, ed. Naomi R. Lamoreaux, Daniel M. G. Raff, and Peter Temin, 19–60 (Chicago: University of Chicago Press, 1999).

31. Peter V. Marsden and Noah E. Friedkin, "Network Studies of Social Influence," *Sociological Methods and Research* 22 (1993): 127; Ed Steinmuller, "Will New

Information and Communication Technology Improve the 'Codification' of Knowledge?," *Industrial and Corporate Change* 9 (2000): 361–76.

32. Olav Sorenson, Jan W. Rivkin, and Lee Fleming, "Complexity, Networks, and Knowledge Flow," *Science Direct Research Policy* 35 (2006): 994.

33. Jaffe, Trajtenberg, and Henderson, "Geographic Localization of Knowledge Spillovers," 577.

34. Harry M. Collins, "Tacit Knowledge and Scientific Networks," in *Science in Context: Readings in the Sociology of Science,* ed. Barry Barns and David Edge, 44–64 (New York: Open University Press, 1982).

35. Zoltan J. Acs, David B. Audretsch, and Maryann P. Feldman, "R&D Spillovers and Recipient Firm Size," *Review of Economics and Statistics* 76 (1994): 336–40.

36. AnnaLee Saxenian, *Regional Advantage: Culture and Competition in Silicon Valley and Route 128* (Cambridge: Harvard University Press, 1994); Bruce Fallick et al., "Job-Hopping in Silicon Valley: Some Evidence Concerning the Microfoundations of a High-Technology Cluster," *Review of Economics and Statistics* 88 (2006): 472.

5. TOP SECRET—NOT SECRET!

1. Robert M. Sherwood, *Intellectual Property and Economic Development* 58 (San Francisco: Westview Press, 1990).

2. David Friedman, William Landes, and Richard Posner, "Some Economics of Trade Secret Law," *Journal of Economic Perspectives* 5, no. 1 (1990): 61–72.

3. *Kewanee Oil Co. v. Bicron Corp.,* 416 U.S. 470, 481 (1974).

4. General Agreement on Tariffs and Trade, October 30, 1947, 55 U.N.T.S. 187 (as amended).

5. *Wyeth v. Natural Biologics, Inc.,* 2003 U.S. Dist. LEXIS 1771.

6. *Hilton Davis v. Warner Jenkinson,* 62 F. 3d 1529 (Fed. Cir. 1995).

7. *Keane v. Fox Television Stations, Inc.,* 75 U.S.P.Q. 2d 1061 (5th Cir. 2005).

8. *All Pro Sports Camp v. Walt Disney Co.,* 717 So. 2d. 363.

9. *Lexar Media, Inc. v. Toshiba Corp.,* no. 11–02-CV-812458, 2005 WL 5872071, at 1 (Cal. App. Dep't Super. Ct. Oct. 14, 2005).

10. Christopher Andrew, *For the President's Eyes Only: Secret Intelligence and the American Presidency from Washington to Bush* (New York: HarperCollins, 1995), 356–57.

11. Karl F. Jorda, "Trade Secrets and Trade Secret Licensing," in *Intellectual Property Management in Health and Agricultural Innovation: A Handbook of Best Practices,* ed. Anatole Krattiger et al. (Oxford: MIHR, 2007).

12. *Cong. Rec.* S12 (Oct. 2, 1996) (Statement of Senator Specter).

13. House of Representatives, Subcommittee on International Economic Policy and Trade, *Corporate and Industrial Espionage and Their Effects on American Competitiveness* (September 13, 2000).

14. *US v. Malhotra,* no. 5:08-CR-00423-JF (N.D. Cal 2008).

15. *US v. Dimson* (ND Ga. 2006).

16. *Bancroft-Whitney Co. v. Glen* (1966) 64 Cal. 2d 327, 353. Alternatively, employers may be held liable even if they had no knowledge of the misappropriation.

Under the doctrine of *respondeat superior,* as long as the activity was performed in the course of employment and was primarily intended to benefit the new employer, the company would incur liability for the consequences of the employee's tortious acts. *MicroStrategy, Inc. v. Business Objects, S.A.,* 331 F. Supp. 2d 396. Therefore, competitor self-reporting of trade secret theft is fairly common.

17. USDOJ, http://www.usdoj.gov/criminal/cybercrime/mcmenaminPlea.htm.
18. Edmund Kitch, "The Expansion of Trade Secrecy Protection and the Mobility of Management Employees: A New Problem for the Law," *South Carolina Law Review* 47 (1996): 659–72.
19. *Open Magnetic Imaging, Inc. v. Nieves-Garcia,* 826 So. 2d 415, 419 (Fla. Dist. Ct. App. 2002); *Platinum Mgmt., Inc. v. Dahms,* 666 A.2d 1028, 1038, 1041 (N.J. Super.Ct.Law Div. 1995); *EMC Corp. v. Allen,* no. 97–5972-B, 1997 Mass. Super.3–9; *Markovits v. Venture Info Capital, Inc.,* 129 F. Supp. 2d 647 (S.D.N.Y. 2001).
20. *Donald McElroy, Inc.,* 389 N.E.2d at 1304–05; *Unisource Worldwide, Inc. v. Valenti,* 196 F. Supp. 2d 269, 279 (S.D.N.Y. 2002) ("While the precise way in which Matrix obtained the information remains murky, it is clear to the court that every customer serviced by Matrix is a former customer of Unisource and that all of Matrix's pricing is the same as or better than Unisource's").
21. James Pooley, *Trade Secrets,* § 1.01 (New York: Law Journal Seminar Press, 2006).
22. *FMC Corp v. Cyprus Foote Mineral Co.,* 899 F. Supp. 1477, 1484 (W. D.N.C 1995).
23. *7's Enterprises, Inc. v. Del Rosario,* 143 P.3d 23, 23–37 (2006).
24. *SI Handling Sys., Inc. v. Heisley,* 753 F.2d 1244, 1244–69 (3d Cir., 1985).
25. *Hapney v. Central Garage, Inc.,* 579 So.2d 127, 132 (Fla. App. 1991).
26. Timothy P. Glynn, Charles A. Sullivan, and Rachel Arnow-Richman, *Employment Law: Private Ordering and Its Limitations* (New York: Aspen Publishers, 2007).
27. Charles T. Graves, "Trade Secrets as Property: Theory and Consequences," *J. Intell. Prop. L.* 15 (2007): 39.
28. *Klamath-Orleans Lumber, Inc. v. Miller,* 87 Cal. App. 3d 458
29. *Commercial Plastics* (1965) 1 QB 623.
30. *Boch Toyota, Inc. v. Klimoski,* no. 04–966, 2004 Mass. Super. LEXIS 258, at *9–11 (Mass. Super. Ct. June 24, 2004).
31. *Serv. Ctrs. of Chi., Inc. v. Minogue,* 535 N.E.2d 1132, 1137 (Ill. App. Ct. 1989); *Phoenix Renovation Corp.,* 439 F. Supp. 2d at 521–22.
32. Chris Montville, "Reforming the Law of Proprietary Information," *Duke Law Journal* 56 (2007): 1159.
33. *Reed, Roberts Assocs., Inc. v. Strauman,* 353 N.E.2d 590, 594 (N.Y. 1976).
34. *BDO Seidman v. Hirshberg,* 712 N.E.2d 1220, 1224–25 (N.Y. 1999).
35. *AMP, Inc. v. Fleischhacker,* 823 F.2d 1199, 1205, n.3 (7th Cir. 1987).
36. *Merck & Co.* 941 F. Supp 1461.
37. *Double Click v. Henderson,* 1997 WL 731413 (N.Y. Sup. Crt., Nov. 7, 1997).
38. *Rockwell Graphic Systems, Inc. v. DEV Indus.,* 925 F.2d 174, 180 (7th Cir. 1991)
39. Richard Posner and William M. Landes, *The Economic Structure of Intellectual Property Law* (Cambridge: Harvard University Press, 2003), 364.

40. Bart Los and Bart Verspagen, "Technology Spillovers and Their Impact on Productivity," in *Elgar Companion to Neo-Schumpeterian Economics,* ed. Hanusch and Pyka, 574–93 (Cheltenham, U.K.: Edward Elgar 2003).

41. *Morlife Inc. v. Perry,* 56 Cal. App. 4th 1514, 1520, 66 Cal. Rptr. 2d 731, 735.

42. *Intermedics, Inc., v. Ventritex, Inc.,* 822 F. Supp. 634 (N.D Cal. 1993) at 652.

43. Robert Milgrim, "1 Milgrim on Trade Secrets § 5.01" (LexisNexis 1994).

44. AnnaLee Saxenian, *Regional Advantage: Culture and Competition in Silicon Valley and Route 128* (Cambridge: Harvard University Press, 1994), 149.

45. Mark C. Suchman, "Dealmakers and Counselors: Law Firms as Intermediaries in the Development of Silicon Valley," in *Understanding Silicon Valley: The Anatomy of an Entrepreneurial Region,* ed. Martin Kenney, 71–97 (Stanford: Stanford University Press, 2000).

46. David Angel, "High Technology Agglomeration and the Labor Market: The Case of Silicon Valley," *Environment and Planning* 23 (1991): 1501.

47. Alan Hyde, *Working in Silicon Valley: Economic and Legal Analysis of a High Velocity Labor Market* (Armonk: M. E. Sharpe 2003).

6. SHARING AND THE MIRACLE OF COGNITIVE FREEDOMS

1. Robert Presthus, *The Organizational Society* (New York: Vintage Books, 1962), 316.

2. *Steenhoven v. College Life Insur. Co. of America,* 460 N.E. 2d 973 (Ind.App. 1984).

3. *E. W. Bliss Co. v. Struthers-Dunn, Inc.,* 408 F.2d 1108, 1112 (8th Cir. 1969).

4. Robert G. Bone, "A New Look at Trade Secrets Law Doctrine in Search of Justification," *California Law Review* 86 (1998): 541.

5. David D. Friedman, William M. Landes, and Richard A. Posner, "Some Economics of Trade Secrets Law," *J. Econ. Perspectives* 5 (1991): 61.

6. Ben Rich and Leo Janos, *Skunk Works: A Personal Memoir of My Years at Lockheed* (New York: Little Brown, 1994), 79–80.

7. *Wall Street Journal,* April 4, 1995.

8. Pete Mortensen, "Apple Hones 'One More Thing' Hype," *Wired,* October 12, 2005.

9. Ibid.

10. Brad Stone, "Apple's Management Obsessed with Secrecy," *New York Times,* June 22, 2009, http://www.nytimes.com.

11. Daniel Eran, "Why Is Apple So Secretive?," Roughly Drafted, August 29, 2006, http://www.roughlydrafted.com/RD.

12. Malcolm Moore, "Four Suicide Attempts in the Last Month at Foxconn, Makers of the IPad," *Telegraph* (UK), April 7, 2010; Ting-I Tsai, "Employee's Suicide Puts Hon Hai, Apple in Spotlight," *Wall Street Journal,* July 23, 2009, http://online.wsj.com.

13. Erick Schonfeld, "P&G's Growth Wizard," *Business 2.0* (Jan.-Feb. 2005): 48; Nabil Y. Sakkab, "Connect & Develop Complements Research & Develop at P&G," *Res.-Tech. Mgmt.* (Mar.-Apr. 2002): 38; Patricia Sellers, "P&G: Teaching an Old Dog New Tricks," *Fortune,* May 31, 2004, 166; Procter & Gamble, "Connect & Develop: Creating a Global Innovation Network to Better Serve

Customers," 7 (2003), available at http:// www.scienceinthebox.com/en_UK; "At P&G, It's '360-Degree Innovation,'" *Bus. Wk. Online,* October 11, 2004, http:// www.businessweek.com/magazine (interview by Robert D. Hof with P&G Chief Technology Officer Gilbert Cloyd).

14. Clayton M. Christensen and Michael E. Raynor, *The Innovator's Solution* (Cambridge: Harvard Business School Press, 2003), 31–71.

15. The longer version of Linus's law, named in honor of Linus Torvalds and formulated by Eric S. Raymond in *The Cathedral and the Bazaar,* is as follows: "Given a large enough beta-tester and co-developer base, almost every problem will be characterized quickly and the fix will be obvious to someone."

16. Ralph Katz and Thomas J. Allen, "Investigating the Not Invented Here (NIH) Syndrome," *R&D Management* 12, no. 1 (1982): 7–19.

17. Ajay Agrawal et al., "Not Invented Here? Innovation in Company Towns," NBER Working Paper no. 15437 (2009).

18. Henry W. Chesbrough, *Open Innovation: The New Imperative for Creating and Profiting from Technology* (Cambridge: Harvard Business School Press, 2003), 43–62.

19. Alexander Kandybin and Martin Kihn, "Raising Your Return on Innovation Investment," *Booz-Allen-Hamilton Strategy and Bus.,* May 11, 2004, available at http://www.strategy-business.com.

20. http://www.catb.org.

21. Joel Spolsky, "In Defense of Not-Invented-Here Syndrome" http://www.joelonsoftware.com/ (2001).

22. Jennifer S. Lerner and Philip E. Tetlock, "Accounting for the Effects of Accountability," *Psychol. Bull.* 125 (1999): 255, 259.

23. Donald C. Langevoort, "Monitoring: The Behavioral Economics of Corporate Compliance with Law," *Colum. Bus. L. Rev.* 1 (2002): 71–118.

24. Robert Cialdini, "Social Influence and the Triple Tumor Structure of Organizational Dishonesty," in *Codes of Conduct: Behavior Research and Business Ethics,* ed. D. M. Messick and A. Tenbrunsel (New York: Russell Sage, 2005).

25. John P. Meyer et al., "Organizational Commitment and Job Performance: It's the Nature of the Commitment that Counts," *J. Applied Psychol.* 74 (1989): 152.

26. Lawrence E. Mitchell, "Trust and Team Production in Post-Capitalist Society," *J. Corp. L.* 24 (1999): 869.

27. Andrew Hargadon and Robert Sutton, "Building an Innovation Factory," *Harvard Business Review* 78, no. 3 (2001): 59.

28. Norbert L. Kerr et al., "Bias in Judgment: Comparing Individuals and Groups," *Psychol. Rev.* 103 (1996): 687; Benjamin F. Jones, Stefan Wuchty, and Brian Uzzi, "Multi-University Research Teams: Shifting Impact, Geography, and Stratification in Science," *Science* 322 (2008): 1259–62.

29. Benjamin F. Jones, Stefan Wuchty, and Brian Uzzi,, "The Increasing Dominance of Teams in Production of Knowledge," *Science* 316 (2007): 1036–39.

30. Lee Fleming, Charles King, and Adam Juda, "Small Worlds and Regional Innovation," *Organ. Sci.* 18, no. 6 (2007): 938–54.

31. William Latham, Claudine Gay, and Christian Le Bas, "Collective Knowledge, Prolific Inventors and the Value of Inventions: An Empirical Study of French, German and British Patents in the U.S. 1975–1999," *Economics of Innovation and New Technology* 17 (2008): 5–22.

32. Roger Guimera et al., "Team Assembly Mechanisms Determine Collaboration Network Structure and Team Performance," *Science* 308, no. 5722 (2005): 697–702.

33. Hargadon and Sutton, "Building an Innovation Factory," 69.

34. L. Fleming et al., "Small Worlds and Regional Innovation."

35. Everett Rogers and Judith Larsen, *Silicon Valley Fever: Growth of High-Technology Culture* (New York: Basic Books 1984).

36. Robin Cowan, Paul David, and Dominique Foray, "The Explicit Economics of Knowledge Codification and Tacitness," *Industrial and Corporate Change* 9, no. 2 (2000): 211–53.

7.   MINE—YOURS (OR OURS)

1. Lincoln's lectures of 1859 on discoveries and inventions, as cited in Catherine Fisk, "Removing the 'Fuel of Interest' from the 'Fire of Genius': Law and the Employee-Inventor, 1830–1930," *University of Chicago Law Review* 65 (1998): 1127–98, at 1129.

2. *Solomons v. United States*, 137 US 342, 346 (1890).

3. *Teets v. Chromalloy Gas Turbine Corp.*, 83 F.3d 403, 408 (1996).

4. *United States v. Dubilier Condenser Corp.*, 289 U.S. at 188 (1933).

5. Steven Cherensky, "A Penny for Their Thoughts: Employee-Inventors, Preinvention Assignment Agreements, Property, and Personhood," *California Law Review* 81, no. 2 (1993): 597–666.

6. *Dickman v. Vollmer*, 736 N.W.2d 202 (Wis. Ct. App. 2007) (holding that agreements to assign do not need to be in writing; upon sufficient proof, oral preassignments may be upheld); *Larson v. Correct Craft, Inc.*, 537 F. Supp. 2d 1264 (M.D. Fla. 2008).

7. These state statutes include Cal. Lab. Code § 2870 (West 1989) (enacted 1979); Del. Code Ann. tit. 19, § 805 (1995) (enacted 1984); 765 Ill. Comp. Stat. 1060/2 (West 1998) (enacted 1983); Kan. Stat. Ann. § 44–130 (1993) (enacted 1986); Minn. Stat. § 181.78 (1998) (enacted 1977); N.C. Gen. Stat. §§ 66–57.1 to 66–57.2 (1992) (enacted 1981); Utah Code Ann. § 34–39–3 (1997) (enacted 1989); Wash. Rev. Code § 49.44.140 (1990) (enacted 1979). Donald J. Ying, "A Comparative Study of the Treatment of Employee Inventions, Pre-Invention Assignment Agreements, and Software Rights," *U. Pa. J. Bus. & Emp. L.* 10 (2008): 763.

8. *Cubic Corp v. Marty*, 229 Cal.Rptr. 438 (Cal.Ct.App.1986); *Cadence Design Systems, Inc. v. Bhandari*, 2007 WL 3343085 (N.D.Cal.,2007) (holding that under Cal. Labor Code § 2870, inventions that are "related to" an employer's business interest are not limited to the smallest business division in which the employee actually works; inventions within the general scope of the employer's business may be preassigned).

9. *Ingersoll-Rand Co. v. Ciavatta*, 110 N.J. 609, 615 (1988).

10. Catherine Fisk, "The Story of Ingersoll-Rand v. Ciavatta: Employee Inventors in Corporate Research & Development—Reconciling Innovation with Entrepreneurship," in *Employment Law Stories*, ed. Samuel Estreicher and Gillian Lester, 143–74 (Eagan, Minn.: Foundation Press, 2010).

11. German Law on Employee Inventions, http://www.wipo.int/clea/docs. Roland Kirstein and Birgit Will, "Efficient Compensation for Employees' Inventions," *Eur. J. Law Econ.* 21 (2006): 129–48.

12. Vai Io Lo, "Employee Inventions and Works for Hire in Japan," *Temp. Int'l & Comp. L.J.* 16 (2002): 279, 306.

13. *United States v. Dublier Condenser Corp.*, 289 US 178 (1933).

14. Bayh-Dole Act, 35 USCS § 200–212.

15. "Innovation's Golden Goose," *Economist*, December 12, 2002.

16. David C. Mowery, "The Bayh-Dole Act and High-Technology Entrepreneurship in U.S. Universities: Chicken, Egg or Something Else?," in *University Entrepreneurship and Technology Transfers*, ed. Gary Liebcap, 40 (Amsterdam: Elsevier, 2005).

17. Peter Lattman, "Critics Take Aim at California's Patent Shield," *Wall Street Journal*, November 17, 2007.

18. Technology Transfer Commercialization Act of 2000 U.S.C. § 3710c(a).

19. Pat K. Chew, "Faculty-Generated Inventions: Who Owns the Golden Egg?," *Wis. L. Rev.* (1992): 259

20. Harvard Patent Policy: http://www.techtransfer.harvard.edu/resources.

21. UC Patent Policy: http://www.ucop.edu/ott/genresources.

22. Stanford University, Research Policy Handbook: http://www.stanford.edu/dept.

23. Yale University Patent Policy: http://www.yale.edu/ocr/pfg/policies/patents; Columbia University Faculty Handbook: http://www.columbia.edu/cu/opg/policies.

24. Johns Hopkins and Harvard: Inventor(s) 35 percent, Department 15 percent.

25. An example of university contract dispute is *Shaw v. Regents of the Univ. of Cal.*, 58 Cal App 4th 44, 53 (1997), upholding agreed royalty-sharing plan where preemployment contract was reasonable.

26. *New York Times*, July 18, 2008.

27. http://www.usatoday.com/money/industries/retail/2008–08–26-mattel-bratz-dolls_N.htm.

28. *Sony Corp. of Am v. Universal City Studios*, 464 U.S. 417, 477 (1984).

29. *Mazer v. Stein*, 347 U.S. 201, 219 (1954).

30. *Graham School and Dance Foundation, Inc., et al. v. Martha Graham Center of Contemporary Dance, Inc., et al.*, Case no. 02–9451, 2004 U.S. App. LEXIS 17452 (2d Cir. Aug. 18, 2004).

31. *Eldred v. Ashcroft*, 537 U.S. 186 (2003).

32. Lawrence Lessig, *Free Culture: The Nature and Future of Creativity* (London: Penguin, 2005), 242.

33. Robert Darnton, "A Republic of Letters," *New York Times Sunday Book Review*, August 20, 2010.
34. Stephen Breyer, "The Uneasy Case for Copyright: A Study of Copyright in Books, Photocopies, and Computer Programs," *Harv. L. Rev.* 84 (1970): 281, quoting T. Macaulay, *Speeches on Copyright* 25 (C. Gaston 1914).
35. James Boyle, *Shamans, Software, and Spleens: Law and the Construction of the Information Society* (Cambridge: Harvard University Press, 1996); Rosemary J. Coombe, *The Cultural Life of Intellectual Properties: Authorship, Appropriation, and Law* (Durham: Duke University Press, 1998), 58; Susan Scafidi, *Who Owns Culture? Appropriation and Authenticity in American Law* (New Brunswick: Rutgers University Press, 2005); Keith Aoki, "Adrift in the Intertext: Authorship and Audience 'Recoding' Rights—Comment on Robert H. Rotstein, *Beyond Metaphor: Copyright Infringement and the Fiction of the Work*," *Chi.-Kent L. Rev.* 68 (1993): 805.
36. S. Colum Gilfillan, *The Sociology of Invention* (Cambridge: MIT Press, 1970), 78.
37. A. Hargadon and R. Sutton, "Building an Innovation Factory," *Harvard Business Review on Innovation* (2001): 55.
38. Wesley M. Cohen and Daniel A. Levinthal, "Innovation and Learning: The Two Faces of R&D," *Econ. J.* 99 (1989): 569–70.
39. John Locke, *Two Treatises of Government* (1690), Peter Laslett, ed. (Cambridge: Cambridge University Press, 1988), 285–302.
40. Robert P. Merges, "Locke for the Masses: Property Rights and the Products of Collective Creativity," *Hofstra L. Rev.* 36 (2009): 1179, 1180, 1182.
41. Jennie Erdal, *Ghosting: A Double Life* (Edinburgh: Canongate Books, 2003).

8. OWNERSHIP AND THE MIRACLE OF INNOVATION MOTIVATION

1. Arthur Miller, "What I've Learned," *Esquire*, July 2003, 110.
2. J. S. G. Boggs, "Who Owns This?" *Chi.-Kent L. Rev.* 68 (1993): 889.
3. Roger Sessions, "The Composer and His Message," in *The Creative Process*, ed. Brewster Ghiselin, 133–34 (Berkeley: University of California Press, 1952).
4. Rebecca Tushnet, "Economies of Desire: Fair Use and Marketplace Assumptions," *Wm. & Mary L. Rev.*, 51 (2009): 533, citing Lyrastar, "The Source of the Mississippi: What Was First?," in *Legacy* 1 (2007): 144.
5. Eric Von Hippel, *Democratizing Innovation* (Cambridge: MIT Press, 2005), 124.
6. Jonathan R. Cole, *Fair Science: Women in the Scientific Community* (New York: Free Press, 1987).
7. *Second Lecture on Discoveries and Inventions*, February 11, 1859.
8. Yuval Feldman and Orly Lobel, "The Incentives Matrix: The Comparative Effectiveness of Rewards, Liabilities, Duties and Protections for Reporting Illegality," *Texas Law Review* 87 (2010): 1151–1211; Yuval Feldman and Orly Lobel, "Decentralized Enforcement in Organizations: An Experimental Approach," *Reg. and Governance* 2 (2008): 165–92.
9. Gary P. Latham and Gary A. Yukl, "Effects of Assigned and Participative Goal Setting on Performance and Job Satisfaction," *Journal of Applied Psychology* 61 (1976): 166–71.

10. Edwin A. Locke and Gary P. Latham, *A Theory of Goal Setting and Task Performance* (Englewood Cliffs, N.J.: Prentice Hall, 1990).

11. Edwin A. Locke, Dong-Ok Chah, Scott Harrison, and Nancy Lustgarten, "Separating the Effects of Goal Specificity from Goal Level," *Organizational Behavior and Human Performance* 43 (1989): 270–87.

12. Feldman and Lobel, "The Incentives Matrix"; Feldman and Lobel, "Decentralized Enforcement in Organizations."

13. Leon Festinger and James M. Carlsmith, "Cognitive Consequences of Forced Compliance," *Journal of Abnormal and Social Psychology* 58 (1959): 203–10.

14. Ernst Fehr and Armin Falk, "Psychological Foundations of Incentives," *Eur. Econ. Rev.* 46 (2002): 687, 7714.

15. Teresa M. Amabile, *Creativity in Context: Update to the Social Psychology of Creativity* (Boulder: Westview Press, 1996); Alfie Kohn, *Punished by Rewards: The Trouble With Gold Stars, Incentive Plans, A's, Praise, and Other Bribes* (New York: Houghton Mifflin, 1993).

16. Mark J. Garmaise, "Ties that Truly Bind: Non-competition Agreements, Executive Compensation and Firm Investment," *J. Law Econ. Organ.* 27, no. 2 (2009): 1, 25.

17. Ibid., 1, 7.

18. Viral V. Acharya, "Labor Laws and Innovation," Working Paper, New York University (2009); Viral V. Acharya et al., "Wrongful Discharge Laws and Innovation" (April 2012). Available at SSRN: http://ssrn.com/abstract=1570663 or http://dx.doi.org/10.2139/ssrn.1570663

19. David Leonhardt, "After the Great Recession," *New York Times*, April 28, 2009.

20. Sharon Hannes, "Reverse Monitoring: On the Hidden Role of Employee Stock-Based Compensation," *Mich. L. Rev.* 105 (2007): 1421, 1444 (citing James C. Sesil and Maya K. Kroumova, "The Impact of Broad-Based Stock Options on Firm Performance: Does Firm Size Matter?," 3 [2005], manuscript, available at http://papers.ssrn.com/abstract=717081).

21. The Supreme Court of Connecticut held that permitting a forfeiture clause without a reasonableness assessment is no different than blindly enforcing a noncompete. *Deming v. Nationwide Mutual Insurance Co.*, 905 A.2d 623, 638 (2006). The Massachusetts Supreme Judicial Court similarly tests the reasonableness of forfeitures in analogy to noncompete covenants. *Bohne v. Computer Associates Int'l.*, 514 F.3d 141, 144 (5th Cir. 2008). See also *Rochester Corp. v. Rochester*, 450 F.2d 118, 123 (4th Cir. 1971).

22. Andrew Hargadon and Robert I. Sutton, "Building an Innovation Factory," in *Harvard Business Review on Innovation* (2001), 61–62.

23. Gerard I. Nierenberg, *Fundamentals of Negotiations* (New York: Hawthorn Books: 1973), 107.

24. Julie E. Cohen, "Copyright, Commodification and Culture: Locating the Public Domain," in *The Future of the Public Domain: Identifying the Commons in Information Law*, ed. P. Bernt Hugenholtz and Lucie Guibault, 121, Information Law Series 16 (The Hague: Kluwer Law International, 2006); Neil Netanel,

Copyright's Paradox (Oxford: Oxford University Press, 2008); Lydia Pallas Loren, "The Pope's Copyright? Aligning Incentives with Reality by Using Creative Motivation to Shape Copyright Protection," *La. L. Rev.* 69 (2008): 1.

25. Rebecca Tushnet, "Economies of Desire: Fair Use and Marketplace Assumptions," *Wm. & Mary L. Rev.* 51 (2009): 513.

26. John Quiggin and Dan Hunter, "Money Ruins Everything," *Hastings Comm. & Ent. L.J.* 30 (2008): 214-15.

27. Feldman and Lobel, "The Incentives Matrix."

28. Interestingly, in our experiments we find gender differences. The women in our experiments were far more likely to report corporate misconduct and cared more than men about protection against retaliation rather than monetary incentives.

29. Guy L. Steele and Eric S. Raymond, eds., *The New Hacker's Dictionary*, 3d ed. (Cambridge: MIT Press, 1996).

30. Anne Barron, "Copyright Infringement, 'Free-Riding' and the Lifeworld," in *Copyright and Piracy: An Interdisciplinary Critique*, ed. Lionel Bently, Jennifer Davis, and Jane Ginsburg, 93-127 (Cambridge: Cambridge University Press, 2010).

31. Daniel L. Kahneman, Jack L. Knetch, and Richard H. Thaler, "Fairness as a Constraint on Profit Seeking: Entitlements in the Market," *American Economic Review* 76 (1986): 728.

32. "How to Retain Talent in India," *MIT Sloan Management Review* 50 (2008): 6-7.

33. April Mitchell Franco and Darren Filson, "Spin-outs: Knowledge Diffusion Through Employee Mobility," *Journal of Economics* 37 (2006): 841.

34. Kathleen Gregory, "Signing Up: The Culture and Careers of Silicon Valley Computer People" (Ph.D. diss., Northwestern University, 1984).

9. TALENT WARS AND THE ENTREPRENEURIAL SPIRIT

1. Sampsa Samila and Olav Sorenson, "Noncompete Covenants: Incentives to Innovate or Impediments to Growth," *Management Science, INFORMS* 57, no. 3 (2011): 425-38. For each area the authors gathered data from several sources, including census-based data, patent database, and VentureXpert, a well-established database on venture capital activity. The layered data on investment, growth, and innovation help disentangle the effects of the legal regime from the many other factors that vary across places.

2. Jinyoung Kim and Gerald Marschke, "Labor Mobility of Scientists, Technological Diffusion and the Firm's Patenting Decision," *Rand Journal of Economics* 36 (2005): 298.

3. Gautam Ahuja, "Collaboration Networks, Structural Holes and Innovation," *Administrative Science Quarterly* 45 (2000): 425.

4. Wesley Cohen and Steven Klepper, "Firm Size and the Nature of Innovation within Industries: The Case of Process and Product R&D," *Rev. of Econ. and Stat.* (1996): 232.

5. Stuart and Olav Sorenson, "Liquidity Events, Noncompete Covenants and the Geographic Distribution of Entrepreneurial Activity," *Admin. Sci. Q.* 48 (2003): 175.

6. Melanie Wells, "Lord of the Skies," *Forbes Magazine,* October 14, 2002.

7. Joseph A. Schumpeter, "The Instability of Capitalism," *Econ. J.* 38 (1928): 361, 379.

8. Robert F. Hébert and Albert N. Link, *A History of Entrepreneurship* (London: Routledge, 2009); Thomas F. Hellman, "When Do Employees Become Entrepreneurs?," *Management Science* 53 (2007): 919–33.

9. Amar Bhide, "How Entrepreneurs Craft Strategies That Work," *Harvard Business Review* 72 (1994): 150–61.

10. Joseph Bankman and Ronald J. Gilson, "Why Start-ups?," *Stanford Law Review* 51 (1999): 289–307.

11. James J. Anton and Dennis A. Yao, "Start-ups, Spin-offs, and Internal Projects," *J.L. Econ. & Org.* 11 (1995): 362; Steven N. Wiggins, "Entrepreneurial Enterprises, Endogenous Ownership, and the Limits to Firm Size," *Econ. Inq.* 33 (1995): 58–63; David Garvin, "Spin-offs and the New Firm Formation Process," *California Management Review* 25 (1983): 3–20.

12. Joseph A. Schumpeter, *Capitalism, Socialism and Democracy,* 3d ed. (New York: Harper and Row, 1950).

13. Naomi Lamoreaux and Kenneth Sokoloff, "Inventors, Firms and Market for Technology in the Late Nineteenth and Early Twentieth Centuries," in *Learning by Doing in Markets, Firms, and Countries,* ed. Naomi R. Lamoreaux, Daniel M. G. Raff, and Peter Temin (Chicago: University of Chicago Press, 1999).

14. Naomi R. Lamoreaux and Kenneth L. Sokoloff, "The Rise and Decline of the Independent Inventor: A Schumpeterian Story?," in *The Challenge of Remaining Innovative: Lessons from Twentieth-Century American Business,* ed. Sally H. Clarke, Naomi R. Lamoreaux, and Steven Usselman, 359–92 (Stanford: Stanford University Press, 2009).

15. Moreover, the use and enforcement of intellectual property protections vary systematically in different types of companies. For example, larger companies with sufficient legal and financial resources can be more aggressive in driving out competition even when their legal claims are on weak grounds. Patrick Bolton and David S. Scharfstein, "A Theory of Predation Based on Agency Problems in Financial Contracting," *American Economic Review* 80 (1990): 93–106.

16. Alexis de Tocqueville, *Democracy in America,* ed. J. P. Mayers (New York: HarperPerennial, 1969), 2:552.

17. *Arthur Murray Dance Studios of Cleveland, Inc. v. Witter,* 105 N.E.2d 685, 703–4 (Ohio Ct. Com. Pl. 1952).

18. Alexander E. Silverman, "Symposium Report: Intellectual Property Law and the Venture Capital Process," *High Tech. L.J.* 5 (1990): 157.

19. Mary S. Koen, *Survey of Small Business Use of Intellectual Property Protection: Report of a Survey Conducted by MO-SCI Corporation for the Small Business Administration* (Rolla, Mo.: MO-SCI Corp., 1990).

20. Victoria Slid-Flor, "More Trade Secret Wars," *Nat'l L.J.,* March 22, 1993, 1, 34; Udaya Gupta, "Start-Ups Face Big-Time Legal Artillery," *Wall Street Journal,* October 31, 1988.

21. Rajsdhree Agarwal, Martin Ganco, and Rosemarie H. Ziedonis, "Reputations for Toughness in Patent Enforcement: Implications for Knowledge Spillovers Via Inventor Mobility," *Strategic Management Journal* 30 (2009): 1349–74; Jamal Shamsie, "The Context of Dominance: An Industry-Driven Framework for Exploiting Reputation," *Strategic Management Journal* 24, no. 3 (2003): 199–206.

22. Tim Jackson, *Inside Intel: Andy Grove and the Rise of the World's Most Powerful Chip Company* (New York: Penguin, 1998).

23. Yuval Feldman, "The Behavioral Foundations of Trade Secrets: Tangibility, Authorship and Legality," *Journal of Empirical Legal Studies* 3, no. 2 (2006): 197–236.

24. Lee Fleming and Matt Marx, "Managing Creativity in Small Worlds," *California Management Review* 48 (2006): 6–27.

25. Matt Marx, Jasjit Singh, and Lee Fleming, "Regional Disadvantage? Non-compete Agreements and Brain Drain" (2010). http://ssrn.com/abstract=1654719.

26. Ibid.

27. Samila and Sorenson, "Noncompete Covenants."

28. Dora L. Costa and Matthew E. Kahn, "Power Couples: Changes in the Locational Choice of the College Educated, 1940–1990," *Quarterly Journal of Economics* 115, no. 4 (2000): 1287–1315.

29. Henry Chesbrough, *Open Innovation: The New Imperative for Creating and Profiting from Technology* (Cambridge: Harvard Business School Press, 2003).

30. Pankaj Ghemawat (March/April 2007), "Why the World Isn't Flat." Foreignpolicy.com.

31. Serguey Braguinsky and Steven Klepper, "Worker Mobility and Growth: The Goose that Laid the Golden Eggs," in *Renewing Globalization and Economic Growth in a Post-Crisis World: The Future of the G-20 Agenda*, ed. Alexei Monsarrat and Kiron K. Skinner (New York: Carnegie Mellon University Press, 2009). Indeed, a good analogy to postemployment restrictions from a global perspective is immigration policy. Does the way a country disseminates its visas and immigration rights contribute or curtail regional brain gain? Under a large student visa category, for example, talented students applying for a U.S. visa must promise that they will not seek employment later on in the United States. At the same time, there is a shortage in technical, high-skilled employees. And yet studies show that an increase in the number of U.S. work visas granted to highly skilled employees strongly correlates with an increase in the number of patent applications filed in the United States and a rise of entrepreneurial activity and job creation. Peter Schuck and John Tyler, "Making the Case for Changing U.S. Policy Regarding Highly Skilled Immigrants," *Fordham Urban Law Journal* 38, no. 1 (2011): 327–62.

32. Paul Romer, "Increasing Returns and Long-Run Growth," *J. Pol. Econ.* 94 (1986): 1002.

10. WIN–WIN–WIN

1. Early on Harvey Goldschmid used the same phrase. See Harvey J. Goldschmid, "Antitrust's Neglected Stepchild: A Proposal for Dealing with Restrictive Covenants under Federal Law," *Colum. L. Rev* 73 (1973): 1193.

2. Steve Johnson, "Google Recruiter: Company Kept 'Do Not Touch' in Hiring Lists," *Mercury News,* June 3, 2009.

3. TelecomTV One (September 17, 2010).

4. The Statute of Artificers enacted in 1562 made it a crime to hire another's servant.

5. Christopher Dyer, *Making a Living in the Middle Ages: The People of Britain, 850–1520* (New Haven: Yale University Press, 2002).

6. N. Rosenberg, "Why Do Firms Do Basic Research (With Their Own Money)?," *Res. Policy* 19 (1990): 165–74.

7. M. Kenney and U. Von Burg, "Technology, Entrepreneurship and Path Dependence: Industrial Clustering in Silicon Valley and Route 128," *Ind. and Corp. Change* 8, no. 1 (1999): 67–103.

8. L. Fleming and K. Frenken, "The Evolution of Inventor Networks in the Silicon Valley and Boston Regions," *Advances in Complex Systems* 10, no. 1 (2007): 53–71.

9. Scott Stern, "Do Scientists Pay to Be Scientists?" *Management Science* 50 (2003): 835–53.

10. Lee Fleming and Matt Marx, "Managing Creativity in Small Worlds," *California Management Review* 48, no. 4 (2006): 6–27.

11. Ibid.

12. W. Cohen and D. Levinthai, "Absorptive Capacity: A New Perspective on Learning and Innovation," *Administrative Science Quarterly* 35, no. 1 (March 1990): 128–52.

13. T. Jackson, *Inside Intel: Andy Grove and the Rise of the World's Most Powerful Chip Company* (New York: Penguin, 1998), 138.

14. Phillips, "A Geological Approach to Organizational Life Chances: The Parent-Progeny Transfer Among Silicon Valley Law Firms, 1946–1996," *Administrative Science Quarterly* 47 (2002): 474.

15. Filippo Wezel, Gino Cattani, and Johannes Pennings, "Competitive Implications of Inter-Firm Mobility," *Organization Science* 17 (2006): 691.

16. Deepak Somaya, Ian O. Williamson, and Natalia Lorinkova, "Gone But Not Lost: The Different Performance Impacts of Employee Mobility between Cooperators Versus Competitors," *Academy of Management Journal* 51 (2008): 936.

17. Rafael Corredoira and Lori Rosenkopf, "Should Auld Acquaintance Be Forgot? The Reverse Transfer of Knowledge Through Mobility Ties," *Strategic Management Journal* 31, no. 2 (2010): 159–81; Michael S. Dahl and Olav Sorenson, "The Migration of Technical Workers," *Journal of Urban Economics* 67 (2010): 33–45.

18. Harhoff finds that "high-technology firms react more sensitively to spillovers in terms of their research and development spending, and their direct marginal productivity gain from spillovers in excess to the effect from enhanced R&D spending is considerably larger than the respective gain for less technology-oriented firms." Dietmar Harhoff, "R&D Spillovers, Technological Proximity, and Productivity Growth: Evidence from German Panel Data," *Schmalenbach Bus. Rev.* 52 (2000): 238, 258; Jeffrey I. Bernstein and M. Ishaq Nadiri,

"Research and Development and Intra-Industry Spillovers: An Empirical Application of Dynamic Duality," *Rev. Econ. Stud.* 56 (1989): 249, 257–58.

19. Gilles Duranton and Diego Puga, "Nursery Cities: Urban Diversity, Process Innovation, and the Life Cycle of Products," *American Economic Review* 91, no. 5 (2001): 1454–77.

20. Daron Acemoglu, "A Microfoundation for Social Increasing Returns in Human Capital Accumulation," *Quarterly Journal of Economics* 111, no. 3 (1996): 779–804; Daron Acemoglu, "Training and Innovation in an Imperfect Labour Market," *Review of Economic Studies* 64, no. 3 (1997): 445–64.

21. Letter from Thomas Jefferson to Isaac McPherson, August 13 1813, in *The Complete Jefferson*, ed. Saul K. Padover, 1011, 1015 (New York: Duell, Sloan and Pearce, 1943).

22. Ibid.

23. *Graham v. John Deere Co.*, 383 U.S. 1, 9 (1966), quoting letter from Thomas Jefferson to Isaac McPherson, August 13, 1813.

24. Nancy Gallini and Suzanne Scotchmer, "Intellectual Property: When Is It the Best Incentive System?" *NBER Innovation Policy and the Economy* 2 (2002): 51–78.

25. Gaia Bernstein, "In the Shadow of Innovation," *Cardozo Law Review* 31, no. 6 (2010): 2257.

26. Michelle Boldrin and David K. Levine, *Against Intellectual Monopoly* (Cambridge: Cambridge University Press, 2008), 2.

27. Dotan Oliar and Christopher Jon Sprigman, "There's No Free Laugh (Anymore): The Emergence of Intellectual Property Norms and the Transformation of Stand-Up Comedy," *Virginia Law Review* 94, no. 8 (2008). Disputes over jokes can get rough among comedians, ranging from shaming all the way to physical violence. Allegations about joke stealing result in reputational harm and risk damaging one's career. The social norms in the standup world are relatively new. In the past, comedians considered joke stealing as part of the nature of the business. With the rise of social norms against such stealing, the nature of innovation in the comedy industry itself changed: jokes became more focused on the originality of the text, more observational, personal, and narrative driven, with fewer one-liners and less performance-driven comedy.

28. Robert C. Allen, "Collective Invention," *Journal of Economic Behavior and Organization* 4, no. 1 (1983): 1–24.

29. Doron Ben-Atar, "Hollywood Profits v. Technological Progress," *Chronicle of Higher Education*, April 1, 2005.

30. Eric Von Hippel, "Cooperation Between Rivals: Informal Know-How Trading," *Research Policy* 16 (1987): 291–302.

31. Ibid., 295.

32. Robert P. Merges, "Property Rights Theory and the Commons: The Case of Scientific Research," *Social Philosophy and Policy* 13 (1967): 145–67.

33. Harry M. Collins, "Tacit Knowledge and Scientific Networks," in *Science in Context*, ed. Barry Barns and David Edge (Cambridge: MIT Press, 1982).

34. Orly Lobel, "The Paradox of Extralegal Activism: Critical Legal Consciousness and Transformative Politics," *Harvard Law Review* 120 (2007): 937–88.
35. Steven Klepper and Sally Sleeper, "Entry by Spinoffs," *Management Science* 51 (2005): 1291; Richard Nelson, "Recent Evolutionary Theorizing about Economic Change," *J. Econom. Lit.* 33 (1995): 48–90.
36. Klepper and Sleeper, "Entry by Spinoffs," 1291.
37. Gordon Moore and Kevin David, "Learning the Silicon Valley Way," in *Building High-Tech Clusters: Silicon Valley and Beyond,* ed. Timothy Bresnahan and Alfonso Gambardella (Cambridge: Cambridge University Press, 2004).
38. Steven Klepper, "Entry, Exit, Growth and Innovation over the Product Life Cycle," *American Economic Review* 86 (1996): 562–83.